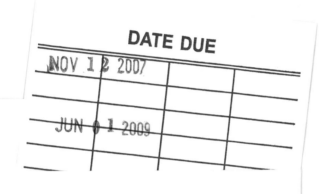

DATE DUE

NOV 1 2 2007			
JUN 0 1 2009			

WHO BENEFITS FROM
SPECIAL EDUCATION?

(Fixing)
Remediating ∧ Other
People's Children

STUDIES IN CURRICULUM THEORY
William F. Pinar, Series Editor

Brantlinger (Ed.) • Who Benefits From Special Education?: Remediating (Fixing) Other People's Children

Pinar/Irwin (Eds.) • Curriculum in a New Key: The Collected Works of Ted T. Aoki

Reynolds/Webber (Eds.) • Expanding Curriculum Theory: Dis/Positions and Lines of Flight

Pinar • What Is Curriculum Theory?

McKnight • Schooling, the Puritan Imperative, and the Molding of an American National Identity: Education's "Errand Into the Wilderness"

Pinar (Ed.) • International Handbook of Curriculum Research

Morris • Curriculum and the Holocaust: Competing Sites of Memory and Representation

Doll • Like Letters in Running Water: A Mythopoetics of Curriculum

Joseph/Bravman/Windschitl/Mikel/Green • Cultures of Curriculum

Westbury/Hopmann/Riquarts (Eds.) • Teaching as a Reflective Practice: The German Didaktic Tradition

Reid • Curriculum as Institution and Practice: Essays in the Deliberative Tradition

Pinar (Ed.) • Queer Theory in Education

Huebner • The Lure of the Transcendent: Collected Essays by Dwayne E. Huebner. Edited by Vikki Hillis. Collected and Introduced by William F. Pinar

jagodzinski • Postmodern Dilemmas: Outrageous Essays in Art & Art Education

jagodzinski • Pun(k) Deconstruction: Experifigural Writings in Art & Art Education

WHO BENEFITS FROM SPECIAL EDUCATION?

(Fixing)
Remediating ∧ Other
People's Children

Edited by

Ellen A. Brantlinger
Indiana University, Bloomington

LEA LAWRENCE ERLBAUM ASSOCIATES, PUBLISHERS
2006   Mahwah, New Jersey   London

Lawrence Erlbaum Associates, Inc., Publishers
10 Industrial Avenue
Mahwah, New Jersey 07430
www.erlbaum.com

Cover design by Kathryn Houghtaling Lacey

Library of Congress Cataloging-in-Publication Data

Who benefits from special education? : remediating (fixing) other people's children /
    edited by Ellen Brantlinger.
        p.   cm. — (Studies in curriculum theory)
    Includes bibliographical references and index.
    ISBN 0-8058-5528-9 (c. : alk. paper)
    ISBN 0-8058-5529-7 (pbk. : alk. paper)
        1. Children with disabilities—Education—United States.   2. Special education—
United States.   I. Brantlinger, Ellen A.   II. Series.

LC4031.W53   2005
371.9—dc22   2005040017
                                                                              CIP

Books published by Lawrence Erlbaum Associates are printed on acid-free paper,
and their bindings are chosen for strength and durability.

Printed in the United States of America
10 9 8 7 6 5 4 3 2 1

Contents

Preface

Special education for students with substantial disabilities was very much the vision of parents. They were the ones who brought forward the court cases (e.g., PARC, 1971) based on equal protection clauses of the constitution that mandated that education was a right of all American children regardless of their unique characteristics. Nevertheless, over time parents lost control as the field of special education has become increasingly dominated by a professional class of specially trained teachers, teacher educators, therapists, psychometrists, and funded researchers. Clearly, the number of influential parents was always insignificant compared with the less powerful parents of students identified with high-incidence disabilities (learning disabilities, emotional disturbance, mild mental retardation). These children had regularly been classified as *disabled* and excluded from mainstream education without their own or their parents' consultation (see Mercer, 1973).

Unfortunately, parents inevitably see the personalized and unique attributes of their children and think in terms of what is best for them, whereas professionals are likely to have a more abstract and disconnected view, and thus may fail to see other people's children as individuals. Furthermore, they tend to understand disability from a medical model perspective; that is, they see disability as a problem or deficit in certain children, rather than as an artifact of the general structure of schooling. Based on the prevailing ideology of the necessity of expertise, these professionals may assume that, because of their specialized training, they know what is best for other people's children.

A related issue is the lack of direct contact between scholars and families or between scholars and school-based personnel. Attendance at special education conferences, for example, is dominated by scholars at research centers or faculty in teacher education programs. Similarly, the myriad of journals that have sprung up in the past few decades are oriented toward university-affiliated professionals, many of whom have little contact with schools or agencies that serve people with disabilities. The authors of journal articles are almost exclusively university professors or members of a complex of individuals paid through "soft monies" (i.e., state, federal, or private grants). The voices of people with disabilities, their families, and even teachers are rarely included in this literature. In this book, we address how researchers and theorists come up with ideas to intervene with (remediate and fix) other people's children. We articulate our concerns about how professionals (a) are not attuned to the real needs and feelings of children with disabilities and their families, and (b) rarely consult with them about their reactions to their labels and where they would like to be educated.

As is the case with many books, the term *fix* in the title has two meanings. Fix can mean to remediate, repair, or make better. Fix can also mean to determine a place for certain individuals such as through classification or specialized classroom assignments. The "other people's children" part of the title is based on Lisa Delpit's (1995) book, *Other People's Children: Cultural Conflict in the Classroom*. Delpit observed that Euro-American, middle-class professionals held ethnocentric assumptions about the low-income, African-American children they taught. Because of the overrepresentation of poor children and children of color identified as disabled, and because these children are most likely to be educated in restrictive circumstances, the idea of the cultural disconnect between those providing services and those receiving services—or those doing the labeling and those being labeled—is highly relevant to special education. Finally, part of the title encompasses Italian Marxist Antonio Gramsci's (1929–1971/1935) recommendation that, when trying to understand social practices, it is essential to ask who benefits from them. The authors of chapters in this book attempt to answer this question by noting how professional practice is often a thing in itself, not linked to the real needs and interests of those for whom the practices presumably are designed.

This book is written from a Disability Studies perspective. This means that the included authors challenge the perception that certain human differences are disabilities. They also are wary of the hegemony of professionals who claim or act as if their technical expertise and ideas about effective remediation of so-called *problems* is more important than the feelings, opinions, and aspirations of those being served through special education. The authors recognize the dangers of normative school practices and structures that rank and sort school children (see Spring, 1989). The book includes fairly diverse chapters that are united under the general claim that tensions exist between professional ideology (and practice) and the wishes and expectations of the recipients of professional practice—children, adolescents, and adults with disabilities and their families. Although the mainstream professional organizations, journals, and textbooks spin their own versions of best practices—now mostly dubbed evidence- or science-based—the voices of those who receive services have rarely taken center stage in formulating important decisions about the quality and characteristics of appropriate education.

The authors of some chapters in *Who Benefits From Special Education?* deconstruct or unmask mainstream special education ideologies and normative practice, even evidence-based suggestions for practice. Other chapters highlight the personal perspectives of students, families, and teachers. Some authors selected to contribute to this volume are scholars known for their critical and postmodern perspectives on disability (Allan, Brantlinger, Danforth, Erevelles, and Ferguson). Others have recently come to higher education after long-term careers as teachers in public schools (de Waal-Lucas, Harvey-Koelpin, Lewis-Robertson, and Stoughton). Their chapters benefit from first-hand, personal knowledge about the nature of schooling, and especially about the impact of special education and related practices on students, parents, and teachers.

The primary audience for this volume is obviously special education/disabilities studies graduate students and faculty. Although some authors integrate complex theory into their chapters to speak to these theoretically sophisticated audiences, their work was intended to be accessible so that the book would also have meaning for teachers, preservice teachers, and individuals with disabilities and their families. Working within the Disability Studies framework, we believe that the recipients' ideas about education should be central to designs for schooling. In addition, because we believe that disability is always contextually bound and the context of special education is clearly general education, it is our hope that general educators will read and profit from this book. It is ultimately general education circumstances that must be significantly changed if all school children are to have a fair, just, responsive, and inclusive education.

Chapters 1 through 4 present theoretical and historical perspectives on special education practices. Chapter 1 by Danforth, Taff, and Ferguson examines the way place, profession, and program weave their way through the history of special education. The authors present a critique of the custodial assumptions that have riddled special education since its onset and continue to interfere with the counterdiscourse that all children can learn. They note that, despite Least Restrictive Education mandates, certain children from less powerful families are still most likely to be labeled with stig-matizing names and educated in segregated settings.

A common mindset among professionals is that each successive new spe-cial education law and intervention contributes to progress in the field. In chapter 2, "Failing to Make Progress," Julie Allan addresses how visions re-main unclear and how vague plans for inclusion have meant faltering prog-ress in the field. She clarifies how it is necessary that the social model of dis-abilities take hold to counter the destructive trends that accrue from the currently widespread deficit model of disability. Allan confronts the dis-abling barriers within school environments and the exclusionary pressures that dominate practice.

In chapter 3—on how special education textbooks socialize preservice teachers to adopt restrictive dominant special education viewpoints and scripts for teaching—Brantlinger presents an analysis of 14 current college textbooks designed for the ubiquitous "introduction to exceptional chil-dren" course found on campuses across the United States. In this chapter, Brantlinger argues that children become categories and curriculum be-comes techniques aimed at remediating the deficits of particular categories of learners. She concludes that these textbooks are neither helpful nor rele-vant to teaching, but rather are hazards and barriers in terms of teachers eventually providing a democratic, just, and humanistic education for all children.

In chapter 4, Erevelles, Kanga, and Middleton return to the classic ques-tion posed to African Americans by DuBois (1901/1065)—"How does it feel to be a problem?" These authors note that scholars' habit of research-ing poor children and children of color and their families perpetuates the idea that it is these oppressed individuals who are to blame for discrepan-cies in the school conditions and school outcomes documented for African-American and Euro-American and for rich and poor students. They untan-gle the racist and ablest politics of common schools and suggest ways to dis-mantle racial and disability oppression.

Chapters 5 through 8 are all reports of narrative and interpretive re-search conducted in classrooms and schools, or with students identified as disabled, their families, and their teachers. The four authors of these chap-ters have all recently been instructors in public school classrooms, with teaching experience ranging from 3 to 17 years. Three of the authors re-turned to their schools or former students to do their research.

Ashley de Waal-Lucas (chap. 5) looks at how social studies is taught in a wealthy, predominantly White suburb. She notes that her four teacher par-ticipants rarely include topics about race, class, gender, or disabilities in their social studies classrooms. She argues that this omission means that these privileged children are not led to understand the nature of their ad-vantages or the difficult situations facing American children in less affluent areas. Although her chapter does not directly relate to special education, her findings about the self-absorbed character of schooling for wealthy children reveal the tendency toward selfishness and exclusiveness in American schooling as well as the fallout of this self-centered education for other people's children.

In chapter 6, Sally Harvey-Koelpin returns to an inner-city elementary school where she taught for 16 years to interview teachers about the impact of the No Child Left Behind Act on their teaching and their students. Sadly, she documents that well-meaning, dedicated teachers who previously enthusiastically participated in the voluntary inclusion of children with disabilities at their schools had begun to refuse to have these children in their classrooms on the grounds that their low scores on tests would jeopardize their own teaching careers in the unforgiving climate of high-stakes testing.

Edy Stoughton (chap. 7) taught for 17 years, and her last several years were in a self-contained middle-school classroom for students identified as emotionally disturbed. She draws from her study of former students, who at the time were young adults or high school students, and their parents to focus specifically on Harriet and Marcus. This mother–son duo had intense feelings about the latter's schooling and articulated these poignantly to Stoughton. The chapter title, "Living on the Edge in School and Society," highlights the vulnerability of both mother and son as they try to secure a satisfactory place in a racist and classist society.

In chapter 8, "No Place Like Home," Genell Lewis-Robertson, like Stoughton, follows a former student who is expelled from elementary school as a result of a draconian zero tolerance policy regarding being caught in school with a small amount of drugs stolen from his father. Based on multiple interviews with the child, his mother, and his home school teacher, Lewis-Robertson documents a healing process that, unfortunately, was not available to the child in school. In this case, even school-based remediation was dismissed, and the family was left on its own to cope with a multitude of family problems related to poverty and a history of substance abuse.

In chapter 9, "Winners Need Losers," Brantlinger expands on the "who benefits" question to explicate the nature of meritocracy in U.S. schools. She points to the standards and accountability movement that pushes a narrow academic purpose for schooling. Brantlinger details a number of parties—many in high and influential places—who benefit from this academic intensification, while the usual suspects—poor children and children of color—continue to be left further and further behind. In chapter 10, "Conclusion: Whose Labels: Whose Norms? Whose Needs? Whose Benefits?", Brantlinger concludes the volume by deconstructing professional buzz words (e.g., *special needs, service delivery*) current in special education and by confounding the normative practices that undergird labeling and exclusion phenomenon. She notes that as schools rely more and more on legalized and bureaucratized systems, which in turn demand professional expertise, they become increasingly severed from the voices and realities of affected people and from humanistic moralities that should also guide interactions among people in democratic schools.

REFERENCES

Delpit, L. (1995). *Other people's children: Cultural conflict in the classroom.* New York: The New Press.

DuBois, W. E. B. (1901/1965). *The souls of black folk.* New York: Avon.

Gramsci, A. (1971). *Selections for prison notebooks* (Q. Hoare & G. N. Smith, Eds.). New York: International Publishers. (Original publication 1929–1935)

Mercer, J. R. (1973). *Labeling the mentally retarded.* Berkeley: University of California Press.

PARC (Pennsylvania Association for Retarded Children v. Pennsylvania), 334 F. Supp. 1257 (E. D. Pa. 1971).

Spring, J. H. (1989). *The sorting machine revisited: National educational policy since 1945.* New York: Longman.

Acknowledgments

As editor of this volume, I would first like to acknowledge the caring parents and teachers of students identified as disabled who have always put children's feelings and opinions first and who have worked hard to ensure that their genuine needs were met and that they were included in comprehensive school settings. Criticism of the system certainly was not meant to undermine the value of their conscious and difficult efforts on behalf of children.

I would like to thank the included authors for contributing valuable and insightful chapters that will, I believe, make a meaningful contribution to the fields of Disability Studies and Special Education.

I am especially grateful to Bill Pinar, Special Series Editor, who suggested that I put this volume together. He was generous in meeting with me on different occasions to convey his ideas about the book and encourage me to get it done when other obligations seemed more pressing. I also want to thank Naomi Silverman, acquisitions editor at Erlbaum, who, along with Erica Kica, patiently worked with me as I bumbled along trying to get the manuscript in shape for publication. I am appreciative of Heather L. Jefferson's careful editing of the manuscript. Of course I must acknowledge the anonymous reviewers who, although somewhat critical of initial drafts, helped us get our chapters ready for final publication. Along with Bill, Naomi, and Erica, these reviewers saw promise in the volume and gave Erlbaum the go ahead for publication.

—*Ellen Brantlinger*
December 16, 2004

Chapter 1

Place, Profession, and Program in the History of Special Education Curriculum

Scot Danforth
Steve Taff
Philip M. Ferguson
University of Missouri, St. Louis

One does not have to go that far back into the history of curriculum in special education before confronting an earlier, more fundamental topic. Curriculum comes into play only when teaching is attempted, and teaching is attempted only when learning is thought possible. Only then does the question of "What do I teach?" arise. So, before a curriculum or "course of study" becomes relevant, there must be a presumption that learning can occur. However, it is precisely this presumption that was late to emerge in the history of the education of children with disabilities. Even in its gradual emergence over the last two centuries or so, the presumption has been granted and withdrawn with waves of professional optimism soon followed by new proclamations of irremediability for an unteachable remnant. A largely custodial discourse would then replace the aggressive tone of experimental treatment and active instruction. Certainly each cycle would leave a smaller group consigned to failure than before, but the cycle of optimistic intervention to pessimistic neglect has remained remarkably durable. Even today, while the federal mantra is to have "No Child Left Behind," and the legislative mandate is that *all* children can learn and are, therefore, entitled to a "free, appropriate public education," the course of study for students with disabilities is often governed in practice by a system of presumptive labels that determine what they will be taught, by whom, and in what type of educational setting.

Throughout history, then, the questions asked about the education of children with disabilities have often had a kind of time lag quality about them, distorted echoes of questions already asked and answered for most children. Although the discussion of public support of private schools through vouchers continues among politicians and policy analysts, there has been a consensus for a century or more that school of some sort is the proper place for children to spend their days. Equally universal is the assumption that in school the children should receive instruction from professional educators. Finally, while debate rages over how standardized and measured it should be, most would agree that there is a broad program of study that schools should follow: a general curriculum that designates in broad strokes what we hope all of our children come to know, value, and use as educated citizens. However, for students with disabilities, these shared assumptions are precisely what seem most contentious. The assumptions become topics of heated debate and conflicting proposals. (a) Where should students with disabilities be taught? Are self-contained schools or classrooms preferred, or should we emphasize general education classrooms? (b) Who should teach these students? Are only those specialists trained to work with specific types of disabilities suitable for teaching such children? Or can elementary and secondary teachers take an active role in their instruction as well? (c) What should these students learn? Should educators focus on a set of functional survival skills and individually designed programs or should we assume that these students should also have access to the general curriculum that their nondisabled peers explore?

In this chapter, we explore how these three topical threads—referred to here as questions of *place, professionalism,* and *program*—have woven their way through the history of special education. We argue that these themes have played out over the last 200 years in the United States in a way that provides a helpful explanatory narrative for the evolution of our policies and practices for children with disabilities.

Our narrative looks at three key eras. First, we look at the influence of the French Enlightenment on American social activists in the middle of the 19th century. This was a time when the theme of place held sway as the dominant narrative thread. The optimism of a new generation of doctors and educators emphasized what might be called a *curative geography,* where the placement of children with disabilities was determinative of outcome. There was a strong belief that new specialized asylums and residential schools would reveal a capacity to learn by children who were deaf, blind, or *idiotic.* This separation, which began as curative, however, became quickly custodial—the optimism of intervention was replaced by the burden of control and maintenance.

Next we move to the Progressive era and the dominance of the theme of a bureaucratic professionalism and rampant specialization of expertise.[1] In

---

[1] By the term *progressive era* we refer to something much broader than the Progressive movement within education associated with Dewey and his followers, and instead follow the practice of most historians of the early 20th century in referring to a complicated time of dramatic industrial expansion, governmental reform, and academic specialization. In the words of a

public schools, we see the rise and administrative recognition of special education classrooms with specially trained teachers to staff them. As with the
earlier period (probably all periods), the reforms of the Progressive era, in
how we responded to children with disabilities, reflected the larger culture,
with a faith in social engineering as the common answer to both fears of social decay and demands on social conscience.

Finally, we look briefly at the period running roughly from 1975 to 2000,
and we review how the final thematic strand of our triad gained prominence.
If the middle of the 19th century was led by the creation of new places for
children with disabilities, and the Progressive era was strongly characterized
by a proliferation and empowerment of professionalization, then the last
quarter of the 20th century, and specifically the changes associated with the
implementation of the *Individuals With Disabilities Education Act (IDEA)*, can
be approached as an era when programmatic elaboration came to encompass both place and profession in the context of a mandated and expanded
system of public special education. It is this consolidation of place and profession within the purview of the special education system that represents the
most fundamental development of the most recent decades.

Our framework is, of course, an idealization of a much messier and complex process. Moreover, our point is not that each era we examine is totally
defined by only one of the three themes we identified. We want to emphasize throughout our discussion of all three eras that our three themes—
where we should teach children with disabilities, *who* should teach them, and
what they should be taught—may be seen as interweaving threads in the history of special education. Each thread is always present, but more visible in
some patterns of official response than in others.

THE THEME OF *WHERE* IN SPECIAL EDUCATION: CURATIVE GEOGRAPHY AND THE INSTITUTIONAL STATE, 1800–1850

The historical development of special education in the United States began
in Europe. Prior to the mid-19th century, there was no distinctly American
tradition regarding the public care and education of persons with disabilities. Professionals in the United States initially appropriated the majority of

---

recent interpreter of this era: "Although concern for order was not new in American history, a
characteristic feature of Progressive movements was their tendency to see social control not as
a moral or political problem, but primarily as an administrative problem. Progressives sought
to depoliticize the growing demands for the protections of a welfare state by promoting
reforms that emphasized administrative efficiency and professional expertise rather than
substantive changes in the allocation of rights and economic resources" (Sutton, 1988, p. 124).

their approaches from European sources, especially the traditions and methodologies of the French. In particular, it was the dramatic developments of the French Enlightenment and its applications to practice in some of the earliest *experiments* in special education that have relevance for subsequent U.S. efforts. Indeed in many ways, it is the Enlightenment culture of revolutionary France that first delineated the three themes that, we argue, have dominated the discourse of special education for the last 200 years. It was the French who first viewed their disabled children and adults and thought it worthwhile to ask the central questions of treatment and education: *Who* does *what* and *where* should they do it?

Place, Profession, and Program: The Emergence of Intertwining Concepts

By 1800, France had a well-established tradition of public custodial care for their mentally ill and disabled populations dating back to 1656 and the establishment of the *Bicetre* and *Salpetriere* hospitals (Shorter, 1997). Previously cared for mainly by the family in the home, children with disabilities began in increasing numbers to move into institutions and specialized schools for the deaf or blind. Although many of these institutions' schools remained purely custodial in nature, a shift also occurred in how these places were portrayed by the specialists who ran them. Knowing *where* to treat or teach was the essential evidence of *who* was qualified to deliver that treatment or instruction. The new facilities were now put forth as convenient laboratories for the great Enlightenment experiment—"improving" people via education (primarily of the senses) and "moral treatment." An intertwining process of mutual reinforcement developed. The new institutions and schools needed a new generation of trained professionals for appropriate staffing while the burgeoning cadre of specialists needed an equally specialized setting to demonstrate their expertise. Both simultaneously demanded an ongoing elaboration of exactly what would be done by the professionals once established in their specialized settings.

However, in this early era of special education and curative treatment, the trinity of intervention was unified in the obsession with therapeutic placement. Cure could be found through careful arrangement of a specialized environment: a curative geography, as it were. It was this *where* of intervention that initially subsumed the *who* and the *what* in the rhetoric of Enlightenment reforms. Here we see the genesis of a theme that appears consistently throughout the history of special education: the notion that "place"—the location of "treatment" and education—emerges as the first key to remediation and the surest evidence of professional expertise: Control the setting and you can control the mind.

The Delineation of Place

In the first half of the 19th century, the place or location of early special education—as practiced primarily by the emerging profession of psychiatry—
was in most cases a specialized institution for "the insane" or "idiots" (as
these two groups were called) or perhaps a specialized school for the blind
or deaf. It was in the institution—both geographically and functionally—
that the notion of a "therapeutic community" developed. In this self-
contained and often out-of-the-way setting, professionals and patients acted
out the theater of Enlightenment ideology. It is important to remember
that, with few exceptions, the customary view held that existence in this
place—the segregated therapeutic community—was a tremendously vital
contributor toward the "perfectibility" of the residents (Shorter, 1997).
Certainly protopsychiatrists (usually physicians with a special interest in
mental illness) practiced in small numbers outside the auspices of the institutions, but it was the creation of therapeutic *places* that truly carried the
Enlightenment worldview from abstract intellectualism to concrete practice. Thus, we see the early origins of a "curative geography," where place
single-handedly acts as both a social reform and an individual remedy. It is
ironic, however, that the classic therapeutic setting was not so much a *community* as it was an isolated, artificial, and professionalized *configuration*—
one that came simultaneously to espouse both Enlightenment ideals of perfectibility and equality and their antithesis of deviance and exclusion.[2]

Before 1800, professional specialization within the medical field was
practically nonexistent (Shorter, 1997). Prior to the intellectual and social
shift forced by the Enlightenment, mental illness and disability were considered predestined—an innate distortion of nature. As such people with disabilities were "incurable," at least in the sense of being largely beyond the
help of human intervention (miracles were always possible). This limited
any possible impetus for the development of medical professional special-
ties (Winzer, 1993). However, in the early 1800s, things began to change.
The uniquely human attribute of rationality gained acceptance as a force
that could literally "change the world" for the better. The consequences of
human action on the world became, as it were, more consequential. There
was a socially responsible prerogative to meet the scientific and social standards set by the Enlightenment worldview. To meet the needs of a newly
egalitarian society imbued with the responsibility of uplifting the weak and
disadvantaged, specialized expertise was needed as well as ways to dissemi-
nate that expertise on a widespread basis. In France (soon to be followed in

---

[2]A similar and equally influential development occurred with the Quakers and the development of moral treatment at the York Retreat at the end of the 18th century in England. The
work of Anne Digby (1985) is the best source here.

the United States), the first major medical specialty to rise to the challenge of the Enlightenment project was psychiatry (Rothman, 1971; Shorter, 1997).

Professional Developments: The Emerging Claims
of Specialized Knowledge

Psychiatrists in early 19th-century France concentrated on "perfecting" those with disabilities via sense education and moral treatment, as introduced most notably by Pinel. Moral treatment as a form of therapy was eminently compatible with the concept of therapeutic community because it both appeared benevolent and sanctioned institutional isolation (Dowbiggin, 1991). Enlightenment thinking provided the "therapeutic optimism" (Goodson & Dowbiggin, 1997) that drove early psychiatrists. However, the professionalization of psychiatry was even further advanced by the struggle to allege a somatic or biomedical cause for insanity and "idiocy." To claim legitimacy in the medical field, a bodily pathology was essential. If madness had no physical basis, then matters of the insane fell into the province of competing groups such as academic psychologists and the Catholic Church. As *physicians*, psychiatrists had been "granted important privileges in the diagnosis and treatment of madness, even though they had displayed no conclusive competence in either capacity" (Dowbiggin, 1991, p. 8). Dowbiggin (1991) referred to the professionalization of French psychiatrists as a continual struggle against marginalization due, in large part, to a glaring gap between bestowed social power (as physicians) and their own lack of technical effectiveness in curing the insane.

By the 1850s, therapeutic optimism began to diminish, gradually replaced by a renewed pessimism regarding the curability of madness. In the context of this pessimism, psychiatry experienced a shift in purpose toward a "collectively oriented moral treatment that stressed surveillance and conformity to moral norms rather than activist therapy" (Goodson & Dowbiggin, 1997, p. 88). This shift in professional function necessitated that psychiatrists become less attentive to residents' mental health and more concerned with protecting others from the mad through classification, segregation, and other forms of control. Next to this shift, there occurred a subsequent recognition by the psychiatric profession that their legitimacy as physicians was in imminent danger. To combat this legitimacy crisis, psychiatry increasingly catered to those with political and social power, in an attempt to ensure that resources for sustaining the institutional system did not go the way of therapeutic optimism (Goodson & Dowbiggin, 1997).

**Programmatic Developments: Curriculum,
Methodologies, and Purpose**

As we undertake a basic sketch of programmatic strategies utilized in the
first half of the 19th century, one must remember that "place" played a defining role in the development of such strategies and provided an environmental context conducive to the type of controlled experimentation that
would not have been possible in individual homes. We now turn our attention to perhaps three of the most prominent and influential early professionals who worked with the mentally ill and/or disabled: Jean-Marc Itard
and Edouard Seguin in France, and Samuel Gridley Howe in America. In
this section, we briefly discuss the curricular approaches and pedagogical
methods that each one utilized. We also touch on the extent to which they
believed persons with disabilities could be educated, and the purposes of
such an education. To begin to answer these questions, we must again journey back to France, where Itard (1801/1962) accepted the challenge of educating the "Wild Boy" of Aveyron (see also Lane, 1976; Shattuck, 1980).

Itard. The Wild Boy of Aveyron embodied all the attributes necessary
for the quintessential Enlightenment experiment, supposedly putting
Locke's (1975) theory of *tabula rasa* to the test. For the French empiricists
and the burgeoning scientific community, the capture of an apparently fe-
ral child (whom Itard later named Victor) granted access to what had been
largely theoretical: an original human—Rousseau's "Noble Savage," uncon-
taminated by the civilizing and corrupting experiences of human society.
Itard hoped to prove that Victor's savagery was not due to some innate inferiority, but to isolation from society (Winzer, 1993). Due to this crucial lack
of socialization, Victor needed to be "reeducated" as a human being (Shattuck, 1980). Enlightenment optimism tinted Itard's belief that what appeared superficially as insanity or idiocy could be replaced by an educated,
functional human, perfected if you will through the careful introduction of
social experience and training. Itard set out to educate Victor using a five-
pronged strategy: socialization, training of the senses, concept development, speech, and transfer of learning (Ball, 1971). Socialization was the
prerequisite for any education, as contact with others stimulated the senses.
Itard utilized a wide variety of means in working with Victor, traces of
which remain in special education (and Montessori) classrooms to this day.
Taken as a whole, Itard based much of his pedagogy on Pinel's concept of
"moral treatment," especially in the deemphasis of physical restraints and
harsh punishment. However, because Victor was starting at a much more
basic developmental level than the inmates of the insane asylum where
Pinel first elaborated his theories, many of the activities and tools used by

Itard were of his own invention. He made use of extensive drill and repetition, manipulatives, games, gestural communication (although not the sign language learned by the deaf children in the other wings of Bicetre during this same time period and with which Itard was certainly familiar; Lane, 1976), and physical modalities (e.g., hot and cold baths; Shattuck, 1980).

Itard felt that the tools of learning—particularly speech and writing—were based on imitation of sensory input provided to the learner. Therefore, frequent imitation played a central role in the educational process. Observation paired with comparison was another favored pedagogical technique. In fact, this is what Itard considered thinking to be. Comparison served as a type of innovation or concept formation (Shattuck, 1980), in what would today be viewed as a version of social learning theory elaborated by Albert Bandura in the 1960s. Indeed due to his belief in the malleability of humans, his emphasis on close observation, and a systematic use of rewards and punishments in response to Victor's actions, Itard is often considered an early forebear of behaviorism, although he appeared to be much more holistic in the application of shaping principles than his more modern colleagues (Shattuck, 1980).

Seguin.   Edouard Seguin—a student of Itard—initially plied his trade at the Salpetriere and, later, Bicetre hospitals. After leaving the Bicetre, Seguin spent roughly the next 6 years running his own private school before emigrating to America, where he would later briefly work in Samuel Gridley Howe's "experimental school" for idiots, which was the first American public institution specifically intended for this segment of the population (Trent, 1994).

Behind Seguin's educational strategies were three major influences: moral treatment as espoused by his mentors Itard and Esquirol, a revised Condillacan sensualism, and a thrust toward the educability of idiots (and, although not quite as clearly, to somehow integrate them back into society) garnered from the Christian socialism of the Saint-Simonians (Trent, 1994). Seguin differed in philosophy from the pure sensualism of Itard, however, by suggesting that "notions," or categories and names, mediated between sensation and knowledge (Seguin, 1866; Trent, 1994).

Seguin's approach to curriculum and instruction (termed *physiological education*) consisted broadly of three objectives: muscular education, sense education, and moral treatment. *Muscular education*, the first stage of Seguin's pedagogy, employed a variety of tools, including gymnastic equipment, weights, ropes, swings, and balance equipment (Seguin, 1866; Trent, 1994). Seguin also utilized the muscular component of physiological education, often done in groups, to foster social skill development. Seguin focused on touch as the conduit to the other senses, whereas Itard, for example, concentrated more on sight. Tactile experience afforded students an awareness of their sensations and environment. Thus "awakened," the senses paved the way for the student to develop notions, which in turn could extend into active ideas (Trent, 1994).

Seguin's pedagogy also utilized imitation (although he disdained repetition), music, oral communication with deaf students, oral-motor exercises, "eye training," and instruction in daily living skills. Seguin strongly believed that the definitive goal of education was independence. To Seguin, independence meant the freedom to associate with other human beings. Therefore, what we now call *community-based instruction* was a prominent component of his educational system. Once again here we see the influence of the Saint-Simonians, if only vaguely, implying the merits of integrating so-called idiots into the greater society.

Howe. Samuel Gridley Howe was a charismatic figure who led a life filled with philanthropic struggles for the disadvantaged waged on many shores (Winzer, 1993). A physician by training, Howe was also powerfully swayed by Protestant religious principles; key among these was the importance of striving for the betterment of fellow citizens (Winzer, 1993). Moreover, prominent in these religious overtones was an optimism analogous to Enlightenment secularism, but emanating from a distinctly different source. The notion of an immaterial mind was popular with the American clergy at the time, which defined the soul in the same manner (Gitter, 2001; Menand, 2001). Howe took mind–body dualism and applied it to the concept of disability, asserting that a damaged body (e.g., blindness) did not necessarily mean a damaged mind.

Howe, while involved in many facets of educating those with disabilities, is perhaps best known for his work with the blind, particularly his famous pupil, Laura Bridgman (Gitter, 2001). As did Seguin, Howe concentrated on the sense of touch to free Laura's unimpaired, but dormant, mind. Despite this, Howe was vehemently opposed to the French sense empiricists (such as Condillac). In fact his success with Laura Bridgman was (in his view) proof that the assumptions of the sensualists were mistaken—for how could she have learned language successfully without being able to see or hear (Gitter, 2001)?

As time passed, however, Howe became more pessimistic regarding the educability of disabled children and came to accept the principles of hereditary determinism (Winzer, 1993). The role of heredity in disability melded agreeably with Puritan religious ideology in positing that the "sins of the father" could be the cause of disabling conditions, including idiocy (Howe, 1858/1993). The belief in the heredity of disability carried on even more forcefully into the Progressive era, where the social utility of such concepts was invaluable in addressing the new national crises of immigration, industrialization, urbanization, and the dangerously increasing heterogeneity of the population.

The first half of the 19th century, then, saw the emergence of institutions as healing agents for those with disabilities. Above all, however, there were now state-endorsed *places* for disabled individuals of all ages, but especially for children who were still capable of education and development. Although this section highlights the primacy of place in our triad of place, profession, and programs, we have also argued that there is an ongoing and intricate interweaving of the three threads throughout the history of special education. Now we shift our attention to the Progressive era, a time in which the geography of special education also situates the soaring ascent of professionalization.

THE THEME OF *WHO* IN SPECIAL EDUCATION: THERAPEUTIC EDUCATION AND PROFESSIONALISM, 1890–1925

The educational and cultural developments of the Progressive Era in the United States continued Enlightenment themes by enacting an optimism concerning the secular perfectibility of the human condition and society through the application of rationality. Running roughly from 1890 through the first quarter of the 20th century, the Progressive Era was a time when programmatic solutions to complex social problems were built on the promises of social science, efficiency, and the expertise of new helping professions. These solutions provided the theoretical and organizational foundation for the development of the helping professions that we know well today—special educators, social workers, psychologists, psychiatrists, and others—in relation to disabled, disadvantaged, or otherwise troubling children and youth. Although the 19th-century institutions housing people with a variety of disabilities continued to operate, the location of the dramatic development of special education programs occurred within the rapidly changing public schools.

The public schools in the early 20th century transformed in the social and political context of an American society marked by a series of striking characteristics. These characteristics combined in the minds of progressives into an understanding of social problems concerning primarily poor or working class, immigrant children and families living in American cities. The three main characteristics of American society at the beginning of the Progressive Era were (a) industrialization and intensification of social class conflict, (b) urbanization and immigration, and (c) expansion of science from physical to social. The progressive agenda in the public schools and the creation of new professions cannot be understood in isolation of the influential social context surrounding and propelling the social changes of the era.

Industrialization and the Intensification
of Social Class Conflict

During the early to mid-1800s, the primarily agrarian America of the colonial period shifted to an economy based on industrial production. The development of machines to power factories, foundries, and plants led to systems of mass production that quickly replaced slower, more costly practices of craft work. Corporations reaped profits while workers (including women and children) labored long hours under dangerous and dirty conditions for low wages. Workers in many industries countered by forming unions. During the latter years of the 19th century, a number of dramatic and ultimately violent strikes demonstrated the degree and scope of the conflict between workers and corporations.

Urbanization and Immigration

The population core of the United States migrated from rural to urban areas in the late 1800s. Following the lure of industrial jobs, a great proportion of the population shifted to the industrial ghettoes of the major cities. Urban factories employed both rural transplants and vast numbers of European immigrants. Factory workers and their families filled the urban ghettoes, overcrowded neighborhoods typically lacking adequate sewer systems, electrical power, running water, and garbage collection. Families lacked basic dental and health care. Disease, malnutrition, crime, and discontent often filled the impoverished neighborhoods of the factory-worker class. Immigrant families struggled with language barriers, the difficulties of understanding and assimilating into a strange new culture, and multiple forms of prejudice (Addams, 1910, 1972; Katz, 1996).

Expansion of Science From Physical to Social

The 19th century in America was an age of mechanical invention—a time when the application of scientific principles to the control of the physical environment yielded astounding results. By the end of the century, railroad trains carried passengers and freight to the far corners of the country. Industrial plants with massive engines produced products thousands of times faster than ever before. Enormous bridges spanned some of the nation's greatest waterways. Electric power was produced by enormous generators and delivered through wires to homes in many cities and towns. The advanced development of the physical sciences allowed humans to conquer and control nature, molding the physical world to human needs.

If a science of the physical world brought about such fantastic feats of mastery, then imagine what we might do with a similar science of the social world. Imagine a sociology of urban areas, a psychology of vice and immorality, and administrative science based on the certainty of social engineering. The progressives set their minds to the tasks of building, using, and selling the new human sciences as the solutions to the variety of problems of the urban, industrialized poor.

Immigration and the Public School

To turn-of-the-century public schools, especially those in urban areas, the complex array of social changes in American society came down to a single issue: too many immigrant students. The public schools struggled to deal with the challenges of booming enrollments and growing linguistic and ethnic diversity. According to a 1909 U.S. Immigration Commission study, 57.8% of all students in urban public schools were the offspring of foreign-born parents (Cremin, 1961). A majority of these immigrants came from southern and eastern Europe. In New York City, school enrollment rose 57% between 1900 and 1910. At that time, three fourths of the city population consisted of first- or second-generation immigrants (Chapman, 1988). Similar immigration patterns and enrollment growth impacted other large cities. More than half of all students in major urban public schools were immigrants or the children of immigrants. Although English was the language of schooling, most spoke a foreign language at home (Richardson, 1999). To make matters more complex, by 1921, all states had passed a compulsory school law requiring that children attend public school until a specified age (usually 14). Increasingly, public school classrooms were filled with students whom educators simply did not know how to educate.

The schools generally enacted the common ethnic prejudice of the times that favored prior generations of northern and western Europeans over the most recent influx of southern and eastern Europeans. In many cases, students' and parents' inability to speak English or understand American cultural norms were interpreted by public schools as indications of laziness, stupidity, and immorality. The all-too-common economic poverty that marked the lives of these children and families only further contributed to the general impression of these immigrants as ethically and intellectually deficient.

Early Public School Special Education

One of the main ways that public schools handled the enormous number of seemingly deficient immigrant students was through the creation of special classes. The first special education class specifically for "mental defectives" was founded in Providence, Rhode Island, in 1896. Most urban school districts soon followed. By 1922, at least 133 school systems provided special education classes for over 23,000 students considered "mentally deficient" (Lazerson, 1983; Osgood, 2002).

These special education classes in the public schools demonstrated central beliefs of the Progressive Era. A top–down approach to social change united the science of psychological measurement with the efficiency of educational administration. Behind the cool rationality of science and efficiency was a deep prejudice based on ethnicity, race, and class that focused the professional energies on the apparent deficiencies of immigrant youth. The end result was a system of special education that sorted students on the basis of psychological measures and placed inferior students—primarily immigrant, working-class boys—in separate classrooms and schools.

The practice of sorting students based on academic ability or moral standing was not new. In the 1870s and 1880s, a variety of specialized classes—"steamer" and "industrial" classes for new immigrants, programs for "incorrigibles," "industrial classes" and "ungraded classes" for "laggards"—were created in public schools. According to a study by noted educator Edward Cubberly (1919), public schools in many areas had created ability tracks by the 1890s and segregated programs for "juvenile delinquents," deaf students, blind students, "cripples," the "feebleminded," and non-English-speaking immigrants by 1900.

Classification and segregation practices received a boost of legitimacy and expanded in number when educational administrators started to rely on psychological measurements. Leading psychologists such as Henry Goddard, Lewis Terman, Robert Yerkes, and Edward Thorndike, expanding from Binet's first intelligence test in 1906, developed the American field of mental measurement as the cornerstone of scientific psychology. At every turn, notions of race or ethnicity and intellectual ability inhered. During World War I, the army hired many top university psychologists to develop and administer intellectual ability scales to military recruits for the purposes of assignment. According to these data, White soldiers were far more intelligent than African-American soldiers, and soldiers of Anglo-Saxon heritage were far more intelligent than eastern and southern Europeans (Brigham, 1923; Yerkes, 1921).

Similar results were found when psychologists administered intelligence tests in public school students. For example, in Terman's work with the schools in Oakland and San Jose, it was discovered that northern Europeans generally scored well, whereas southern Europeans and Latin students showed high levels of mental retardation (Chapman, 1988). The widespread application of intelligence tests as a scientific method of classification produced school tracks that segregated immigrants, minority culture, and working-class students in special programs.

Springing forth within and in conjunction with public schooling were a host of new professions claiming a legitimacy of science, including psychology, social work, psychiatry, and special education. By 1900, scientific ways of viewing social issues and possible solutions had become increasingly popular in the media and the public. The human service professions believed that the problems of poverty and social deviance could be solved by professionals whose practical expertise was based in science (Baritz, 1960; Cremin, 1988; Danforth, 1997).

Working hand in hand with the mental measurement psychologists were the "administrative progressives" (Tyack & Hansot, 1982, p. 105), turn-of-the-century schoolmen who claimed that schools should be run not by local politicians, but by professional leaders who could make decisions through scientific means. Prior to the development of the professional administrator and the science of management, schools answered directly to local political leaders—to mayors, city councils, ward bosses, and so on. This made for a highly politicized way of managing schools. Teachers got jobs through insider favors. Curriculum was created through the battle of disparate social classes, ethnic groups, and political organizations. The new professional administrators said they would pull the schools out of politics by managing them in an objective and unbiased way.

Behind their claims of objectivity and neutrality, the early school administrators were closely linked with the wealthy corporate leaders who served as their advisors and financed the political operations necessary to bring about the switch to the professional management of schools. Many administrators viewed themselves as scientifically reenergizing the traditional educational goal of bringing Protestant values to the poor and immigrant populations. The common value that both the business leaders and the educational administrators gravitated toward was industriousness, the old Protestant work ethic refashioned to meet the personnel needs of factory owners (Cremin, 1988; Tyack & Hansot, 1982).

Psychological measurement provided an apparent degree of certainty in the identification of "mental defectives," while administrative science assured that such students would be placed in classrooms that allowed schools to operate with maximum efficiency and order. In the eyes of the administrative progressives, special education was more than an ethnically based response to immigration and rising enrollments. It was scientific and rational.

Programs and Place: Geography as Curriculum

> We believe that in every community, in every school district and in every graded school there are these children. You teachers know them better than I. There are these children that do not get along, that are taking your time and your attention to an unlimited extent, taking it from other children largely. They are a drag upon you, a drag upon the class, and a drag upon the

school, day after day and year after year; and the State is paying the expense of keeping them in the same class, duplicating the work, and still they don't make progress.

Now we believe that these children must be given that specialized care—in the small special class, that should enable them to attain to that degree of training or education—those things that even the feebleminded can do if they have proper training and have been under proper supervision. (James T. Byers, secretary of the National Committee for Provision of the Feebleminded, 1917; cited in Osgood, 2002, pp. 215–216)

If it were not for the fact that the presence of mentally defective children in the school room interfered with the proper training of the capable children, their education would appeal less powerfully to the boards of education and the tax-paying public. (James Van Sickle, 1979, superintendent of Baltimore Public Schools, 1908-09; cited in Sarason & Doris, p. 263)

There is perhaps no greater demonstration of Rothman's (1980) concept of the Progressive Era tension between "conscience and convenience" than the educational programming and practices developed in the special classes of the public schools. School and professional leaders espoused special classes as a way to provide instruction at a rate and in a manner more suitable for "mental defectives" and other disabled students. At least in part, these curricular reforms emerged from a social conscience committed to educational improvement. This curricular purpose serves as a forerunner to the current emphasis on instruction designed to meet the "special needs" of the individual child. At the same time, however, school leaders consistently articulated the need for special classes as a way of improving instruction in general education classes. By clearing out the weak and disruptive students, schools could become more efficient in the delivery of curriculum to the nondisabled students. The social conscience of addressing the individual needs of the disabled student was conceptually and practically inseparable from the organizational convenience of ability tracking and segregated programs.

The purposes and quality of the curriculum and instruction in early special education classrooms varied greatly. In some cases, these classrooms were clearing houses where students could be screened for possible relocation to institutions and hospitals. In many schools, instruction in special classrooms amounted to a slower, simpler version of the general class curriculum—a combination of "the 3 R's" (reading, writing, arithmetic) and lessons on physical hygiene and cleanliness. Some districts added vocational programs for students who were able to learn industrial or agricultural skills. State "schools for the feebleminded" (as the institutions were commonly named at this point), such as Vineland in New Jersey and Rome in New York, ran summer institutes to prepare teachers for their special education classrooms. Yet most special class teachers had little or no preparation for their work. Districts placed more emphasis on the existence of the special classes than on students' achievement in those classes (Lazerson, 1983; Sarason & Doris, 1979). Overall, it would be difficult not to say that the main focus of early special education programs was on the improved efficiency of general education classrooms left behind after the removal of the difficult students. It was the legitimation of special education as a distinct area of educational specialization that granted the pursuit of this outcome as a basis in professional expertise.

ELABORATING THE *WHAT* OF SPECIAL EDUCATION: BUREAUCRATIZING DISABILITY THROUGH PROGRAMMATIC REGIMENTATION, 1975–2000

If the middle of the 19th century was led by the creation of new *places* for children with disabilities, and the Progressive Era was strongly characterized by a proliferation and empowerment of *professionalization,* then the last quarter of the 20th century—and specifically the changes associated with the implementation of *IDEA*—can be approached as an era where *programmatic* elaboration came to encompass both place and profession in the context of a mandated and expanded system of public special education. As we have emphasized in our discussion of the earlier eras, this characterization does not mean that the threads of professionalism and place did not continue to weave their way through the developments in special education from 1975 to 2000. However, in many ways, the pattern of educational change during these years is dominated by the growth of special education as the *governing system* within which parents, professionals, and children with disabilities have come to define their interactions with each other.

Regardless of the theme of emphasis, however, the last quarter of the 20th century is certainly one of dramatic changes for people with disabilities: the emergence of the disability rights movement (Barnartt & Scotch, 2001; Pelka, 1997); the deinstitutionalization of large numbers of people with psychiatric and cognitive disabilities (Rothman & Rothman, 1988); and the passage of significant antidiscrimination legislation in fields of employment, transportation, and community accessibility (Fleischer & Zames, 2001; Wehman, 1993). For most children with disabilities and their families, however, the single most influential event during this period has to be the passage and implementation of what is now called the *Individuals With Disabilities Education Act* (*IDEA;* Turnbull & Turnbull, 1998). Passed in 1975 and fully implemented by 1978, this law in some ways simply represented a federal recognition and consolidation of changes that had been emerging at the state level and through a number of important court decisions, consent decrees, and model statutes over the previous decade (Crockett &

Kauffman, 1999; Lippman & Goldberg, 1973). However, in many other ways, the law stands as a clear demarcation point for a dramatic new era for special education.

Some accounts of this most recent era in special education have focused on the provision of the new education law for students with disabilities to be educated in the *least restrictive environment*. The interpretation of this phrase has led to an ongoing debate about where along the cascade or continuum of placement options children with disabilities should be educated (Reynolds & Birch, 1977; Taylor, 1988). Indeed in one such review, the placement issue is seen as superseding all others in importance during the last quarter of the 20th century.

> The hottest issue in special education during the 1980s and 1990s was where, not how, students with disabilities should be taught in the schools and classrooms they should attend, not the instruction they should receive. (Crockett & Kauffman, 1999, p. 1)

Although we agree that the discourse around the implications and applications of such terms as *mainstreaming* and, more recently, *inclusion* have generated at least as much heat as light among special educators and family advocates, we would argue that in the long run the era can be viewed more helpfully as one in which the power of the special education system as a whole became institutionalized. So while the discussions over the appropriate *place* for disabled children to receive their education did rage, the truly new context was that the entire range of placements was now the legal responsibility of local and state school districts for the first time. It is in the "post-IDEA" environment that the *placement* of children—whether largely custodial and self-contained or optimistically remedial and inclusive—was permanently located within this continuum of public school services that was supposed to match the educational needs of the child with the least restrictive setting possible. Equally important, we also acknowledge that this last era has also seen the continued growth and specialization of special education as a fully elaborated profession. However, what is truly remarkable is how that professional development has in many ways become the fuel that feeds the ever-growing demands for specialists of the special education system. The *profession* of special education not only became segmented into proliferating subspecializations, but now came to include all types of therapeutic specializations as well as part of mandated, interdisciplinary teams within school systems coordinating the whole array of services and instructional technologies provided to each child. In many ways, the tensions of previous eras were not so much overcome as overwhelmed—subsumed under a bureaucratic umbrella of rules, rights, procedural safeguards, and systemic structures that inevitably shaped what was taught, by and to whom, and where that instruction was to occur.

The Evidence of Expansion

A few indicators of the dimensions of the changes suggest how all encompassing the special education system has become in a fairly short time. Prior to the passage of *IDEA* (originally called the *Education of All Handicapped Children Act or* PL 94-142), most states continued to exclude significant numbers of children from attending public school programs of any kind. In many states, there were provisions of minimum abilities without which a child was deemed unable to benefit from a public education (e.g., one state's "permissive" legislation said that a child could be excluded from public school if he or she was not ambulatory, continent, and able to follow simple directions). More important, those who were served by the public schools were covered by a crazy quilt of different laws, programs, and eligibility criteria across the 50 states. However, with the passage of IDEA, there was a new federal mandate that states must provide a "free appropriate public education" to all children regardless of the type or severity of the disability. If states wanted to continue to receive federal funding, they had to adopt a zero reject policy for children with disabilities up through the age of 21.

By 1979 (1 year after the full implementation of all provisions of IDEA), the federal government reported that almost 4,000,000 (3,919,000) children between the ages of 3 and 21 were being served by the special education system (U.S. Department of Education, 1980). By 2000, that number had grown some 62% to almost 6,254,000 students (U.S. Department of Education, 2001). If one looks at only the 6 to 21 year age range, the percentage of children receiving special education for 2000 has grown to 11.4% of the total school population. Within that general heading, there has been a dramatic shift in terms of the percentage distribution by disability category. So in 1979, less than 30% of the children in special education were said to be learning disabled (LD), with another 31% identified as speech impaired and 23% mentally retarded. By 2000, these percentages showed the dramatic growth in the use of the LD label, with over 50% of the school-age children in special education having this label. Speech impairment actually slipped in percentage to slightly less than 20%, and mental retardation was more than halved to just under 11% (U.S. Department of Education, 2001).

In terms of placement, we see a movement of children into regular class placements. By 2000, almost all children (96%) were educated in regular school buildings, with almost 50% (47.4%) spending most of their time in regular classes.

Three Dimensions: Complicating the Numbers

However, as you break down these aggregate percentages by disability category, the picture shows that most of this movement in placement has occurred among those children identified as having a specific learning or speech disability. The placement patterns for children labeled *mentally re-tarded* have remained largely unchanged for at least the last decade, and the story is similar for other categories of children. Although placement has seemingly been at the forefront of change in special education since 1975, there are several strands or dimensions along which it is clear that, instead of dramatic reform, we have seen the illusion of change in the midst of bu-reaucratic sprawl. It has been a period of history that is described by the his-torian David Fischer (1978) with the label, *involutionary change*, where things become "more elaborately the same" (p. 101). We briefly identify three of these strands of elaborate sameness.

1. *Disproportionality: the displacement of racial segregation into special educa-tional programming.* Although place as a theme in special education has moved within the context of the public school system, the demarcations within that context continue to play out the social tensions of whether chil-dren should be taught together or separately. Indeed the impetus to move children with disabilities into more inclusive settings and give them access to the general curriculum that exclusion had previously denied them has inevitably invested the remaining self-contained placements with at least a tinge of the educational failure that came to characterize the institutional placements of earlier eras.

This is most clearly seen when one uses the lens of race and ethnicity to look at the pattern of special education placement. The overlap of racism and ableism has been a constant within U.S. history (e.g., Gould, 1996). Al-though there has been some progress in the last 25 years in the statistics of overrepresentation, the disparity remains troublingly large. A recent study noted the persistence:

> After more than twenty years [of tracking by the federal government], black children constitute 17 percent of the total school enrollment and 33 percent of those labeled mentally retarded. . . . During this same period, however, disproportionality in the area of emotional disturbance (ED) and the rate of identification for both ED and specific learning disaabilities (SLD) grew sig-nificantly for blacks. (Losen & Orfield, 2002, p. xvi)

Not only are African-American students disproportionately labeled for spe-cial education services, but, once receiving those labels, also spend dispro-portionately more time in more segregated settings than students from any other racial category. According to the most recent federal data available, while over half of the White students in special education spend most of their time in regular class settings (defined as 80% or more of the school day), that percentage drops to 34.8% for African-American students (U.S. Department of Education 2001).

2. *The apparent conflict of professionalism and inclusion: untrained in special, but also uncertified in the classroom.* Professionalism in special education also continues to play out the assumptions noticed most clearly emerging in the Progressive Era. As with issues of place, these issues of professionalism now occur within the context of *IDEA* and its call for inclusive programs whenever appropriate. Faced with the prospect of having children with disabilities included in their classrooms, general education teachers reflect their own preparation by complaining that they have not been professionally trained to educate such children. From this perspective, it is not only difficult to manage children with disabilities in general education classrooms, it is simply unprofessional. The cult of expertise inherited from the Progressives defines *educational professionalism*, in part, as the possession of a specialized knowledge particularly suited to teach specific types of children.

> This strand of resistance to inclusion as unprofessional can be seen in the words of a set of teachers from different eras. In a survey from 1913, general education teachers opposed what we now call inclusion as distracting her from what she was trained to teach: "The teacher's time is wasted in maintaining discipline with the defective." . . . "Mingling the backward with normals is a drag on everybody." (A. Johnson, 1913, pp. 100, 101)

Some 66 years later, faced with the "least restrictive environment" clause of *IDEA,* an elementary teacher made much the same complaint: "I hear rumors about these changes. Someone in the building told me I would be responsible for language arts for all the handicapped kids. I said, 'You've got to be kidding! I'm not trained for that'" (U.S. Dept. of Education, 1980, p. 48).

This mixed message of professionalism as specialized expertise and inclusion as preferred educational policy is compounded by this classroom reality: Huge numbers of those providing the instruction in special education are not certified as professionals in that field. According to the *23rd Annual Report to Congress on the Implementation of the Individuals with Disabilities Education Act* (U.S. Department of Education, 2001), the national shortage has produced a situation where over 10%—or almost 40,000 teachers—of those employed to provide special education services to students with disabilities were not certified in any area of special education. Indeed in many cases, the instructors had no teacher certification of any kind. The situation is often worse in the most rural and urban districts. In the city of St. Louis, a reasonably typical example, there are some 6,500 students identified as eligible for special education and some 850 special education teaching positions. In its most recent announcements, the district reports that some 135 of these positions are filled by individuals with "emergency" teaching certifications (Missouri Department of Elementary and Secondary Education,

2002). This means that 34% of the special education teaching positions in this urban district are filled by officially unqualified persons. One recent study found that, as of October 1, 1999, there were over 12,000 special education positions left vacant or filled by a substitute. The same study found that another 33,000 special education teachers were categorized as not fully certified for their main teaching assignment (Carlson, Brauen, Klein, Schroll, & Willig, 2002). The message to the parent and the child with a disability, then, is an educational Catch-22: You cannot have access to inclusive programs because you need specialized professionals for your instruction, but you may not have access to this specialized instruction because of the shortage of certified teachers.

3. *The imposition of the IEP: the individualistic bias in the planning process.* At the center of the programmatic dominance of the special education *system* over the last 25 years is the document demanded by *IDEA* to be in place and updated annually for every child with a disability: the Individualized Education Plan (IEP). It is through the process that produces the IEP (as well as the document) that all of the key elements of special education programming as we know it today are demonstrated: categorical definitions, family involvement, least restrictive placement, measurable objectives, ancillary supports, therapeutic services, and so on. The IEP process has been instrumental in establishing a standard of accountability and individualized curriculum design that have undeniably benefited the quality of instruction received by a generation of students with disabilities. It is through the IEP and its due process features that parent advocates have been able to negotiate with school systems from a position of strength (at least in principle) and identified rights.

However, in its ubiquity, the IEP process has also obscured for many years the programmatic individualism that it has in essence required of teachers and administrators. It is ironically through this programmatic individualism that the *system* of special education has come to dominate the era and resist the structural reforms that some have promoted. A partial list of the ways in which this individualism plays out in the programmatic decisions for children would include the following:

- The IEP often drives families and educators to think of inclusive placements as something to be accomplished one child at a time, without disturbing the larger control of the special education bureaucracy.
- The IEP context tends to push a diagnostic/prescriptive paradigm based on a "defect" of "medical" model of disability.
- The IEP demands a continued reliance on behavioral objectives that have the appearance of individualized learning goals while substantively endorsing a programmatic bias in how we choose curricular goals and design

instructional methods. Instead of beginning by asking how can we help this student access the general education curriculum, the IEP structure encourages us to ask, "How can we fix what's wrong with the child?"

• Finally, the IEP fosters an overreliance on specialized discourse that effectively denies effective participation in the planning by general education teachers.

We are left with a situation where the system of special education has swallowed whole the debates and dilemmas of previous eras without resolution of the underlying tensions that originally produced them. The tensions of where children with disabilities should be educated (place) and by whom (professionalism) have been, in a sense, superficially trivialized by the terms with which the special education system requires those tensions to be discussed. The tensions are real and fundamental, but remain trapped and obscured within a programmatic bureaucracy that distorts the debate.

CONCLUSION: RECONCILING THE TENSIONS

Our intention in the preceding discussion was to illustrate the historical progression of, and exchanges between, the three recurring themes of place, profession, and programs within the context of the American special education system. That the tensions surrounding student placement, professional roles, and programs persist today in assorted ways is not in doubt. Rather, the question that remains is, "Where do we go from here?" Perhaps the most obvious answer to this question would be to eradicate the tensions created by the interactions of our three threads. However, the history of special education reform is one of change that is often illusory and superficial and still arises under (and is limited by) the watchful eye of the governing structure that drives the profession. Within this context, the tensions surrounding place, profession, and programs tend to be static and, at times, destructive.

The special education system has been—and continues to be—compelled by an overarching philosophy of programmatic individualism. This philosophy narrows and constricts the focus of potential reforms by placing them in a milieu where they are void of connections to the larger social world. Caught in the social vacuum of programmatic individualism and the "cult of expertise" that drives it, special education has marginalized and isolated itself from the greater arenas of education and society.

So how can we address these issues? We have room for only the sketchiest of responses to this crucial question. Instead of attempting to eliminate the tensions, we suggest a different approach. We do not advocate dissolution of tensions (or the governing system that produces them) because this would amount to what Marcuse (1964) referred to as the "grand unification of opposites" (p. 225)—a situation that tends to stifle the possibility of qualitative change. Eliminating the tensions, if possible in the first place, would not result in a scenario more receptive to reform. In our opinion, the key is to further illuminate the fundamental nature of existing tensions and facilitate a shift from static and destructive toward dynamic and less antagonistic. To accomplish this, we must first create spaces for discourse within the governing system of special education *and* the larger framework of school and social reform. Inside these discourse spaces, the destructive tendencies of the tensions could be more carefully understood.

In practical terms, that probably means moving further toward the unification of special education and general education at the "central office" level of district administration. It means that conversations about school restructuring, curricular reform, authentic assessment, and accountability for student achievement need to incorporate those who are familiar with students with disabilities—not as an adjunct to the larger conversation, but as an organic part of the conversation about helping diverse learners succeed in the classroom. It probably also means that students with disabilities, their families, and their advocates need to develop a better vocabulary for talking about the need for specific techniques and supports without isolating through language what is being integrated in practice. Individualizing education to meet student needs does not have to be covered by a specialized jargon that only specific professionals understand.

Finally, reform must not be initiated primarily from the individual level. Because the programmatic elements of the special education system have subsumed all other aspects of that system, the more appropriate center would be at the macro level, where there is a transformation from an individual focus to a vision of systematic reform at the convergence of social, school, and disability agendas. Just as we would want disability viewed in terms of diversity, special education should be considered as just one of many players within the arena of whole school reform, not as an isolated entity that utilizes its history of professional expertise as the vehicle for segregation from the larger community. Such a challenge is immense, but nothing less will adequately engage the tensions inherent in the place, professionalism, and programs that surround the education of children with disabilities.

REFERENCES

Addams, J. (1910). *Twenty years at Hull-House: With autobiographical notes.* New York: Macmillan.
Addams, J. (1972) *The spirit of youth and the city streets.* Urbana, IL: University of Illinois Press.
Ball, T. S. (1971). *Itard, Seguin, and Kephart: Sensory education—a learning interpretation.* Columbus, OH: Merrill.

Baritz, L. (1960). *The servants of power: A history of the use of social science in American industry.* Middletown, CT: Wesleyan University Press.

Barnartt, S., & Scotch, R. (2001). *Disability protests: Contentious politics, 1970–1999.* Washington, DC: Gallaudet University Press.

Brigham, C. C. (1923). *A study of American intelligence.* Princeton, NJ: Princeton University Press.

Carlson, E., Brauen, M., Klein, S., Schroll, K., & Willig, S. (2002, July). *Study of personnel needs in special education: Key findings.* Rockville, MD: WESTAT.

Chapman, P. D. (1988). *Schools as sorters: Lewis M. Terman, applied psychology, and the intelligence testing movement, 1890–1930.* New York: New York University Press.

Cremlin, L. (1961). *The transformation of the school: Progressivism in American education, 1876–1957.* New York: Knopf.

Cremin, L. A. (1988). *American education, the metropolitan experience, 1876–1980.* New York: Harper & Row.

Crockett, J. B., & Kauffman, J. M. (1999). *The least restrictive environment: Its origins and interpretations in special education.* Mahwah, NJ: Lawrence Erlbaum Associates.

Cubberly, E. P. (1919). *Public education in the United States: A study and interpretation of American educational history; an introductory textbook dealing with the larger problems of present-day education in the light of their historical development.* New York: Houghton-Mifflin.

Danforth, S. (1997). On what basis hope? Modern progress and postmodern possibilities. *Mental Retardation, 35,* 93–106.

Digby, A. (1985). *Madness, morality and medicine: A study of the York Retreat, 1796–1914.* New York: Cambridge University Press.

Dowbiggin, I. R. (1991). *Inheriting madness: Professionalization and psychiatric knowledge in 19th century France.* Berkeley: University of California Press.

Fischer, D. H. (1978). *Growing old in America: The Bland-Lee lectures delivered at Clark University.* New York: Oxford University Press.

Fleischer, D. Z., & Zames, F. (2001). *The disability rights movement: From charity to confrontation.* Philadelphia: Temple University Press.

Gitter, E. (2001). *The imprisoned guest: Samuel Howe and Laura Bridgman, the original deaf-blind girl.* New York: Farrar, Straus & Giroux.

Goodson, I. F., & Dowbiggin, I. R. (1997). Docile bodies: Commonalities in the history of psychiatry and schooling. In I. F. Goodson (Ed.), *The changing curriculum: Studies in social construction* (pp. 83–112). New York: P. Lang.

Gould, S. J. (1996). *The mismeasure of man* (rev. ed.). New York: Norton.

Howe, S. G. (1993). "The causes of idiocy" with an introduction by Edgar Miller. *History of Psychiatry, 4,* 587–603. (Original publication 1858)

Itard, J.-M. G. (1962). *The Wild Boy of Aveyron* (G. Humphrey & M. Humphrey, Trans.). New York: Appleton-Century-Crofts. (Original publication in 1801/1806)

Johnson, A. (1913). Backward children and forward teachers: A symposium. *The Training School Bulletin, 10*(7), 97–104.

Katz, M. B. (1996). *In the shadow of the poorhouse: A social history of welfare in America.* New York: Basic Books.

Lane, H. (1976). *The Wild Boy of Aveyron.* Cambridge, MA: Harvard University Press.

Lazerson, M. (1983). The origins of special education. In J. G. Chambers & W. T. Hartman (Eds.), *Special education policies: Their history, implementation, and finance* (pp. 15–47). Philadelphia: Temple University Press.

Lippman, L., & Goldberg, I. I. (1973). *Right to education: Anatomy of the Pennsylvania case and its implications for exceptional children.* New York: Teachers College Press.

Locke, J. (1975). *An essay concerning human understanding.* New York: Oxford University Press.

Losen, D. J., & Orfield, G. (2002). Introduction: Racial inequity in special education. In D. J. Losen & G. Orfield (Eds.), *Racial inequity in special education* (pp. xv–xxxvii). Boston: Harvard Education Press.

Marcuse, H. (1964). *One-dimensional man.* Boston: Beacon.

Menand, L. III (2001). *The metaphysical club.* New York: Penguin Books.

Missouri Department of Elementary and Secondary Education. (2002). *Missouri Special Education Self-Assessment.* Jefferson City, MO: Author.

Osgood, R. L. (2002) From "public liabilities" to "public assets": Special education for children with mental retardation in Indiana public schools, 1908–1931. *Indiana Magazine of History, 98,* 203–225.

Pelka, F. (1997). *The ABC-CLIO companion to the disability rights movement.* Santa Barbara, CA: ABC-CLIO.

Reynolds, M. C., & Birch, J. (1977). *Teaching exceptional children in all America's schools.* Reston, VA: Council for Exceptional Children.

Richardson, J. G. (1999). *Common, delinquent, and special: The institutional shape of special education.* New York: Falmer.

Rothman, D. J. (1971). *The discovery of the asylum: Social order and disorder in the New Republic.* Boston: Little, Brown.

Rothman, D. J. (1980). *Conscience and convenience: The asylum and its alternatives in progressive America.* Boston: Little, Brown.

Rothman, D. J., & Rothman, S. M. (1988). *The Willowbrook wars: A decade of struggle for social justice.* New York: Harper & Row.

Sarason, S. B., & Doris, J. (1979) *Educational handicap, public policy, and social history: A broadened perspective on mental retardation.* New York: The Free Press.

Seguin, E. (1866). *Idiocy and its treatment by the physiological method* (rev. by E. C. Seguin). New York: W. Wood.

Shattuck, R. (1980). *The forbidden experiment: The story of the Wild Boy of Aveyron.* New York: Farrar, Straus & Giroux.

Shorter, E. (1997). *A history of psychiatry: From the era of the asylum to the age of Prozac.* New York: Wiley.

Sutton, J. R. (1988). *Stubborn children: Controlling delinquency in the United Statese, 1640–1981.* Berkeley: University of California Press.

Taylor, S. J. (1988). Caught in the continuum: A critical analysis of the principle of the least restrictive environment. *The Journal of the Association for Persons with Severe Handicaps, 13,* 41–53.

Trent, J. W. (1994). *Inventing the feeble mind: A history of mental retardation in the United States.* Berkeley, CA: University of California Press.

Turnbull, H. R. III, & Turnbull, A. P. (1998). *Free appropriate public education: The law and children with disabilities* (5th ed.). Denver: Love.

Tyack, D., & Hansot, E. (1982). *Managers of virtue: Public school leadership in America, 1820–1980.* New York: Basic Books.

U.S. Department of Education. (1980). *2nd annual report to Congress on the implementation of the Education of All Handicapped Children Act.* Washington, DC: Author.

U.S. Department of Education. (2001). *23rd annual report to Congress on the implementation of the Individuals with Disabilities Education Act.* Washington, DC: Author.

Wehman, P. (1993). *The ADA mandate for social change.* Baltimore: Paul Brookes.

Winzer, M. A. (1993). *The history of special education.* Washington, DC: Gallaudet University Press.

Yerkes, R. (1921). *Psychological examining in the United States Army.* Washington, DC: Government Printing Office.

Chapter 2

Failing to Make Progress?
The Aporias of Responsible Inclusion

Julie Allan
University of Stirling, Scotland

Dear Mr Blair,

We are a group of disabled and nondisabled young people and supporters who believe we should all have the right to go to our local mainstream school. We feel that children in special schools miss out on a decent academic and social education and those in mainstream schools, who hardly ever see disabled people, miss out on the opportunity to learn about and appreciate differences, rather than only seeing disabled people through the patronizing view of the media.

We feel we deserve each other's friendship and that the segregated education system denies us the chance to be together and see each other for what we really are. We are asking you to put an end to compulsory segregation by changing the law. We want to be together!

Yours sincerely, the Young People of Great Britain, c/o Young and Powerful. (Shaw, 2002)

Progress toward inclusion has either been celebrated (Lipsky & Gartner, 1997; Mittler, 2000) or seen as something that we are taking steps toward (Ainscow, 2000; Berres et al., 1996). Some have claimed to have found the "essential ingredients for successful reform" (Kugelmass, 2001, p. 1) or to have pinpointed the characteristics of inclusive schools (Rose, 2001). Although it is claimed that we are "not yet there," we speak as if we know where the *there* of inclusion is (Slee & Allan, 2001). There is little evidence, however, to suggest that inclusion has made much of an impact on the lives of young people and their families, and there is little idea about what *good* (as opposed to effective) inclusion might look like. Frustration with the fal-

27

tering rate of progress toward full inclusion has prompted the authors of the earlier letter to proclaim, simply, "We want to be together." Much of the failure to make progress with inclusion has been recognized as lying with the continued malevolent influence of a special needs paradigm, with its medical and charity discourses, and which engenders deficit oriented practices (Allan, 1999; Fulcher, 1989). The scientific basis of special education knowledge has been questioned (Gallagher, 1998), and the work of disabled writers (e.g., Barnes, 1996; Oliver, 1996) has been crucial in helping us escape from the epistemological hole of "special needs" knowledge. In particular, the social model of disability, which separates the individuals' impairment from disabling barriers within the environment, structures, and attitudes of institutions, has been important in helping educators understand the kinds of exclusionary pressures that have to be removed. There has been some frustration, however, that the social model of disability has not had a significant impact on the inclusion agenda, either in teaching or research (French, 1994; Oliver, 1999). Furthermore, there remains an "astonishing lack of reflexivity by special education researchers and an appalling ignorance of the scope of inclusive education" (Slee, 2001a, p. 121). Although Slee's criticism is directed at the special education researchers within the United States, this could be leveled more widely at educationists who have failed to respond to the inclusion imperative.

In this chapter, I offer some reflections on what has impeded progress toward inclusiveness, and I explore the destructive features in some detail. I then offer some speculations on what it will take to be inclusive. This is intended neither as a definitive analysis of where we have gone wrong nor as a template for change. Rather it is offered as a means to disrupt the complacency with which we continue to mythologize progress toward inclusion and as a stimulus for further debate along these lines.

DESTRUCTIVE PRACTICE: WHAT GETS IN THE WAY?

Much of what takes place in schools at present is destructive and exclusionary, leading Slee (1996) to question the assumption that "regular school provides an education worth being included into" (p. 110). Identifying the elements of knowledge and practice that speak against, and ultimately destroy, inclusive possibilities represents a major step toward becoming inclusive.

THE TEACHER TRAINING AND SKILLS ACQUISITION IMPERATIVE

Inclusive education now forms part of the curriculum in most teacher education programs, either replacing "special needs" provision or coexisting uneasily with it. According to Slee (2001b), inclusive education has been adopted enthusiastically by special educators because it has enabled them to continue their practices from a publicly acceptable base and to convert the student teacher into a "card carrying designator of disability" (p. 171). Gender, ethnicity, and social class are rarely acknowledged as arenas of exclusion within teacher education. Instead these are silenced within establishments that are race blind (Almeida Diniz & Usmani, 2001) by individuals who cannot handle multiple oppressions and who are intent on equipping new teachers (only) with skills. This "teacher-training imperative," as it is presently configured, is far from inclusive, and so student teachers have few examples to draw on. Furthermore, the policies that drive Teacher Education Establishments (TEIs) and the universities in which many of them are housed espouse values of inclusivity and participation while actively discouraging these in practice.

New teachers are required to rehearse the "official scripts" (Smyth & Hattam, 2002, p. 392), which are "dominant and restrictive" and emphasize "the physical control of students' bodies . . . that is their movements, whereabouts and silence" (Gutierrez et al., 1995, p. 413). The "conservative incrementalism" (Slee, 2001b, p. 173) within teacher training, which involves transmitting regulated chunks of traditional special education knowledge to student teachers, enables professionals to retain their authority and ensures that classroom teachers can chant the "mantras for those constructed as other" (Evans, 2002, p. 35) and "are not so spooked" (Slee, 2001b, p. 173) when they enter their classrooms. The message received by new teachers, however, is that they can never know enough about students' pathologies to be able to deal effectively with them. Thus, they come to regard their responsibilities toward disabled students with guilt, fear, and the sense they will inevitably let them down.

THE WILL TO CERTAINTY

The quest for certainty within education generally creates closure in practices and profound injustices for particular individuals. Derrida (1997) suggested that injustice is a product of the pressure to reach a just decision, and the instant when this occurs is a "madness" (Derrida, 1990, p. 967). Furthermore, he argued, the certainty with which recommendations (e.g., about what constitutes good practice) need to be made allows for the evasion of responsibility. This irresponsibility extends to the kind of guarantees and assurances (of quality, value added, or enhancement) required within education, which Derrida (2001a) claimed set up an inertia from which it is impossible to break away:

> Any presumption of guarantee and of non-contradiction in so paroxystic a situation . . . is an optimistic gesticulation, an act of good conscience and irre-

sponsibility, and therefore indecision and profound inactivity under the guise of activism. (p. 71)

Proponents of the school effectiveness and school improvement movements, in what amounts to little more than a leap of faith, announce that the way forward is certain:

> The challenge for education policy is clear. Now we know what makes a good school, a good department and a good teacher, how do we create the conditions which will make it happen in every school and classroom in the country? (Barber, 1997, p. 17)

The task is viewed here as merely one of dissemination and *roll out,* and there is no acknowledgment of the "series of interlocking constraints" (Gillborn & Youdell, 2000, p. 33) that is experienced by schools, teachers, and pupils. To grasp the problems created by this will to certainty, we need to understand the role of misunderstanding (Biesta, 2001) within educational processes and allow much of what we think we know to be unraveled.

THE "TYRANNY OF TRANSPARENCY"

Education policies, including policies of inclusion, operate within a regime of accountability that is inefficient, ineffective, and socially unjust (Salter & Tapper, 2000; Vidovitch & Slee, 2001). Warnings have been sounded that if accountability frameworks are not problematized, they could become the "midwives of globalization . . . which deliver market ideologies uncritically around the globe" (Blackmore; cited in Vidovitch & Slee, 2001, p. 451), but these appear to have gone unheeded. Much of the problem lies with the emphasis on proving rather than improving, and these performative frameworks create an imperative for fabrication by those under scrutiny (Ball, 2000).

The quest for indicators and outcomes within the quality assurance genre has extended to inclusion. However, the views of disabled youngsters and their parents regarding what the desirable consequences of inclusion should be have been disregarded. Consequently, institutions have been forced to search for "inclusivity indicators" (Nunan et al., 2000, p. 75), which reduce inclusion to a contrived cultural performance by professionals. These symbolic displays of values required of new teachers—for example, that they should "recognise the cultural and social embeddedness of problems with respect to both their conceptualization and solution" (p. 80)—surely cannot be taken as evidence of their existence. Alternatively, attempts have been made to produce indicators that specify increases in the numbers of children present in mainstream schools (Department for Education and Employment, 1997) or even a reduction in the number of children formally assessed as having special educational needs (Scottish Executive, 1999). These are quite simply inept.

DISABLING RESEARCH

According to Oliver (1999), disability research is characterized by two main approaches, both of them problematic and exclusionary. Oliver labeled the first of these the *emancipatory approach*, whereby researchers seek to obtain "faithful accounts of individual experience" (p. 186) and assume that this is enough. According to Oliver, it leaves us without "the faintest idea of how to produce collective accounts of collective experience" (p. 186). It also presents the ethical question of who is entitled to appropriate individuals' experiences. Oliver pondered over whether disability researchers "are *shitting* disabled people when they write about experiences that they have no access to save through their own research techniques" (p. 187; italics original), but considered the researcher's positioning in the relations of research production, rather than the presence or absence of an impairment, to be a crucial factor in determining the answer to this question. A more significant problem with experiential research is that standpoint epistemology is merely assumed without a more concrete connection to a politics of action or praxis (Denzin, 1997). Oliver said this is unsurprising from a research paradigm, which privileges investigation over emancipation.

The second, equally problematic, approach is participative research. This involves sharing the responsibility for research with disabled people, but in a closely circumscribed way and "short of overall control over resources and agendas" (Oliver, 1999, p. 187). This tokenistic involvement of disabled people does not enable oppression to be tackled. Worse still, it often contributes to oppression by the way disabled people are positioned within the relations of research production.

Oliver argued that both experiential and participative research approaches have been ineffective and, in many cases, disabling; he called for a new epistemology for research praxis, which relocates the existing discourses of disability research with an emancipatory discourse. This requires the relations of research production to be scrutinized in terms of their disabling potential. Such reified calls to change the discourses is bound to have little impact on researchers already resistant to change and who may welcome the deflected focus on the discourses, rather than on them, the speakers of the discourses. Nevertheless, Oliver's accumulated pain needs to be felt and reacted to.

The role of nondisabled people in research has been a key issue, which has at times descended into a *them and us*—oppressed and oppressors—dichotomy (Barnes, 1992; Davis, 2000). Connolly (1996) attempted to break into this disabled/nondisabled binarism by arguing that the characteristics of who does the research are less important than who they are reflexively, what kind of research they are doing, and why. Walmsley (2001) took a similar line, identifying the problem as lying not so much in who does the research, but in the way the normalization imperative permeates research. This takes the form of types of participation, a focus on service quality and outcomes, the use of normalization ideas as an evaluative yardstick, and an advocacy model that emphasizes attitudinal change and positive imagery. Clear (1999) suggested that so-called *normal* research regulates and disciplines the process and conceals important knowledge. Shakespeare (1993) also attempted to dismantle the oppressed/oppressor dualism by exploring the possibilities for participatory research and establishing a multifaceted oppression matrix.

The oppressed/oppressors dichotomy has been resurrected by Branfield (1998), who questioned whether nondisabled people should be researching disabled people's lives at all. Kitchen's (2000) study of the researched opinions on research concluded that there was a need for both inclusive action-based research involving disabled people as consultants and an exclusive approach in which only disabled people participated. Humphrey (2000), working first as a nondisabled researcher and then as one who subsequently chose to self-disclose as disabled, reported how she was cast by those she was attempting to research as an outsider-cum-oppressor. Her disclosure was viewed with hostility as a form of retrospective accounting to gain privileged access to disabled people—a reaction she found distressing. It also made her critical of how Oliver's messages about nondisabled people's involvement in research leaves them in limbo because it is so ambiguous. She suggested that the nondisabled researcher "has become a kind of trope . . . a symbol of all that is wrong with the disabling society" (p. 80).

The debate on disability research has also centered on the use of a social model developed by disabled people as a means to identify (with a view to removing) disabling barriers that exist within institutions and practices. What is at stake is the extent to which individuals' impairments can be taken into account. On the one hand, it has been argued that acknowledgments of impairments interfere with the process of tackling oppression (French, 1993). On the other hand, it is contended that a social model needs to become more sophisticated if it is to be relevant to the lives of disabled people (Paterson & Hughes, 1999) or at least used more reflexively (Corker, 1999). Humphrey's (2000) experience of working with the social model in research with Unison reveals how it privileges certain impaired identities over others, sanctions a separatist ghetto, and weaves a tangled web around researchers who adhere to the emancipatory paradigm.

WHAT WILL IT TAKE TO BE INCLUSIVE?

As Slee (2001b) reminded us, inclusion starts with ourselves. This means facing up to our own responsibilities as members of an exclusionary and disabling system, as part of its past, and as producers of its future. If we allow ourselves to talk, at a distance, about systemic changes, we risk displacing our own responsibilities and avoid asking ourselves this fundamental question: "What does it mean to create a just classroom" (Edgoose, 2001, p. 119).

GETTING BACK TO POLITICS AND IDEOLOGY

As Gewirtz (2000) contended, there is a need to bring politics back into the educational policy debate. This requires us to "foreground the struggles between competing interest groups over key concepts such as accountability, performance indicators and quality" (Vidovitch & Slee, 2001, pp. 450–451). We need to be vigilant and to "fight against accumulation, concentration and monopoly; in short, against all quantitative phenomena that might marginalize or reduce to silence anything that cannot be measured on their scale" (Derrida, 1992, p. 99). Schools have to be recognized as "spaces of regulated confrontation" (Bordieu, 1991, p. 384), and we need to begin to subvert the power imbalances that exist within them. Education systems are "busy institutions" (Connell, 1993, p. 27), in which much effort is expended on the production of social hierarchies and inequalities. As Gillborn and Youdell (2000) contended, "it is high time this level of activity was refocused toward the achievement of social justice" (p. 222).

There is, of course, no shortage of debate over inclusion. Within the United States, the debate over full inclusion versus traditional special education continues to rage on, with each camp "arguing past each other" (Gallagher, 2001, p. 638) and using ideology as a weapon with which to construct and berate those holding opposing views (Brantlinger, 1997). Dyson (2001) noted that the "inclusion backlash" (p. 26) has been gathering pace in the UK, although he suggested that nostalgia seems to drive some of the arguments and that Garner and Gains' (2000) call for responsible inclusion seems to be little more than a yearning for a return to integration. The negative and often aggressive nature of the debate inevitably limits its possibilities for dialogue and change. As Gallagher (2001) observed, there is something of an impasse between the empiricists, who champion a neutral and scientific resolution to the debate and those for whom inclusion is a "struggle of conscience through free, open and informed moral discourse" (p. 651). This is unproductive politics in which the opposing sides will inevitably beg to differ.

A more successful engagement with politics has been made by Roger Slee, who found himself at the center of politics and policy, seconded as Deputy Director General within the Queensland Government. He made the observation that critique as an outsider was an easier and more straightforward task than policy reconstruction. Nevertheless, from his position as an insider/outsider, he was able to ask some difficult questions of his ministerial and administrative colleagues and, on one memorable occasion, was heard saying, "Minister, with respect, I think you are asking the wrong question." He was given advice by seasoned officials that *inclusive education* was an inappropriate nomenclature because of its unsuccessful history in Queensland, but he pointed out that other principles such as democracy and equity have had troubled histories and needed a redoubling of effort rather than abandonment. During his time in Education Queensland, Slee (2003) "insisted on inclusive education as [their] organising language and closed the special needs chapter" (p. 214). He also inserted the "politics of recognition" (p. 216) into the debate on inclusion, which he contended, "has to be the point of embarkation for a new deal for disabled students, their families and advocates in Queensland" (p. 216).

THE ETHICS OF THE ENCOUNTER

Policy documents regularly contain enjoinders to listen to the voices of children and their parents. A real danger exists, however, in succumbing to a kind of *voice fetishism,* in which the concentration of effort is on listening to the voices of children and their parents without actually engaging with them or with what has been said. In this way, having regard for the other functions only as a form of symbolic representation and is a significant barrier to inclusion. The Western obsession with the other has had a silencing effect, turning it into "an object of enquiry, a surrogate fetish, and mirror for the West's desires and imperialist need for frontiers" (Gregoriou, 2001, p. 136). One consequence of this is that valuing diversity is "on its way to becoming a cliché: nothing but a euphemism for the enduring reproduction of oppressive social relations and consequent material inequalities" (Benjamin, 2002, p. 310).

Following Levinas (1998), teachers have to contend with the ethics of their encounter with the other. The key question facing them is how they engage with the marginalized or silenced other without trying to assimilate or acculturate that other (Levinas, 1998; Moss & Petrie, 2002). This relationship is characterized by an "infinitude of responsibility . . . with regard to the other" (Derrida, 1996, p. 86)—a concern to prevent injustice that is without limits. Concerns about speaking for the other have perhaps gone too far, according to Alcoff (1991–1992), who reminded us that a retreat from speaking for others does not necessarily lead to more receptive listening and may indeed lead to a relinquishing of responsibility for others.

Gregoriou (2001) asked two pedagogical questions, which could be useful for teachers to engage with. First of all, how do we, as "pupal [as in developing] and forgetful learners, listen to others' narratives?" (p. 134). Secondly, how do we, as teachers, "become messengers, to ventriloquize, transfer and recite others' narratives in the context of our classrooms?" (p. 134). Pratt (1992) suggested that we might usefully think about "contact zones" (p. 4) as spaces of engagement with the other. These are:

> Social spaces where disparate cultures meet, clash and grapple with each other, often in highly asymmetrical relations of domination and subordination . . . the spatial and temporal copresence of subjects. (pp. 4–7)

These relations among individuals can be treated as spaces in which trading of modes of representation and the negotiation of self-representation can take place. Gregoriou (2001) emphasized the disruptive nature of this space of contestation:

> Trading and engaging in each other's idioms leaves neither the metropolis's nor the periphery's modes of representation untouched. Rather, it corrupts, distorts and hybridizes both of them. (p. 139)

Gregoriou, drawing on Plato's *Timaeus*, suggested that teachers may become displaced receptacles for others' narratives, acting as traveling mediators or sophists. This requires cultivation of teachers—not through self-reflective critique, tolerance of, or respect for difference, but through an invitation to inhabit new spaces:

> It is a place we *create* when in hosting others we change, hybridize our discourses and identities, and let others teach us, from the beginning, how we are different and multiple *within ourselves*. (p. 146; italics original)

A more succinct rendering of the necessary changes was provided by a teacher who suggested that the teacher had to shift from being the "sage on the stage" to being the "guide on the side."

DOING DISABILITY STUDIES

A number of academics have called for a humanities-based disability studies (Bérubé, 1996; Gabel, 2001; Linton, 1998; Ware, 2001) to be integrated within academic programs of study, providing the "means to hold academics accountable for the veracity and social consequences of their work"

(Linton, 1998, pp. 1–2). However, Barnes (1999) has been highly critical of the way in which U.S. scholars have attempted to reinvent disability studies, which, as he pointed out, has a history within the United Kingdom stretching back to the 1960s. He also questioned the move to locate disability studies in the arts and humanities. He saw this as deeply misguided and unscholarly, arguing that the U.S. writers must look at what has gone before rather than "continually attempt to rewrite history according to their own particular view of the world" (p. 580). Yet those promoting a humanities-based approach advocate, above all, an integration into universities' disciplines and curricula of the sort that has never been achieved on either side of the Atlantic. Linton (1998) contended that what is needed is:

> a broad-based epistemology of inclusion, a knowledge base grounded in the liberal arts that provides the tools that academics and civilians need to make critical social, intellectual and professional changes. (p. 81)

Rather than argue about who got there first, it makes sense to harness all efforts toward this goal and achieve the not insurmountable challenge of insinuating disability studies into academic disciplines. As Ware (2001) contended, "disability is a long overdue conversation among critical theorists, pedagogues, and educationalists, who fail to recognize disability as a cultural signifier . . . [and] as a meaningful category of oppression" (p. 112). Peters (1999) went further to call for educators to break the "culture of silence" (p. 115) that surrounds disability and to begin the task of critical conscientization of themselves and others. Whatever shape or form disability studies take, it needs to be put to use productively to guide schools' reform.

There may need to be a reconsideration of what counts as research so that activities such as disability arts and personal narratives can be used to enable teachers to see the point of change. Bowker (1993) suggested that the age of biography is upon us, and Goodley (2001) contended that stories of impairment can precipitate reform. The power of narrative to generate change lies in its capacity to highlight the storied nature of knowledge and to problematize it as historically and socially contingent (Munro, 1998). It may be difficult for work of this kind to encroach on a highly rigid education system that seems impervious to challenges of any kind, but it is incumbent on academics to promote such accounts. As Linton (1998) pointed out:

> New scholars of all stripes must recognize their moral and intellectual obligation to evaluate gaps and faults in the knowledge base they disseminate to students that result from the missing voices of disabled people. (p. 142)

Disability studies could provoke teacher educators to scrutinize the way in which knowledge about special education disables. It could also invite teacher educators to ask, "What kind of knowledge do we want our teachers to have?" (Linton, 1998, p. 169), and to ensure that student teachers are exposed to this knowledge and helped to examine it critically.

RECONFIGURING RESEARCH: DECONSTRUCTING FOR JUSTICE

Deconstruction has tended not to be associated with inclusion and social justice and has more commonly been dismissed as "wild nonsense and irresponsible play" (Caputo, 1997, p. 36). A closer look at deconstruction as a research tool, however, suggests that it offers not a theory or philosophy to be applied to disability, but a chance to think "again and afresh" (Biesta, 2001, p. 34). Derrida (1997) saw deconstruction as inextricably linked with justice, but paradoxically the very possibility of justice is sustained by its impossibility:

> Justice, if it has to do with the other . . . is always incalculable. . . . Once you relate to the other as the other, then something incalculable comes on the scene, something which cannot be reduced to the law or to the history of legal structures. This is what gives deconstruction its movement. (pp. 17–18)

In this sense, deconstruction operates as a form of "hyper-politicization" (Derrida, 1996, p. 85), allowing us to think its "possibility from another border" (p. 68). Derrida argued that ethics and politics only begin when undecidability is acknowledged:

> I will even venture to say that ethics, politics, and responsibility, *if there are any,* will only ever have begun with the experience and experiment of the aporia. When the path is clear and given, when a certain knowledge opens up the way in advance, the decision is already made, it might as well be said that there is none to make; irresponsibly, and in good conscience, one simply applies or implements a program. . . . It makes of action the applied consequence, the simple application of a knowledge or know how. It makes of ethics and politics a technology. No longer of the order of practical reason or decision, it begins to be irresponsible. (pp. 41–45; italics original)

Deconstruction allows us to examine the trajectory of the human right (Derrida, 2001b; Egéa-Kuehne, 2001) and how it functions as an ideal. It helps us to be alert to the institutional powers that force us to neutralize education "through a translating medium which would claim to be transparent, metalinguistic and universal" (Derrida, 1992, p. 58). Deconstruction is disruptive and subversive, but is also highly responsible and affirmative: "going further, displacing *changing*, changing the world, or changing society, changing the state of things, in terms of human rights, for instance; it is not simply reconstructing. It is . . . an ethics" (Derrida, 1990, p. 180; italics original). The ethical stance of deconstruction takes the form of speaking against closure, by offering us not a choice, but a series of aporias that highlight dual responsibilities:

> That is not easy. It is even impossible to conceive of a responsibility that consists in being responsible *for* two laws, or that consists in responding *to* two contradictory injunctions. No doubt. But there is no responsiblility that is not the experience and experiment of the impossible. (Derrida, 1990, pp. 44–45; italics original)

These "double duties" (Egéa-Kuehne, 2001, p. 202) are conflicting, but must, according to Derrida (1992), remain equally binding and not become subject to choice. As soon as a choice is made, injustice and irresponsibility are inevitable. The following example given by Derrida (1992) relates to ethnicity and the necessity to:

> respect differences, idioms, minorities, singularities, but also the universality of formal law, the desire for translation, agreement and univocity, the law of the majority, opposition to racism, nationalism and xenophobia. (p. 78)

Such an aporetic reconfiguration of disability may go some way to challenge those who have blamed inclusion for some of the problems within the educational system (Fuchs & Fuchs, 1994) or who wish to count the cost of inclusion. It challenges such positions because it does not present inclusion or the removal of disabling barriers as something we choose to do, but as part of our dual responsibilities as educators. One obvious aporia confronting educators is how to raise achievement *and* be inclusive. The aporetic features arise not because the goals are contradictory. Rather the problem arises in the implementation of reforms aimed at raising standards, which Gillborn and Youdell (2000) observed have led to deepening inequality, and they contended that these reforms "seem relentlessly to embody an increasingly divisive and exclusionary notion of education" (p. 41).

Rather than seeking to reduce these double-edged responsibilities to a single set of recommendations, with the inevitable erasure this will generate, it is more responsible to acknowledge the divergent nature of these obligations. Therefore, we might ask:

1. How can teachers be helped to acquire *and* demonstrate the necessary competences to qualify as a teacher and understand themselves as in a continuous process of learning about others?

2. How can teachers develop as autonomous professionals *and* learn to depend on others for support and collaboration?
3. How can teachers be supported in maximizing student achievement *and* ensuring inclusivity?
4. How can teachers be helped to understand the features of particular impairments *and* avoid disabling individual students with that knowledge?
5. What assistance can be given to teachers to enable them to deal with the exclusionary pressures they encounter *and* avoid becoming embittered or closed to possibilities for inclusivity in the future?

Thus, we do not have to make a choice between one policy imperative and another, nor do we need to devote our energies to wishing the standards agenda away to enable us to get on with inclusion. Rather we face a set of dual responsibilities. These "double contradictory imperatives of a continuum of *double duty*" (Egéa-Kuehne, 2001, p. 204; italics original) provide a challenge that takes "the impasse of the dilemma seriously and offers educators better understanding of the dilemma itself" (Edgoose, 2001, p. 125).

CONCLUSION: UNENDINGS AND DOUBLE ENTRIES

In this chapter, I considered some of the failures associated with a lack of progress in inclusion, and I examined some of the frustration this has provoked among disabled people. In my exploration of the possibilities for achieving inclusion, I have identified a series of dual imperatives facing educators and researchers today, and the *impossibility* is to avoid reducing these to a single course of action, consensus, or compromise. These suggestions—and that is all they amount to—speak to an "enabling conception of justice" (Young, 1990, p. 40), one that goes beyond distribution to address oppression, "a terrible caricature of obedience" (Weil; cited in Young, 1990, p. 40) and domination within disability research and, more generally, within education. The challenge comes from others' inability to see what we ourselves think we see so clearly and from our own inability to see our own selves as complicit:

> Someone who does not see a pane of glass does not know that he does not see it. Someone who, being placed differently, does see it, does not know the other does not see it. When our will finds expression outside ourselves in actions performed by others, we do not waste our time and our power of attention in examining whether they have consented to this. This is true for all of

40

us. Our attention, given entirely to the success of the undertaking, is not claimed by them as long as they are docile. (Weil; cited in Young, 1990, p. 40)

Responsible inclusion, then, involves opening our eyes.

REFERENCES

Ainscow, M. (2000). The next step for special education: Supporting the development of inclusive practices. *British Journal of Special Education, 27*(2), 76–80.
Alcoff, L. (1991–1992, Winter). The problem of speaking for others. *Cultural Critique,* pp. 5–32.
Allan, J. (1999). *Actively seeking inclusion: Pupils with special needs in mainstream schools.* London: Falmer.
Almeida Diniz, F., & Usmani, K. (2001). Changing the discourse on race and special educational needs. *Multicultural Teaching, 20*(1), 25–28.
Ball, S. (1998). Educational studies, policy entrepreneurship and social theory. In R. Slee, G. Weiner, & S. Tomlinson (Eds.), *School effectiveness for whom?* London: Falmer.
Ball, S. (2000). Performativities and fabrication in the education economy: Towards the performative society? *The Australian Educational Researcher, 27*(2), 1–23.
Ballard, K. (1997). Researching disability and inclusive education: Participation, construction and interpretation. *International Journal of Inclusive Education, 1*(3), 243–256.
Barber, M. (1997, September 12). Why tackling poverty is simply not enough. *Times Educational Supplement,* p. 17.
Barnes, C. (1992). Qualitative research: Valuable or irrelevant? *Disability, Handicap and Society, 7*(2), 115–124.
Barnes, C. (1996). Theories of disability and the origins of the oppression of disabled people in Western society. In L. Barton (Ed.), *Disability and society: Emerging issues and insights.* London: Longman.
Barnes, C. (1999). Disability studies: New or not so new directions? *Disability and Society, 14*(4), 577–580.
Barton, L. (1993). The struggle for citizenship: The case of disabled people. *Disability, Handicap and Society, 8,* 235–248.
Benjamin, S. (2002). "Valuing diversity": A cliché for the 21st century? *International Journal of Inclusive Education, 6,* 309–323.
Berres, M., Ferguson, D., Knoblock, P., & Wood, C. (Eds.). (1996). *Creating tomorrow's schools today: Stories of inclusion, change and renewal.* New York: Teachers College Press.
Bérubé, M. (1996). *Life as we know it: A father, a family and an exceptional child.* New York: Pantheon.
Biesta, G. (2001). "Preparing for the incalculable": Deconstruction, justice and the question of education. In G. Biesta & D. Egéa-Kuehne (Eds.), *Derrida & education.* London: Routledge.
Bordieu, P. (1991). Epilogue: On the possibility of a field of world sociology. In P. Bordieu & J. Coleman (Eds.), *Social theory for a changing society.* Boulder, CO: Westview.
Bowker, G. (1993, January). The age of biography is upon us. *Times Educational Supplement, 8,* 9.
Branfield, F. (1998). What are you doing here? "Non-disabled" people and the disability movement: A response to Robert F. Drake. *Disability and Society, 13*(1), 143–144.
Brantlinger, E. (1997). Using ideology: Cases of nonrecognition of the politics of research and practice in special education. *Review of Educational Research, 67*(4), 425–459.

Caputo, J. (1997). *Deconstruction in a nutshell: A conversation with Jacques Derrida.* New York: Fordham University Press.

Clear, M. (1999). The "normal" and the monstrous in disability research. *Disability and Society, 14*(4), 435–448.

Connell, R. (1993). *Schools and social justice.* Philadelphia: Temple University Press.

Connolly, P. (1996). Doing what comes naturally? Standpoint epistemology, critical social research and the politics of identity. In E. Lyon & J. Busfield (Eds.), *Methodological imaginations.* Basingstoke: Macmillan.

Corker, M. (1999). New disability discourse, the principle of optimization and social change. In M. Corker & S. French (Eds.), *Disability discourse.* Buckingham: Open University Press.

Davis, J. (2000). Disability studies as ethnographic research and text: Research strategies and roles for promoting social change? *Disability and Society, 15*(2), 191–206.

Denzin, N. (1997). *Interpretive ethnography: Ethnographic practices for the 21st century.* London: Sage.

Department for Education and Employment. (1997). *Excellence for all children: Meeting special educational needs.* London: Author.

Derrida, J. (1990). Force of law: The mystical foundation of authority (M. Quaintance, Trans.). *Cardozo Law Review, 11,* 919–1070.

Derrida, J. (1992). *The other heading: Reflections on today's Europe* (P. Brault & M. Naas, Trans.). Bloomington and Indianapolis: Indiana University Press.

Derrida, J. (1996). Remarks on deconstruction and pragmatism. In C. Mouffe (Ed.), *Deconstruction and pragmatism.* London: Routledge.

Derrida, J. (1997). The Villanova roundtable: A conversation with Jacques Derrida. In J. Caputo (Ed.), *Deconstruction in a nutshell: A conversation with Jacques Derrida.* New York: Fordham University Press.

Derrida, J. (2001a). "A certain 'madness' must watch over thinking": Jacques Derrida's interview with François Ewald. In G. Biesta & D. Egéa-Kuehne (Eds.), *Derrida & education.* London: Routledge.

Derrida, J. (2001b). Talking liberties: Interview with Alan Montfiore. In G. Biesta & D. Egéa-Kuehne (Eds.), *Derrida & education.* London: Routledge.

Dyson, A. (2001). Special needs in the twenty-first century: Where we've been and where we're going. *British Journal of Special Education, 28*(1), 24–29.

Edgoose, J. (2001). Just decide! Derrida and the ethical aporias of education. In G. Biesta & D. Egéa-Kuehne (Eds.), *Derrida & education.* London: Routledge.

Egéa-Kuehne, D. (2001). Derrida's ethics of affirmation: The challenge of educational rights and responsibility. In G. Biesta & D. Egéa-Kuehne (Eds.), *Derrida & education.* London: Routledge.

Evans, R. (2002). Ethnography of teacher training: Mantras for those constructed as "other." *Disability and Society, 17*(1), 35–48.

French, S. (1993). Disability, impairment or something in between? In J. Swain, V. Finkelstein, S. French, & M. Oliver (Eds.), *Disabling barriers—enabling environments.* London: Sage/Open University.

French, S. (1994). Equal opportunities . . . yes please! In L. Keith (Ed.), *Mustn't grumble: Writing by disabled women.* London: The Women's Press.

Fuchs, D., & Fuchs, L. (1994). Inclusive schools movement and the radicalization of special education reform. *Exceptional Children, 60*(4), 294–309.

Fulcher, G. (1989). *Disabling policies? A comparative approach to education policy and disability.* London: Falmer.

Gabel, S. (2001). Problems of methodology in cross-cultural disability studies. *Exploring Theories and Expanding Methodologies, 2,* 209–228.

Gallagher, D. (1998). The scientific knowledge base of special education: Do we know what we think we know? *Exceptional Children, 60,* 294–309.

Gallagher, D. (2001). Neutrality as a moral standpoint, conceptual confusion and the full inclusion debate. *Disability and Society, 16*(5), 637–654.

Garner, P., & Gains, C. (2000, Autumn). The debate that never happened. *Special!,* pp. 8–11.

Gewirtz, S. (2000). Bringing the politics back in: A critical analysis of quality discourses in education. *British Journal of Educational Studies, 48,* 352–370.

Gillborn, D., & Youdell, D. (2000). *Rationing education: Policy, practice, reform and equity.* Buckingham: Open University Press.

Goodley, D. (2001). "Learning difficulties," the social model of disability and impairment: Challenging epistemologies. *Disability and Society, 16,* 207–232.

Gregoriou, Z. (2001). Does speaking of others involve receiving the "other"? A postcolonial reading of receptivity in Derrida's deconstruction of *Timaeus.* In G. Biesta & D. Egéa-Kuehne (Eds.), *Derrida & education.* London: Routledge.

Gutierrez, K., Larson, J., & Kreuter, B. (1995). Cultural tensions in the scripted classroom: The value of the subjugated perspective. *Urban Education, 29,* 410–442.

Humphrey, J. (2000). Researching disability projects, or, some problems with the social model in practice. *Disability and Society, 15*(1), 63–86.

Kitchen, R. (2000). The researched opinions on research: Disabled people and disability research. *Disability and Society, 15*(1), 25–48.

Kugelmas, J. (2001). Collaboration and compromise in creating and sustaining an inclusive school. *International Journal of Inclusive Education, 5*(1), 47–65.

Levinas, E. (1998). *On thinking of the other: Entre nous.* London: Athlone.

Linton, S. (1998). *Claiming disability: Knowledge and identity.* New York: New York University Press.

Lipsky, D., & Gartner A. (1997). *Inclusion and school reform: Transforming America's classrooms.* Baltimore, MD: Brookes.

Mittler, P. (2000). Profile. In P. Clough & J. Corbett (Eds.), *Theories of inclusive education: A students' guide.* London: Paul Chapman.

Moss, P., & Petrie, P. (2002). *From children's services to children's spaces: Public policy, children and childhood.* London: RoutledgeFalmer.

Munro, P. (1998). *Subject to fiction: Women teachers' life history narratives and the cultural politics of resistance.* Buckingham and Philadelphia: Open University Press.

Nunan, T., George, R., & McCausland, H. (2000). Inclusive education in universities: Why it is important and how it might be achieved. *International Journal of Inclusive Education, 4*(1), 63–88.

Oliver, M. (1992). Changing the social relations of research production? *Disability, Handicap & Society, 7*(2), 101–114.

Oliver, M. (1996). *Understanding disability: From theory to practice.* Basingstoke: Macmillan.

Oliver, M. (1997). Emancipatory research: Realistic goal or impossible dream? In C. Barnes & G. Mercer (Eds.), *Doing disability research.* Leeds: The Disability Press.

Oliver, M. (1999). Final accounts and the parasite people. In M. Corker & S. French (Eds.), *Disability discourse.* Buckingham: Open University Press.

Paterson, K., & Hughes, B. (1999). Disability studies and phenomenology: The carnal politics of everyday life. *Disability and Society, 14*(5), 597–611.

Peters, S. (1999). Transforming disability identity through critical literacy and the cultural politics of language. In M. Corker & S. French (Eds.), *Disability discourse.* Buckingham: Open University Press.

Pratt, M. (1992). *Imperial eyes: Travel writing and transculturation.* New York: Routledge.

Rose, N. (2001). Primary school teacher perceptions of the conditions required to include pupils with special educational needs. *Journal of Educational Studies, 53,* 147–156.

Salter, B., & Tapper, T. (2000). The politics of governance in higher education: The case of quality assurance. *Political Studies, 48,* 66–87.

Scottish Executive. (1999). *New Community Schools Prospectus.* Edinburgh: Author.

Shakespeare, T. (1993). Disabled people's self organisation: A new social movement. *Disability and Society, 8*(3), 249–264.

Shaw, L. (2002). *"We want to be together."* Retrieved July 22, 2003, from http://inclusion. uwe.ac.uk/inclusionweek.articles.together.htm.

Slee, R. (1996). Disability, class and poverty: School structures and policing identities. In C. Christensen & F. Rizvi (Eds.), *Disability and the dilemmas of education and justice.* Buckingham: Open University Press.

Slee, R. (2001a). Inclusion in practice: Does practice make perfect? *Educational Review, 53*(2), 113–123.

Slee, R. (2001b). Social justice and the changing directions in educational research: The case of inclusive education. *International Journal of Inclusive Education, 5*(2/3), 167–178.

Slee, R. (2003). Teacher education, government and inclusive schooling: The politics of the Faustian waltz. In J. Allan (Ed.), *Inclusion, participation and democracy: What is the purpose?* Dordrecht: Kluwer.

Slee, R., & Allan, J. (2001). Excluding the included: A reconsideration of inclusive education. *International Studies in the Sociology of Education, 11*(2), 173–191.

Smyth, J., & Hattam, J. (2002). Early school leaving and the cultural geography of high schools. *British Educational Research Journal, 28*(3), 375–398.

Vidovitch, L., & Slee, R. (2001). Bringing universities to account? Exploring some global and local policy tensions. *Journal of Educational Policy, 16,* 431–453.

Walmsley, J. (2001). Normalisation, emancipatory research and inclusive research in learning disability. *Disability and Society, 16*(2), 187–206.

Ware, L. (2001). Writing, identity and the other: Dare we do disability studies? *Journal of Teacher Education, 52*(2), 107–123.

Young, I. (1990). *Justice and the politics of difference.* Princeton: Princeton University Press.

Chapter 3

The Big Glossies: How Textbooks Structure (Special) Education

Ellen Brantlinger
Indiana University, Bloomington

Representatives from major textbook publishing companies regularly come by my office to convince me to buy their big glossy wares. In the past, conforming to academic routines, I required such texts for undergraduate courses. A walk through the bookstore at the beginning of the semester reveals that most of my colleagues use textbooks, especially for undergraduate and master's level courses. Similar to the customs of elementary school teachers who use basal readers and workbooks rather than a whole language approach to literacy and high school teachers who teach from subject matter texts, these fully packed textbooks do make the difficult task of teaching a bit easier. New take-over-your-course versions of textbooks are not only convenient, but make decision making on the part of faculty and students virtually unnecessary. Textbook packages are equipped with such enticements as teachers' guides, test item banks, templates to make overheads for lectures that follow textbook themes, and supplementary CDs with step-by-step instructions for writing individual educational plans or doing curriculum-based assessments. Given the similarities among all these expanded textbooks, perhaps uniformity has been brought to university teacher education methods and survey courses across the country.

THE NONRANDOMNESS OF RESILIENT EDUCATIONAL POLICIES AND PRACTICES

Theorists inform educators that there are hierarchical patterns and structures in society that are reproduced in school; they maintain these are neither random nor meaningless in terms of their influence on human relations (e.g., Apple, 1990, 1995; Ball, 1990; Bowles & Gintis, 1976). Tyack and Tobin (1994) surmised that the grammar of schooling is resistant to internal and external pressures for change (see also Britzman, 1991; Fullan, 1993; Sarason, 1990). This structural resiliency is likely to be precisely because those who wield power do not want change (Brantlinger, 2003). The particular pattern that I address in this chapter is the ubiquitous teacher education practice of requiring what I call *big glossy* textbooks for use in survey and methods courses and, in turn, for these texts to have an impact on preservice teachers' thinking about education, and hence on the eventual nature of practice. In addition to analyzing textbook content and the control aspects of textbook usage, I illustrate that textbook use is counterproductive in preparing future teachers for their lives in classrooms and schools.

I reviewed 14 textbooks designed for use in introduction to special education courses for special or general education majors (see starred list in reference section and/or Table 3.1). The selection criteria was simple: I included all textbooks sent to me over the past few years. Three textbooks had an inclusion focus and were substantially different from the other 11 (Miller, Peterson & Hittie, Salend). They were included because they were designed for an introductory class. Methods used for this study were document (textbooks, syllabi) or content analysis (Merriam, 1998). It also might be considered a critical discourse analysis (Fairclough, 1992).

FALLING INTO ROUTINE TEXTBOOK USAGE FOR TEACHER EDUCATION PRACTICE

Given the current intensification of demands for productivity and excellence in research, service, and teaching at the university, faculty may feel it necessary to rely on the convenience of comprehensive texts and their prepackaged accouterments. Furthermore, once adopted, an easy next step is to have the course conform to the structure of the text, especially now that the add-ons are available. An inspection of archived syllabi at my institution reveals that, for example, in the introductory exceptionality course the first week, and corresponding chapter, focus on "history of the field," the second on "the law," with subsequent weeks/chapters spent on disability categories—learning disabilities, mental retardation, emotional disturbance, and so forth. This course schedule replicates the table of contents of the required textbooks.

When doctoral students are hired to teach undergraduate courses, which often is at the last minute, they turn to knowledgeable faculty models and mentors and copy their syllabi and adopt the same texts. This quick and dirty induction further cements textbook-oriented traditions in professional teacher education practice. Even graduate students who are fresh out of years of actual classroom teaching experience are likely to come to understand that teacher education is based on standard textual knowledge, rather than the personal knowledge they acquired during teaching. Faced with similar busy schedules and survival needs as faculty, the embellished textbooks are hard to resist. Graduate students may realize that textbook knowledge is mostly irrelevant to actual classroom teaching, but also know they must compete for popularity in course evaluations and prepare preservice teachers for required standardized national exams. Socialized during their public school careers to comply with pressures for accountability through measurable outcomes and to avoid the dangerous consequences of "rocking the boat," these teacher educator inductees quickly learn to conform to demands for safe official knowledge and known practice.

Not only do faculty depend on texts, but, based on their K–12 school experiences, by the time they reach college, students have grown to expect course content to be neatly packaged in and around texts. Furthermore, in today's teach-to-the-test educational climate, preservice teachers must pass national teacher exams that, not coincidentally, include the exact information provided in texts. The circularity is apparent. The test and textbook companies—often one and the same outfit—clearly have a good thing going. Speculations are that text/test conglomerates are responsible for creating the conditions that have culminated in this form of teacher preparation (see Berliner & Biddle, 1995; Kohn, 2003; McNeil, 2000a, 2000b; Metcalf, 2002; Miner, 2003). Moreover, corporations exert continuous efforts to keep us hooked on texts not only by upgrading their products, but by attempting to control or eliminate alternatives. They bring lawsuits against duplication companies for breaking property rights[1] and for using journal articles and book chapters in course packets custom designed by course instructors. Under an "all is fair in love, war—and capitalism" morality/climate, perhaps capitalists have the right to go to extremes to maintain a lucrative trade. The consequence of text publishers' monopoly on producing school knowledge is that knowledge is only as good as the texts used.

To avoid the omnipresent big glossy standard texts for a methods course entitled "Teaching Students With Mental Retardation and Learning Disabilities," for several years I used each updated version of Good and Brophy's (1984) *Looking in Classrooms,* although the book did not mention disabilities. The first edition was published before the idea of inclusion became the norm in schools. Nevertheless, the book incorporated the essential rudiments for developing inclusive, democratic classrooms. Thick and

---

[1]Some conglomerate owners of tests and texts also own journals so they can charge exorbitant prices for use of these articles, which increases the price of course packets, often prohibitively.

dense with information that was, in fact, mostly based on research, and hence was science- or evidence-based, it also included vignettes describing classroom interactions that were so realistic they obviously came from field notes of empirical observations. These were a good source for discussions about the implications of various classroom practices. In retrospect, I think *Looking in Classrooms* does not qualify as a "big glossy," first, because it was written in meaningful narratives not sound bites, and, second, at least the early versions were not packed full of glossy sales catalogue or magazine type pictures.

STRUGGLES WITH BUCKING THE SYSTEM

Texts are convenient for faculty, but, perhaps more important, students are used to them and suspicious of alternatives. When our undergraduate special education program merged to include elementary education courses and certification and the secondary courses (my area of expertise) were no longer offered as in the previous all-grade special education major, I suddenly found my name next to the "Introduction to Learning Disabilities" course. The program coordinator, who taught the course in the past, dropped her copy of the text *Introduction to Learning Disabilities* on my desk, "highly recommending" its use. She asked me to pass it along to the instructor of the other course section, who promptly decided to use it and urged me to do the same "so both sections would seem equivalent to students." In addition to uniformity, my colleague justified his choice by claiming the text would prepare students for the exam required for state certification.

After thumbing through this learning disabilities text, for reasons that will be explained later in this chapter, I decided it would not do. Instead I ordered Rodis, Garrod, and Boscardin's (2001) *Learning Disabilities & Life Stories*, which includes essays by young adults who reflect on their experiences with being classified and specially educated as learning disabled. I combined that insider perspective with Sapon-Shevin's (1999) *Because We Can Change The World*,[2] which provides concrete, creative suggestions for nurturing inclusion in elementary classrooms. I quickly turned in my textbook requisition so I could say, "Sorry, I already ordered my books," in case my colleagues would press the uniformity and test preparation case and pressure me to use the recommended text with its "prerequisite information" for the next course/text in the series, *Teaching Students With Learning Disabilities*, which was written by the same authors.

A few days after crystalizing my book selection, still feeling somewhat guilty about my noncompliance with colleagues' expectations (a common

---

[2]It might be noted that both books are published by Allyn & Bacon.

occurrence, I confess), I was at a social gathering of special education teachers who had become friends during the years I placed and supervised field experience students in their classrooms. I told them of my dilemma and asked whether they thought I should call back my bookstore order and require the text that offered preservice teachers the officially sanctioned versions of learning disabilities. Fortunately, these experienced teachers, many of whom were former students, reinforced the validity of my impression that the knowledge packaged in these texts was largely extraneous to actual teaching.

Despite collegial pressures, as a tenured full professor who does not have to worry much about course evaluations (except for the pain and embarrassment of being criticized or unpopular), I have chosen to venture out and avoid standard texts in my undergraduate courses. However, I have not sunk to the anti-intellectual level of appeasing students by validating their current knowledge as sufficient or by concurring with their opinion that they are already finished products—the good teachers they know they will be simply because that is what they want to be. The slim paperbacks I require—unfortunately also overpriced and some published by the main textbook publishers—convey knowledge that is less standardized. Indeed most of the ones I use take the iconoclastic position of challenging foundational special education knowledge. Initially, some college students are angry that these books or articles imply that, despite their own good intentions and conscientious teaching, they still may be complicit in an oppressive system. Many do not find uncommon knowledge useful or practical, and they wonder what complex theories or radical approaches to inclusive schooling will mean for them as classroom teachers. Given their intense orientation to grades, preservice teachers mostly worry about how they will be tested on these nonstandard and often complex course materials.

Once I used Julie Allan's (1999) Foucaldian analysis of special education, *Actively Seeking Inclusion,* with a senior class. The night before we were to discuss the first chapter in class and students were to turn in short reflection papers, I received a rush of panicked e-mail messages. Students claimed to be confused by the book and "did not know what I wanted" in the required response papers, although I had included a list of ways to approach these papers in the course syllabus. Some already worried about how the book would figure in the midterm exam.

In class the next morning, a feisty student, who I will call Rochelle, confronted me with the announcement that the book was full of jargon that she and others did not understand. I clarified the difference between jargon (highly extracted or particularistic terms that substituted rather artificially for familiar words that have the same meaning and are more common to experience) and difficult but useful terminology that was necessary to meaningfully convey unique ideas. Rochelle persisted in mutiny, announcing that she was speaking for the whole class in expressing her opinion that I had required an inappropriate book. With her outspoken, confrontational manner, Rochelle had the potential to be a feminist; however, in conveying her desire not to be challenged or even taught, she unfortunately fell more into the category of whiner. In an attempt to appease the furious masses squeezed into my class (fully awake and, because of the exciting mood of rebellion, also uniformly attentive perhaps for the first time that semester), I smiled at Rochelle and said I would make a stab at defining the "p" word that she complained was repeated continuously in the text but not defined. She could not recall the word, but opened her book and found it: *pedagogy*. I tried not to look shocked as I glanced around the room for a volunteer to define it. Heads shook in admission that they did not know the word. Often when I ask questions I get blank stares or, as I scan the class for a potential respondent, students look downward to signal they do not want to be called on. This time I got well-choreographed and exaggerated back-and-forth head shake motions. A helpful person, who already had come across as a venturesome risk-taker not to be intimidated by me or her peers, blurted out that she had "heard the word before" and thought it had "something to do with teaching or curriculum." I put a blank sheet on the overhead and wrote a definition. Students knew that anything I wrote on the Formica board or a transparency might be on a test, so they dutifully copied my definition.

To be transformed from villain to helpful professor, I countered class resistance with a routine they understood, suggesting we identify complex words in the book and work together to define them. Most seemed satisfied with this solution. Rochelle was not happy to have lost her following and tried to reclaim the hostile mood with this challenge: "I don't understand why you picked this book if we are all having so much trouble reading it. Besides the author is not American. What does she know about special ed in this country?" I confessed that I selected the book because I thought it was unusual, interesting, informative, and had a new take on special education, albeit foreign. Drawing on the "because-it-is-going-to-be-on-high-stakes-test" rationale, I also argued, "if you decide to get a master's degree, having an improved vocabulary as a result of reading this book, you will do well on the GRE," then mumbled, "then you will thank me." Rochelle's peers were satisfied with my explanation and proceeded to outdo each other to find big words and strange names and ideas in Allan's book. They stayed alert and surprised themselves by identifying ways that Foucault's mechanisms of surveillance—hierarchical observation, normalizing judgments, and the examination—applied to their experience in school. As we hypothesized about word definitions, meanings, and applications or significance to real-life classrooms, and especially special education practice, the students stayed interested. At the end of the class session, as one cheerful student walked past me to leave the room, she whispered, "That was fun!" At the end of the course, expecting the worst, I did not read my course evaluations for several weeks. To my delight, many praised the Allan book as "unique," "exciting," and "hard but interesting"—only 2 of the 31 checked the category "Never use this book again."

REVELATIONS OF A CLOSE TEXTBOOK READ

I suspect that busy faculty often select textbooks without carefully reading them. Instead they glance at the table of contents and pictures and gauge their potential for guiding lectures and providing testable content. One way to thoroughly get to know a textbook is to review it for a publisher, which I recently did for a text undergoing revision as well as a unique manuscript being considered for publication. In the case of the former, I was asked to focus especially on the high-incidence chapters, which the publishers perceived as my area of expertise. As I read about disability etiology, I was alarmed at the pervasiveness of the cultural deficit perspective. Overrepresentation of racial and ethnic minorities in special education was not addressed, and there was no hint that the structure of school practice or school personnel might have an intrinsic social class and racial/ethnic bias.

The second textbook manuscript I reviewed balanced the focus on societal structure, including social class and racial/ethnic bias, and students' and teachers' perspectives about the meaning of school and typical special education practice. Despite my own glowing review, the manuscript was not accepted. The publisher perceived that, because of its nonstandard format and content, its audience would be too small—it would not be viable in the competitive textbook market. An additional comment on the rejection letter was that the proposed text, which was based on actual situations of students, parents, and teachers, was not science-based. In other words, it did not contain the results of a host of mostly inane studies that boast conclusive evidence about best special education practice. It is important to note here that the same scholars whose evidence is routinely found in textbooks complain about the gap between research and practice. Apparently, teachers do not find the evidence included in texts compelling enough to use as a basis for classroom instruction. Despite their preference for the use of standard textbooks because they know what is expected of them in terms of content and course grades, informal checks with some of my undergraduate classes reveal that many students think textbook information will not be relevant to their teaching—that it is not useful. Evidence for the accuracy of these brief surveys is that most students promptly sell the texts at the end of the semester. Because of my own disgust at the price of textbooks, when I use cheap books or course packets, I expect students to be pleased to be saving money. It turns out most charge the textbooks to their parents at the beginning of the semester and pocket the refund when they resell the book.

TEXTBOOK CONSTRUCTIONS OF DISABILITY

All but 3 of the 14 reviewed textbooks were organized around disability category chapters (see Table 3.1). In these categorically focused textbooks, each disability category or disabling condition was outlined as including students who were clearly distinctive from students with other types of disabilities and students without disabilities. It was inferred that consistencies and regularities exist among students with the same disability. Conditions were described as remaining stable over time and context—an idea that Mercer (1973) debunked three decades ago in her theory of the "6-hour-a-day retarded" child.

Disability studies theorists have identified distinctive discourses about disability that take place in the special education community and in general. Based on his review and analysis of the literature, Danforth (2001) delineated three models of disability that undergird research and service provision. With an emphasis on individual imperfection and abnormality, the "functional limitations" (i.e., medical, deficit) model frames disability as a condition of biophysical essence and origin within certain individuals that renders them unable to perform expected, valued, or normal human activities. This has also been called the "epidemiological model" (Richardson, Casanova, Placier, & Guilfoyle, 1989, p. 3). In England, Ball (1990) contended that the medical model portrays certain children as having technical trouble so they need professional intervention to become normal or the same as peers. Ball also named a "charity" model, in which disabled people are tragic figures—either objects of pity or sources of inspiration. Tomlinson (1982) claimed that the benevolent humanitarianism surrounding special education permeates both medical and charity discourses.

In addition to the medical (deficit) and charity models, Ball (1990) named a "market" model, in which the language of choice, efficiency, and management are deployed. Such terms as *due process*,[3] *most appropriate environment*, and *evidence-based practice* reveal the legalistic, technorational, supposedly scientific, and also the market model permeation into special education discourse and practice. The language of evidence-based practice is consistent with Giroux's (1994) idea that education, including teacher education, is seen as a matter of being able to use techniques. According to the conservative ideal of market efficiency, manageable teachers are to rely

---

[3]This has elements of legal language and so might also be called a *legal* model.

TABLE 3.1
Reviewed Textbooks

Author, Date	Categorical Chapter Organization	Universal Design	Ethnic/ Racial Overrepresentation	Social Class or Structural Issues	Poverty in At-Risk Context	Disability Studies or Rights	Includes Unrealistic Pictures	Stereotyped or Staged Pictures
Blackbourn et al., 2004	Yes	No	Yes, brief	Some	Yes (label a problem)	No	No (black & white)	No
Culatta et al., 2003	Yes	No	No	No	Yes	No	Yes (black & white)	Staged (pp. 115, 121)
Hallahan & Kauffman, 2003	Yes	Mentions briefly	No	Some	Cultural deficit perspective	Yes	Yes	Stereotyped (pp. 235, 243, 353)
Hardman et al., 2002	Yes	Mentions briefly	No	No	Yes	No	Yes	Stereotyped (pp. 239, 263, 265)
Heward, 2003	Yes	No	No	No	Yes	No	Yes	No
Lewis & Doorlag, 2003	Yes	No	No	No	Yes	No	Yes (very unrealistic)	Staged and stereotyped (pp. 407, 411)
Miller, 2002	No	Some	No	Yes	Sensitive discussion	No	No (black & white)	No
Peterson & Hittie, 2003	No (some within chapters)	Yes, excellent coverage	No	No	Mentions	Yes	Some (black & white)	No
Salend, 2001	No	One paragraph	No	No	Sensitive discussion	No	Some	Yes (p. 83)
Smith, 1989	Yes	No	No	No	Mentions	No	No pictures	No pictures
Smith, 2004	Yes	Mentions	Yes	No	Mentions	No	Very few	No
Smith et al., 2001	Yes	No	No	Yes (SES)	Yes, at risk	No	Yes	Yes (pp. 352, 362, 393)
Smith et al., 2004	Yes	No	No	Yes (SES)	Yes, at risk	Yes, disabled manifesto	Yes	Staged (pp. 200, 206, 412), stereotyped (p. 395)
Turnbull et al., 2004	Yes	Yes, excellent coverage	No	Yes	Yes	No	No	Stereotyped (p. 12)

solely on standardized techniques that they transmit to docile students. In-
corporation of foundational knowledge and mastery of prescribed techniques is equated with professional competency. The proliferation of specialized techniques and science-based interventions are viewed as progress
in the field. Inspection of special education textbooks indicates that they
are replete with prescribed, standardized, legislatively endorsed, or litiga-
tion-grounded technical knowledge to be learned or mastered by pre- or
inservice teachers. Textbook authors convey that what is detailed in their
books is essential, fundamental, and foundational knowledge—that is,
"what every teacher needs to know" (see Culatta, Tompkins, & Werts,
2003).

In contrast to assessing and classifying deficits, individuals who adhere to
the "minority group" model view people with disabilities as an oppressed
group subjected to dominant groups' prejudices and biased practices (Danforth, 2001). This model is grounded in an assumption of the prevalence of
biased attitudes, institutional barriers, and exclusionary practices—for example, ability-based reading groups, secondary school tracking or stream-
ing, special education pullout, class/race segregated schools, property
tax–based school funding, segregated living and working arrangements,
disparate wages, nonprogressive taxes, public universities requiring tuition,
within-district disparities in school funding, and material and human resource distribution. These traditions, structures, and barriers have distinctive outcomes for dominant and subordinate group members. Subordinates inevitably are at the bottom of school and society's hierarchical
structure. Despite the huge amount of evidence of discrimination and disparities in school and society, there is little account of structural bias perspectives in the textbooks I examined. A few touch on the theme of minority ethnic/racial overrepresentation in special education or the history of
racism and poverty in this country, but this coverage is brief and cursory, especially compared with the detailed overview of individual deficiencies.
The message often is that problems existed in the past, but disappear when
the fair prescriptions offered in the textbooks are faithfully followed.

The third model that Danforth identified is the "social construction of
disability" or "social model," for which Danforth referred to McDermott
and Varenne's (1996) description: "It takes a whole culture of people producing idealizations of what everyone should be and a system of measures
for identifying those who fall short for us to forget that we collectively produce our disabilities and discomforts that conventionally accompany them"
(p. 337). In *Successful Failure*, anthropologists Varenne and McDermott
(1998) described American schools' preoccupation with failure and how
schools "naturalized ways of talking about children as successes and failures" (p. xiii). Claiming that "education is discovering, taming, and transforming our humanity" (p. 154), these authors maintained that certain

words (e.g., *skill, ability, disability, intelligence, competence, proficiency, achievement, motivation, self-esteem, objective test, grade level*) come easily. These supposedly scientifically derived concepts have become the content of big glossy texts.

There is little evidence of a constructivist viewpoint in textbooks. Those with categorical chapters are firmly embedded in medical or deficit models. Apparently, however, some textbook writers have become aware of the hazards of these models. At the beginning of a chapter on mental retardation, the commentary accompanying a picture of an elderly woman (apparently retarded) nuzzling a guinea pig states: "Professionals are more cautious than they once were about identifying and labeling mental retardation due to the concerns about the consequences of misidentification, and the idea that some definitions may have been socially constructed" (Hallahan & Kauffman, 2003, p. 113). Their use of *some* (instead of *all*) definitions is indicative of their lack of understanding of the social construction model.

Those who subscribe to minority group or social models of disability highlight structural inequalities in institutional and societal hierarchies. They tend to be in disability or cultural studies or they are critical theorists attuned to power differentials. Disability studies theorists, who often have disabilities, recently emerged in a number of fields (e.g., Charlton, 1998; Corbett, 1996; Gabel, 1999, 2001; Garland Thomson, 1997; Grandin & Scariano, 1986; Hahn, 1983, 1997; Linton, 1998; Oliver, 1990). Cultural study scholars who have contributed insightful essays of disabilities from a constructivist perspective include Baker (1999, 2002), Barton and Oliver (1997), Christensen and Rizvi (1996), Davis (1995, 1997), Linneman (2001), Mitchell (1997), Rogers and Swadener (2001), Trent (1994), and Ware (2001). Those from within special education who fell away from the behaviorist orthodoxy or studied first-person views of being disabled include Bogdan (1988), Bogdan and Taylor (1976, 1994), Duplass and Smith (1995), Erevelles (2000, 2002a, 2002b), Gabel and Danforth (2002), Harry (1992), Heshusius (1995), Skrtic (1995a, 1995b, 1995c), Slee (1993, 1996, 1998), Sleeter (1986), Taylor (1988), and Ware (2001). Some psychologists and educational psychologists have critiqued the labeling frenzy of recent decades (Armstrong, 1993; Caplan, 1995; Capshew, 1999; Kutchins & Kirk, 1997).

Critical theorists highlight the oppressively negative identity constructions for subordinate groups claiming that it is not an unintentional by-product of useful practice, but a purposeful way to retain social hierarchies that benefit dominant groups. One critical British scholar, Tomlinson (1995), claimed her radical structuralist theories point out how powerful social groups control and dominate weaker social groups as they treat them differentially and unequally. Tomlinson gave the example of IQ testing as a prevalent mechanism used to label and separate children in school and le-

gitimize inequality between socioeconomic groups. Confirming Tomlinson's claim about the prominence of IQ's role in distinction-making processes, the indexes of categorically organized textbooks reviewed for this
chapter include multiple references to IQ.

Critical theorists take an openly value-oriented or political stand in scru-
tinizing power differentials in order to eliminate them in current educational practices. In contrast to the touted objectivity, neutrality, and scientific basis of the medical/deficit or market models, critical theorists are
dubbed uniquely political (e.g., Walker et al., 1998). These mainstream
scholars claim to their own apolitical stance is naive. Informed theorists
(Thompson, 1990; Zizek, 1994) pointed out that those who endorse status
quo practices in hierarchical societies are the most political because they retain power discrepancies between the most and least advantaged. Because
there is so much consensus about the validity of the prevalent deficit models, however, their political aspects remain relatively opaque (see Ryan,
1971; Valencia, 1997; Wright, 1993). Tomlinson (1995) claimed that fault-
ing context rather than individuals identified with disabilities is not popular in Western democratic societies, where citizens like to think schools are
harmonious, ordered places organized around a consensus of values.

Apple and Christian-Smith (1991) wrote that textbooks selectively frame
and organize the vast universe of possible knowledge into specific narratives
for specific audiences; experts who write textbooks tell a certain way to interpret classroom phenomena. Textbook authors conceptualize some children
as inferior and label them—a labeling that places value on certain kinds of
students. An example of this is the commentary by a picture of racially/ethni-
cally diverse students in a classroom, which states: "The dynamics of a classroom are determined by many different student factors" (Smith, Polloway,
Patton, & Dowdy, 2001, p. 383); teacher or structural factors are not mentioned. The caption by a picture of two dark-haired boys writing on a graffiti-
covered wall states: "Researchers define the externalizing dimension of disordered behavior as striking out against others, for example fighting, disruptive
behavior, or damaging property" (Hallahan & Kauffman, 2003, p. 227). An
alternate interpretation of graffiti as creative expression is not suggested. In
this picture, one of the boys sits on a skateboard—a prompt present in many
at-risk and behavior-disordered textbook illustrations. Another picture in the
same textbook is of three boys standing by an angry-looking youth. This picture is accompanied by the statement: "Children who act out aggressively or
impulsively with frequent negative confrontations are not well liked by their
peers" (p. 243). Again, here, the personal pathology description of origin-
free anger trumps the peer pressure for conformity explanation for violence.
Stoughton (2003) found that children with what their peers perceive as odd
characteristics are ostracized and bullied, hence they become frustrated, depressed, and angry as a result of their peers' persistent abusive actions.

SELECTIVITY OF TEXTBOOK GAZE

Clearly, textbook authors' conceptualization of disability influences how children and adults are portrayed in their books. Unfortunately, a perusal of current textbooks indicates that authors are securely situated in the medical model, with shades of Ball's charity and market discourses infused as well. Like other authority sources, special education textbooks assume representational politics that reduce or abolish the complexity of human acts; that is, they function as myth (Barthes, 1972). By excluding the potentially damaging aspects of school structures in their diagnostic gaze, special education text authors reinforce the notion that disability is intrinsic to the child and not the system and sustain the myths of special education helpfulness to classified students and technical progress in the field (Slee, 1998). Instead disability should be seen in terms of uneven power relations and privilege. Slee suggested schools should pathologize themselves to acknowledge their own failures, thus speaking of political rather than individual pathologies. Little of the friction endemic to professional and consumer relations or conflict among scholars regarding assessment, classification, and the best ways and places to educate students makes it into these texts. Court cases are summarized, however, the included cases are always ones that have established landmark practices such as access to education, least restrictive environments, and due process in decision making. The current slew of consumer-initiated court cases against school districts are not detailed or even summarized. In these textbooks, the world of special education is a peaceable kingdom of consensus and cooperation—what Barthes and Slee would call a *myth*.

It is particularly noteworthy that for decades many educational journals have included articles that address social class, race/ethnicity, and gender bias issues in schools and society. Nevertheless, in contrast to the strictly technical publications, little of this scholarly evidence has made it into textbook print. This politics of selective content and silencing of certain information and perspectives is addressed in subsequent sections of this chapter.

THE THIRD-PERSON VOICE OF TEXTBOOK AUTHORITY

Textbooks are written as authoritative documents. A text title touts the ultimate authority of having "the fundamentals of special education" (Culatta, Tompkins, & Werts, 2003). Perhaps the most effective way to claim authority is to write and state things as if they were not coming from a particular human perspective. The third-person style common to scholarly writing—what Nagel (1986) called "the voice from nowhere" and Haraway (1988) the "God trick"—prevails in texts. With this rendering, authors' position and perspective vanish. Textbook content appears as not necessarily based on any particular slant on the social world or unique experience in the field. Impersonal narratives create an aura of universal or eternal truth. Barthes (1972) argued that such written words effuse a simplicity of essences as they do away with dialectics and organize a world without contradictions to establish a blissfully clear, but detached reality so that things seem to mean something by themselves. Using the third-person voice, texts transmit ideas about people and practice that seem technical, scientific, and, hence by implication objective, neutral, and free of subjectivity. According to Giroux (1994), content is presented as "seamless, disinterested, and authoritative and their hierarchies of value as universally valid, ecumenical, and effectively consensual" (p. 44).

VISUAL RHETORIC OF IDEAL PRACTICE

The clichéd phrase, "Pictures say it better than words," is relevant to messages gleaned from the glossy, colorful photographs that dominate textbook pages. When initially examining a book, reviewers might be pleased that illustrations show diverse children eagerly working in well-lit, modern classrooms and, with the exception of pictures in behavior disorder or at-risk chapters, playing cooperatively in playground settings. Advanced technology is apparent. Books and other supplies and equipment look new.

Pictures show teachers and students constructively participating in one-on-one or small-group instruction with an ideal teacher-to-pupil ratio (rarely more than four students are shown together). A long-term myth of special education—one that perhaps convinced me and others to enter the field and parents to allow their children to become part of the system—is that classified and placed children receive individualized instruction by expert teachers so they catch up with peers and are subsequently successful in school and postschool life. Textbook illustrations capture that story line well. Unfortunately, the staged conditions in pictures in many textbooks do not resemble the reality of schools and classrooms. During more than 40 years of teaching and field supervision, except occasionally in wealthy suburban schools, I rarely saw such positive school conditions. Instead I saw that instruction in pull-out or inclusion settings takes place in groups that have large student-to-adult ratios—never one on one and rarely fewer than eight even in resource settings. Regardless of the actuality of school life, text pictures show clean, well-equipped classrooms with contented children and calm teachers. The contrived portrayals give a false impression of special education. Based on textbook images, preservice teachers would gain little idea about the reality of sites where they will teach.

Textbook pictures represent a diverse array of students in various class-room, school, family, and neighborhood contexts. Most, but not all, teachers and other professionals shown in these pictures are White—something that accurately represents the current teaching force.[4] A close look at pictures reveals signs that children are middle class, even when racially diverse. Perhaps the biggest deception of these texts' visual rhetoric in illustrations is the clustering of ethnically and racially diverse students together. Based on what I observe in schools, and what statistics indicate (Artiles & Trent, 1994; Connor & Boskin, 2001; Patton, 1998), special education clientele are mainly low income—often exceedingly poor and racially segregated—especially students, but also faculty. Some pictures are more obviously staged than others. In a supposed gang picture in a chapter called "Teaching Students Who Are at Risk," a group of eight racially diverse adolescents stand on a doorstep holding skateboards (Smith, Polloway, Patton, & Dowdy, 2001). A similar picture in an at-risk chapter of another text shows four racially and gender-mixed teenagers in front of a wall with graffiti (Lewis & Doorlag, 2003). Their faces supposedly reflect a bad attitude; however, a couple of youths appear to be having trouble keeping from laughing.

Perhaps the most problematic textbook picture is actual not staged, although this is unknown because the source was not given. An African-American youth stands with his hands behind his back (perhaps hand-cuffed) surrounded by three serious looking elderly White people, one of whom is pointing at him (Hallahan & Kauffman, 2003). The picture is located in a "Cultural Factors" section. The caption reads: "Questions about the influence of culture on behavior include the degree to which violence in the media affects behavior. This thirteen-year-old boy was convicted of murdering a six-year-old family friend, but said he was only imitating wrestling moves he'd seen on television" (p. 235).[5] The stereotyping in this picture is pernicious. It seems a more appropriate commentary would have been that African-American and other minority youth find themselves controlled by White authority figures who have little empathy for them and little understanding of the impact of race/class privilege/dominance of such public institutions as schools and legal systems.

For legal and ethical reasons, children in pictures that represent high-incidence disabilities may be actors who do not actually receive special services. Often my own children and their friends were recruited to be in videos or illustrations. Recruiting actors is convenient and retains the confidentiality of those classified. Such casting, however, misconstrues the reality

---

[4]An actual count might reveal that there are more teachers of color pictured in proportion to their actual representation in schools across the country.

[5]The authors claimed that, "all the photographs we chose are reproduced with the consent of the individual depicted" (p. xxix), which seems hard to believe in the case of this picture.

of who receives special education services. Using actors and enriched settings indicates such problems as: students who receive special education services may not want it to be known and thus will not be in pictures, authors' contacts are solely with middle-class children, and/or reality must be concealed even to potential special education teachers. Defenders of these deliberately staged pictures might claim that schools should be integrated, that practices related to identifying and teaching low-income and racial/ethnic minority students should be fair, and that all children should attend schools with adequate resources. I agree with these wishes. Nevertheless, class and minority race/ethnic overrepresentation exists in low-status placements just as underrepresentation is common in high-status arrangements. Teachers and other citizens must be made acutely aware that schools and society do not distribute resources equally to all children and low-status school arrangements are resented by students. They need to know that routine classification and placement practices often are biased.

When issues of discrimination are addressed in texts, it is done to reassure readers that it happened in the past or in other places, but is no longer a problem. The message that comes across is that the authors and readers are innocent. The text is clean, neutral, objective, and not complicit in biased practice. Nevertheless, the reality is that American schools are largely segregated by social class and race/ethnicity (Orfield, Eaton, & the Harvard Project on Desegregation, 1996). It is deceitful to pretend otherwise by picturing or describing inaccurate social situations.

It seems valid to conclude that text photographs are a socially conscious art meant to deceive readers into thinking that special education is a beneficial service that results from humanitarian motives. Texts' visual rhetoric is a controlled representation of school conditions and diversity that masks identities and realities and hides power differentials endemic to special education and schools generally. The popular textbooks I reviewed did not trouble the hierarchies or challenge the basic foundations of meritocratic schools or unequal relations within society. Textbook content is euphemized. The subaltern voice is silent except as it is portrayed; asymmetrical and incommensurate cultural spaces are erased (Mohanty, 1994). Text coverage indicates that poverty and low status are comfortable, just as high status and authority are benign.

Although the significance of this pattern is unclear, a trend over time that might be noted is that earlier textbook covers included pictures of children with physical stigmata that made them recognizable as disabled or some showed typical-looking children assumed to be learning disabled or in another high-incidence category. A few newer editions of texts or new textbooks still have photographs of a child or children on the cover, and others have drawings of diverse children that looked somewhat like UNICEF greeting cards. Most new textbook covers have colorful abstract art that is cheerful and upbeat. Because many textbooks were published by the same companies, it might be that their cover designs were done by the same artists.

SOFTENING DISTANCE AND OBJECTIVITY
WITH PERSONALIZATION

A seeming improvement to the most recent textbooks is the personalized touch of inserting short stories about children with disabilities, their families, and professionals. The strictly factual content of earlier texts may have seemed too dry to engage young adult readers. An alternative rationale is that authors became aware of and bothered by children being reduced to labels, traits, and social roles. Now, in addition to details about disabling conditions, personal stories cast a human glow on the texts' subject matter. Voices in these vignettes talk about needed services. Faces smile with pleasure at the helpfulness of special education teachers and supportiveness of peers. Contented parents mention being respected as partners and listened to in case conferences. These personal tangents make the object of texts (i.e., disabled other) seem as one with authors and readers. Although these personalized episodes may seem an improvement, a problem is that all are positive, clean portrayals inconsistent with evidence that students often are not happy about being classified and parents are not satisfied with their interaction with school personnel (see Brantlinger, 1986, 1994; Cook-Sather, 2002; Harry, 1992; Lee, 1999; Stoughton, 2003). The factiousness apparent in the burgeoning of special education-related lawsuits does not appear nor are there traces of the tensions that pervade special education labeling and service delivery.

Personal vignettes are a version of biography. Corbett (1996) argued that the confident authority apparent in portraying others in certain ways (i.e., distorting the subjects' views) serve to restrict thinking and justify the continuation of patronage. When those on the recipient end of special education speak in scenarios scattered through modern textbooks, it is a ventriloquism of the text author's voice. Recipients' perspective and agency are diminished or eliminated. When personalization involves idealized imaginary that pacifies friction and avoids power differentials, the result is the colonization of disabled people by the expert writers of texts. Individuals with disabilities become commodities. Regardless of how classified students may feel about special education, representations of their contentment with the system are dutifully packaged for sale. Moreover, these brief personalized moments in textbooks retain the character of add-ons. Preservice teachers may decide not to read them because they know they will not be covered on tests.

In the revised textbook that I reviewed for the publisher, another new human touch was the author's picture and a short bibliography of his life's work in the preface. The book was dedicated to his parents, which fits the pattern of textbook dedication to authors' family members, particularly children. A single author of a textbook is rare; most have two to four authors and, except for university affiliation, little information is revealed about them. Nevertheless, the short sidetrack about the author in the text I reviewed happened once; the remainder of the text is written with third-person distance and anonymity.

TRANSMOGRIFICATION TO WHAT SELLS

Although this review did not include a historical component of comparing textbooks over time, it is clear that with advances in technology most textbook packages have added to the print components of texts. For instance, the ninth edition of Hallahan and Kauffman (2003) offered the following supplements: student study guide with practice tests, companion Web site plus online study guide, instructor's resource manual and test bank, PowerPoint electronic slide package organized by chapter for lecture use, computerized test bank, six "snapshots" videos (profiles of students), five "professionals in action" videos, package of 100 transparencies, resource guide for the Internet, and a free booklet of case studies. To compete in the lucrative textbook market, publishers have continuously embellished on their product by adding features and somewhat modifying the format or content of texts. Nevertheless, despite these changes, a perusal of recent textbooks reveals that the basic content and categorical chapter organization has remained stable over time.

One thing that has changed is that many texts now appear committed to inclusion, at least rhetorically. There was a notable absence of inclusion content in textbooks for several years after inclusion was advocated by teacher educators and became routine in school districts. Indeed for years after federal legislation prioritized it, inclusion was still omitted in many texts. That has changed. Inclusion has now worked its way into the textbook market, albeit in some rather odd forms. It has gained enough stature to be foregrounded in the title of some texts. Yet despite official support for inclusion, some authors still hold out and fail to recognize its importance. A 2003 textbook published by Merrill Prentice-Hall, *Fundamentals of Special Education: What Every Teacher Needs to Know,* consists of an introductory and 10 categorical chapters. The index reveals that inclusion is mentioned on only four pages, and inspection of those pages reveals that this limited coverage includes commentary on resistance to it and why it does not work. This particular text is somewhat of an aberration. Textbook companies apparently have decided that inclusion sells and have encouraged even the most reluctant of authors to recommend its use and provide information on what they see as best inclusion practices. Despite what must have been unrelenting resistance on the part of some authors—prominent special education professors who vehemently criticized inclusion supporters as well as inclusion (see reviews by Brantlinger, 1997; Danforth, 1999)—inclusion is now present in their updated texts, although in rather ambiguous ways. Inclusion makes brief appearances in each categorical chapter in Hallahan and Kauffman (2003). However, the one generic index reference, "inclusive school movement," includes this conclusion:

> More radical reformers . . . call for a single, unified educational system in which all students are viewed as unique and special and entitled to the same quality of education. Although many of the suggested reforms have great appeal and some could produce benefits for exceptional students, the basis for the integration of special and general education and the ultimate consequences they might bring have been questioned. [the authors list themselves a few times in this fairly long list of citations] (pp. 18–19)

Given that federal funding priorities and federal, state, and local legislation emphasize inclusion, these skeptics may realize that, to stay on top of the field (and the textbook market), they must turn into inclusion proponents. The depth and sincerity of their support for inclusion are questionable.

Slee (1993) noted that special education reinvented itself to stake its claim in the so-called *era of inclusion*. A close reading of these modified textbooks reveals that the title and section heads may have changed somewhat, but the content is still slanted toward assessment, identification, classification, and remediation—that is, practices that single out individual students as different and in need of specialized services rather than strategies to create inclusive classrooms that accommodate a wide (i.e., normal) range of diverse learners. The technically focused interventions are illustrated by a section headed "Inclusion Strategies," which goes on to give a bulleted two-page list of "learning strategies including acquisition, storage, and expression levels of learning" (Smith et al., 2001, pp. 480–481).

Textbooks and Conservative Control of Schooling

Proponents of capitalism tout that a benefit of the free market is diversified products and consumer choice. The result of competition in the special education textbook arena has had the opposite effect—texts are remarkably similar. In fact the tables of contents seem hewn from the same template. Apple (1989) observed that K–12 and college-level textbook homogenization has accompanied pressures to regulate curricula and teaching. An increasing emphasis on discipline-centered curriculum and tightening control of all curricula supposedly are done for purposes of efficacy, cost effectiveness, and accountability. Apple claimed the real impact is to reduce text content to narrow technical skills, which he called a "commodifying reorganization convenient for administrative surveillance" (p. 146). Brady (2002) attributed these trends to a "limited modernist, positivist paradigm with an agenda that seeks to define exemplary practices in order to package them for use in schools to 'fix' problems, and control and predict human behavior" (p. 63). Foucault would have seen these phenomena as part of an assimilating gaze that subjugates people and renders them controllable (see Allan, 1999). Techniques of power operate to simultaneously create whole domains of knowledge that are aligned with conservative interests. Pinar (1997) claimed that traditionalists (textbook producers and authors) see curriculum work as service to practitioners, but function under a bureaucratic model with an ameliorative orientation, an ahistoric posture, and an allegiance to behaviorism and technological rationality.

NORMALIZING DISCOURSES

Foucault's writings elucidate subtle aspects of social practice that are particularly relevant to disability studies. In *The Birth of the Clinic*, Foucault (1973) introduced the idea of *governmentality* in reference to the presumption that everything can and should be managed by the appropriate authority. Administering *pastoral* (taking care of others) power and authoritative protectiveness supposedly is done out of concern for others' well-being. Foucault's ideas about the medical gaze relate to this analysis of textbooks: Medical (special education professional) observation allows the construction of an account of what is going on with a patient (student) that connects signs and symptoms (slow acquisition of reading skills, acting out behavior) to diseases (mental retardation, emotional disturbance, attention deficit disorders) that, when identified, can be managed by the right authority.

In *Discipline and Punish*, Foucault (1977) furthered his ideas about the gaze and its relation to disciplinary regimes. Alert to the *deviant*, the gaze uses three mechanisms of surveillance: hierarchical observation, normalizing judgments, and examination. Observations are hierarchical in that only certain credentialed members of society are positioned to determine others' deviance and establish norms for appropriate behaviors. Normalizing judgments become coercive principles that highlight difference (i.e., deviance, abnormality, pathology) and seek to eradicate it through assimilating practices. Standards for normality are incorporated into surveillance instruments or examinations. Foucault delineated three imposing features of examination: (a) compulsory visibility; (b) mechanisms of objectification that facilitate forming categories, determining averages, fixing norms, and classifying individuals; and (c) documentation and description of individual cases so they can be judged, measured, compared with others, and then trained, corrected, and normalized or else excluded.

The usefulness of Foucault's analyses to understanding special education discourse is readily apparent. Once children are declared deficient, they are marked for perpetual surveillance (e.g., regular evaluation is mandatory for the initial classification of children and must be repeated for children to retain the classification and specialized services); and the parents of disabled children and involved professionals are scrutinized as part of the constant review of each case (i.e., case conference and annual review). Correspondingly, special education textbooks detail the nature of deviance and then devote space to mechanisms designed to gauge variation from the norm that have been validated by scientific research (e.g., IQ and a myriad of other tests and evaluation protocols for determining classification and eligibility for special education services). Texts then detail remedial strategies or interventions to correct or control a range of abnormalities. If difference from the norm is extensive or extreme and if modification of abnormality is impossible, then exclusionary practices in the form of the more restrictive options on a cascade of services or placements kick in. Individuals who remain abnormal cannot be part of the mainstream, hence the need for pull-out placements. The inevitable rationale for surveillance, modification, and exclusion is that it is necessary for the sake of the involved children—for their own good. Again teacher education courses and textbooks are the vehicles that socialize preservice teachers into their roles of recognizing deviance, making expert judgments about normality, conducting examinations, and implementing appropriate instruction. Appropriate, like normality, is a key concept in special education; practitioners and clients must do things appropriately—that is, according to the norm.

Foucault (1977) used the analytical technique of reversal or discontinuity to unsettle and subvert categories to make their meaning apparent. All (dis)ability categories are reversals of normed or expected abilities—to see, hear, think, be mobile, behave oneself, and so forth. Because disability is a lack of ability, to understand a society's meaning of disability, its ideas about ability must be clear. Nevertheless, definitions of normality and explanations about why normality is so essential are glaring silences in special education textbooks. For example, in learning disability chapters, reading interventions are provided based on an assumption that it is problematic to read less well than peers. Yet benefits of advanced or equal achievement (i.e., the necessity of normality and the insistence on equating normality with sameness or a statistical average) are not addressed. Special education texts typically allot a chapter to each disability category, constructing each area of diversity as abnormal and problematic rather than natural and acceptable. Yet abnormality is explicated without articulating the nature of normality. "Normal children" are an assumed but insufficiently identified control group. Positivists insist that definitions be operationalized, yet the central concept of normality in special education textbooks and rationale justifying its importance remain elusive. Apple (1995) contended that textual silences reveal much about the ideological interests at work. Special education is not the only field that practices textual exclusions. Anyon (1983) noted the absence of working-class content and perspective in texts, and Kuzmic (2000) echoed Harding's (1993) concern about the dominance of masculine standpoint in texts.

In his early work, Foucault directed attention to forces external to individuals, but by 1988 he noted how the external gaze was internalized so individuals policed themselves. Although Foucault claimed that normality is a fiction, he nevertheless noted that fictions or myths induce the effects of truth. This idea resonates with the well-known medical student syndrome, in which symptoms read about become imagined in self. It seems that disability identities detailed in special education texts are imagined in children who are then referred and their disability status becomes actualized. Because Foucault was gay, it is no coincidence that his *The Care of The Self* (1988) has the subtitle, *The History of Sexuality*, and that he was interested in the surveillance around gender generally and masculinity specifically. He used an *archeological* approach to examine the layers of sediment on which particular ideas or disciplines are built. Layers of special education practice can be traced, perhaps starting with the founding of the common school, to the educational emphasis on academic learning, the development of IQ and achievement tests to measure and sort students, the proliferation of disability categories, the formation of a cascade of placements and service provisions, and, eventually, the measures designed to monitor and modify deviance.

Theories offered by Foucault and his followers should be unsettling to textbook companies and the scholars who publish foundational knowledge about abnormality in these texts. As distributors of disciplinary routines, textbooks' coverage fits into hierarchical schemas that anonymously descend from the authorities who originally research and delineate deviance to school personnel who eventually practice according to the strategies laid out in texts. Conditions and procedures are covered in textbooks as accurate, permanent, and objectively derived policy and practice. Special education law has codified conditions (classifications) that can be treated in schools and also details how procedures should be appropriately applied to school children. New versions of the law are portrayed as superior to previous ones and as part of progress in the field. Professionals are (re)assured that as they classify children at their locales, their observations and judgments are sanctioned by higher, objective but anonymous legal expertise and professional wisdom that have been laid out authoritatively in textbook print. Textbook authors take on the responsibility of interpreting complex systems for naive readers and do so efficiently and succinctly in seemingly neutral and apolitical, but certainly dehistoricized and decontextualized ways. Expanding areas of expertise have been accompanied by increasing reliance on specialized credentials (Troyna & Vincent, 1996), which has meant a lucrative and powerful professionalization of dominant group members just as the neediness and risks, and subsequent powerlessness, of subordinate groups have become more severe.

In contrast to permanent, accumulated, foundational knowledge (e.g., found in textbooks), Foucault recommended that theory be an attitude, ethos, or philosophy that critiques everything in social life, especially limits placed on humans by prefabricated notions of normality. Foucault suggested creating new selves courageous enough to live in uncertainty. His work opened the scholarly world to postmodern and poststructural deconstruction of foundational knowledge and inspection of the dynamic, drifting, impermanent layers and sediments of language and practice.

TEXTBOOKS AS AUTHORITATIVE PURVEYORS OF TECHNICAL KNOWLEDGE

In *Education and Power*, Apple (1995) made assertions consistent with Foucault's claims that the world is discursively constructed by text and that textual discourses—and ideologies infused in these discourses—hide the particular interests they serve and uneven power relationships they maintain. Apple saw modern governments as hierarchical bureaucracies that are dependent on the circulation of ideas that promote their legitimacy. Whereas earlier governments were sanctioned by religious dogma, current ones rely on technical knowledge. Apple argued that bureaucracies are maintained by the development of control mentality, in which those subjected to its rules are to accept only technical authority and expertise as legitimate. Citizens must be oriented to rules and procedures, have compliant attitudes toward authority, and adopt habits of punctuality, regularity, and consistency. Apple claimed that the major function of the educational apparatus in bureaucracies is to maximize the distribution of technical knowledge supposedly so individuals can enhance their chances of attainment in a competitive market. However, drawing from Raymond Williams, Apple argued that the "actual stuff of curriculum" serves to retain hierarchical power relations through its "selective traditions" (p. 28).

In *Teachers and Texts* (1989), and later with Christian-Smith (1991) in the *Politics of the Text*, Apple examined the process by which curriculum gets to teachers, including the politics of textbook production and sales, the ideological and economic reasons behind textbook decisions, and how culture, economy, and governments interact to produce official knowledge. According to Apple, teacher education texts define what should be taught and the nature of legitimate knowledge. He further claimed that textbooks represent the ideas and interests of state-represented policymakers. Apple found that a few large publishers (Prentice-Hall, McGraw-Hill, CBS publishing group, Scott, Foresman) controlled 75% of the total sales of college texts. Metcalf (2002) claimed that numerous politicians, including the current U.S. president and his cabinet members, own substantial shares in test and textbook companies. Thus, because they benefit from test and text sales connected with the tightening of standards around disciplinary knowledge, a conflict of interest is evident in these politicians' educational decisions. Furthermore, the prescribed text and test content preserves the societal hierarchies from which they benefit (Brantlinger, 2003). Academic content is vast and the sanctions for not knowing it extreme, hence alternative curriculum geared toward progressive, democratic, and communitarian-oriented educational reform are squeezed out of schools.

Although teachers have always had relatively little control over their labor, Apple (1989) argued that with increasing state intervention in curriculum development and textbook adoption and the subsequent workload routinization and intensification, teacher autonomy has declined. This announcement was made before the accountability movement was in full swing. Apple noted that teachers (and teacher educators) interpret external pressures as professionalization and so do not protest state interference. This imposed professionalism and the discourse surrounding the need to control teachers relates to class and gender dynamics: A majority of teachers are women and/or first-generation college. This round of professionalization has not meant more power and autonomy, but rather the opposite; teachers must increasingly rely on highly educated experts.

Control-oriented trends change teachers' relations with students and students' status in schools. In the 1970s and 1980s, teachers were encouraged to be attuned to children's feelings and life conditions. This emphasis on caring and multicultural sensitivity meant a rejection of meaningless rote learning. Teachers were to eliminate the ranking practices in schools. Apple claimed that the right-wing educational reform agenda has been aimed at replacing teachers' connections with diverse students with detached practice—to append a formalized agenda in which administrative oversight demands a responsiveness to textual authority and a reemphasis on the traditional western European canon. Text- and test-dominated practice ensures that sorting and ranking children (reproducing social privilege) is the uppermost responsibility of schools.

TEXTBOOK READERS BECOMING EXPERTS
IN SPECIAL EDUCATION

Ball (1990) pointed out that we do not speak the discourse, the discourse speaks us. Not only do textbooks construct the subject (children, adolescents, and sometimes adults with special needs or disabilities), they also construct readers as needing particular knowledge. Readers, however, are even less evident in textbooks than authors. Anonymous textbook consumers are blank slates or open vessels to be filled by text content. Text usage mythology suggests that as pre- or inservice teachers become acquainted with or memorize text content, they are filled with the knowledge necessary to become competent professionals who will benefit students.

In most of the textbooks I reviewed, routines of referrals, prereferral interventions, due process guidelines for handling case conferences, and legalities of assessment and service delivery are covered as depersonalized and even dehumanized events. The implication is that well-trained technical experts know the rules, follow them, and implement special education in a fair, neutral manner. The grand textbook narrative is that (special) education is a peaceable and righteous kingdom where all benefit and none suffer. Therefore, if preservice teachers learn everything in texts and follow provided rules and guidelines, they will become professionals who get it right.

In a high-stakes testing climate, textbooks have facts essential for passing required state certification examinations. However, textbooks were in style before the accountability movement became vogue. Texts have long been accepted as the primal source through which potential special education teachers gain expert knowledge and hence professional stature. Status as specially prepared teachers is dependent on being filled with the special education textbook knowledge that supposedly will transform college students into competent teachers who will be respected by their students, parents, administrators, and peers. Conscientious and erudite potential teachers who receive As in courses are assured that they have the foundational knowledge to implement the best technologies of science-based practice. They know that in their future jobs they will skillfully participate in the texts' versions of meticulous assessments and fool-proof interventions. Schmidt (2000) and Martin (2002) claimed that much of professional socialization in many fields results in closing down the minds of their members.

Teacher educators may buy into the logic of the importance of textbook knowledge, expecting students to draw on texts' essential facts in their teaching practice. In the highly competitive high-stakes atmosphere of academia, by using the big glossy texts, faculty encourage college students to be dependent on packaged knowledge. Preservice teachers become part of the intensified, depersonalized, and commodified world of modern education. Consensus about text accuracy and usefulness is part of the politics of text use that keeps the textbook industry in business. Ironically, when students enter the field, they pronounce much of what they learned in teacher education irrelevant. Rejecting text content and teacher education recommendations, they praise student teacher supervisors and current colleagues as well as their own survival skills for correct and useful induction into the field.

CONTROLLING THE DAMAGE OF TEXTS

College students are likely to see what is encompassed in texts as necessary and important, although a few are skeptical, wondering what the texts' content has to do with actual teaching. Many reject textbook information during their student teaching when they are positioned to maintain classroom order and be accountable for student learning. Others may retain respect for texts and worry about their own competencies as they struggle with the complexities of teaching in the messy context of schools. Some may be concerned that they did not sufficiently incorporate important text content and therefore lack the hoped for professional competency. They may feel let down by the texts' promise of expertise that they do not feel when on the job. The clean, unrealistic textbook portrayals of children and classrooms may do neophytes harm by setting up an expectation that, if the explicit and implicit guidelines in the text are followed, teaching will be smooth and uncomplicated. Hence, those who dismiss textual knowledge may be healthier, happier, and more prepared to teach than those who retain a nagging sense of personal inadequacy. Internalizing beginning teachers doubt themselves rather than the textual construction of special education service delivery as controllable and fairly easy.

REFERENCES

Allan, J. (1999). *Actively seeking inclusion: Pupils with special needs in mainstream schools.* London: Falmer.

Anyon, J. (1983). Workers, labor and economic history, and textbook content. In L. Cronbach, F. Bienstedt, F. McMurray, W. Schramm, & W. B. Spalding (Eds.), *Text materials in modern education* (pp. 51–52). Philadelphia: Temple University Press.

Apple, M. W. (1989). *Teachers & texts: A political economy of class & gender relations in education.* New York: Routledge.

Apple, M. W. (1990). *Ideology and curriculum.* New York: Routledge.

Apple, M. W. (1995). *Education and power* (2nd ed.). New York and London: Routledge.

*References with an asterisk are found in Table 3.1.

Apple, M. W., & Christian-Smith, L. (1991). The politics of the textbook. In M. W. Apple & L. K. Christian-Smith (Eds.), *The politics of the textbook* (pp. 1–21). New York: Routledge.

Armstrong, L. (1993). *And they call it help: The psychiatric policing of America's children.* Reading, MA: Addison-Wesley.

Artiles, A. J., & Trent, S. (1994). Overrepresentation of minority students in special education: A continuing debate. *Journal of Special Education, 27,* 410–437.

Baker, B. (1999). Disabling methodologies. *Pedagogy, Culture, & Society, 7*(1), 91–115.

Baker, B. (2002, Winter). Disorganizing educational tropes: Conceptions of dis/ability and curriculum. *Journal of Curriculum Theorizing,* pp. 47–80.

Ball, S. (1990). *Politics and policy making in education.* London: Routledge.

Barthes, R. (1972). *Mythologies* (A. Lavers, Trans.). New York: Noonday.

Barton, L., & Oliver, M. (1997). Special needs: Personal trouble or public issue? In B. Cosin & M. Hales (Eds.), *Families, education and social differences* (pp. 89–101). London and New York: Routledge, in association with The Open University.

Berliner, D. C., & Biddle, B. J. (1995). *The manufactured crisis: Myths, fraud, and the attack on America's public schools.* Reading, MA: Addison-Wesley.

*Blackbourn, J. M., Patton, J. R., & Trainor, A. (2004). *Exceptional individuals in focus* (7th ed.). Upper Saddle River, NJ: Prentice-Hall.

Bogdan, R. (1988). *Freak show: Exhibiting human oddities for amusement and profit.* Chicago: University of Chicago Press.

Bogdan, R., & Taylor, S. (1976). The judged, not the judges: An insider's view of mental retardation. *American Psychologist, 31,* 47–52.

Bogdan, R., & Taylor, S. (1994). *The social meaning of mental retardation: Two life stories.* New York: Teachers College Press.

Bowles, S., & Gintis, H. (1976). *Schooling in capitalist America.* New York: Basic Books.

Brady, J. (2002). Transformative leadership through alternative curriculum. *Scholar-Practitioner Quarterly, 1*(1), 53–66.

Brantlinger, E. A. (1986). Making decisions about special education: Do low-income parents have the information they need? *Journal of Learning Disabilities, 20,* 95–101.

Brantlinger, E. A. (1994). High-income and low-income adolescents' views of special education. *Journal of Adolescent Research, 9*(3), 384–407.

Brantlinger, E. A. (1997). Using ideology: Cases of non-recognition of the politics of research and practice in special education. *Review of Educational Research, 67,* 425–460.

Brantlinger, E. A. (2003). *Dividing classes: How the middle class negotiates and rationalizes school advantage.* New York: Routledge Falmer.

Britzman, D. (1991). *Practice makes practice: A critical study of learning to teach.* Albany: State University of New York Press.

Caplan, P. J. (1995). *They say you're crazy.* Reading, MA: Addison-Wesley.

Capshew, J. H. (1999). *Psychologists on the march: Science, practice, and professional identity in America, 1929–1969.* Cambridge: Cambridge University Press.

Charlton, J. I. (1998). *Nothing about us without us: Disability oppression and empowerment.* Berkeley, CA: University of California Press.

Christensen, C., & Rizvi, F. (Eds.). (1996). *Disability and the dilemmas of education and justice.* Buckingham: Open University Press.

Connor, M. H., & Boskin, J. (2001). Overrepresentation of bilingual and poor children in special education classes: A continuing problem. *Journal of Children & Poverty, 7,* 23–32.

Cook-Sather, A. (2002). Authorizing students' perspectives: Toward trust, dialogue, and change in education. *Educational Researcher, 31*(4), 3–13.

Corbett, J. (1996). *Bad mouthing: Language of special needs.* London: Falmer.

*Culatta, R. A., Tompkins, J. R., & Werts, M. G. (2003). *Fundamentals of special education: What every teacher needs to know.* Upper Saddle River, NJ: Prentice-Hall.

Danforth, S. (1999). Pragmatism and the scientific validation of professional practices in American special education. *Disability and Society, 14*(6), 733–751.

Danforth, S. (2001). A pragmatic evaluation of three models of disability in special education. *Journal of Developmental and Physical Disabilities, 13*(4), 343–359.

Davis, L. (1995). *Enforcing normalcy: Disability, deafness, and the body.* London: Verso.

Davis, L. (1997). Introduction: The need for disability studies. In L. Davis (Ed.), *The disability studies reader* (pp. 1–8). New York: Routledge.

Duplass, D. (Pseudonym), & Smith, T. (1995). Hearing Dennis through his own voice: A redefinition. *Behavioral Disorders, 20*(2), 144–148.

Erevelles, N. (2000). Educating unruly bodies: Critical pedagogy, disability studies, and the politics of schooling. *Educational Theory, 30*(2), 25–48.

Erevelles, N. (2002a). Voices of silence: Foucault, disability, and the question of self-determination. *Studies in Philosophy and Education, 21,* 1–35.

Erevelles, N. (2002b). (Im)material citizens: Cognitive disability, race, and the politics of citizenship. *Disability, Culture, and Education, 1*(1), 5–25.

Fairclough, N. (1992). *Critical language awareness.* London: Longman.

Foucault, M. (1973). *The birth of the clinic.* London: Routledge.

Foucault, M. (1977). *Discipline and punish.* London: Penguin.

Foucault, M. (1988). *The care of the self: The history of sexuality* (R. Hurley, Trans.). New York: Routledge.

Fullan, M. (1993). *Change forces: Probing the depths of educational reform.* New York: Falmer.

Gabel, S. (1999). Depressed and disabled: Some discursive problems with mental illness. In M. Corker & S. French (Eds.), *Disability discourse* (pp. 38–46). England: Open University Press.

Gabel, S. (2001). "I wash my face in dirty water": Narratives of disability and pedagogy. *Journal of Teacher Education, 52*(1), 31–47.

Gabel, S., & Danforth, S. (2002). Disability studies in education: Seizing the opportunity. *Disability, Culture, & Education, 1,* 1–3.

Garland Thomson, R. (1997). *Extraordinary bodies: Figuring physical disability in American culture and literature.* New York: Columbia University Press.

Giroux, H. A. (1994). Living dangerously: Identity politics and the new cultural racism. In H. A. Giroux & P. McLaren (Eds.), *Between borders: Pedagogy and the politics of cultural studies* (pp. 29–55). New York and London: Routledge.

Good, T. L., & Brophy, J. E. (1984). *Looking in classrooms.* New York: Harper & Row.

Grandin, T., & Scariano, M. M. (1986). *Emergence: Labeled autistic.* Novato, CA: Arena.

Hahn, H. (1983). Paternalism and public policy. *Society, 20,* 36–44.

Hahn, H. (1997). Advertising the acceptably employable image: Disability and capitalism. In L. Davis (Ed.), *The disability studies reader* (pp. 172–186). New York: Routledge.

*Hallahan, D. P., & Kauffman, J. M. (2003). *Exceptional learners: Introduction to special education* (9th ed.). Boston: Allyn & Bacon.

Haraway, D. (1988). Situated knowledges: The science question in feminism and the privilege of partial perspective. *Feminist Studies, 14,* 575–599.

Harding, S. (1993). Rethinking standpoint epistemology: What is "strong objectivity"? In L. Alcoff & E. Potter (Eds.), *Feminist epistemologies* (pp. 49–82). New York: Routledge.

*Hardman, M. L., Drew, C. J., & Egan, M. W. (2002). *Human exceptionality: Society, school, and family* (7th ed.). Boston: Allyn & Bacon.

Harry, B. (1992). Making sense of disability: Low-income, Puerto Rican parents' theories of the problem. *Exceptional Children, 59*(1), 27–40.

Heshusius, L. (1995). Holism and special education: There is no substitute for real life purposes and processes. In T. M. Skrtic (Ed.), *Disability and democracy: Reconstructing [special] education for postmodernity* (pp. 166–189). New York: Teachers College Press.

*Heward, W. L. (2003). *Exceptional children: An introduction to special education* (7th ed.). Upper Saddle River, NJ: Prentice-Hall.

Kohn, A. (2003). Introduction: The 500-pound gorilla. In A. Kohn & P. Shannon (Eds.), *Education, Inc.: Turning learning into a business* (pp. 1–11). Portsmouth, NH: Heinemann.

Kutchins, H., & Kirk, S. A. (1997). *Making us crazy: DSM: The psychiatric bible and the creation of mental disorders.* New York: The Free Press.

Kuzmic, J. J. (2000). Textbooks, knowledge, and masculinity: Examining patriarchy from within. In N. Lesko (Ed.), *Masculinities in school* (pp. 105–126). Thousand Oaks, CA: Sage.

Lee, P. W. (1999). In their own voices: An ethnographic study of low-achieving students within the context of school reform. *Urban Education, 34*(2), 214–244.

*Lewis, R. B., & Doorlag, D. H. (2003). *Teaching special students in general education classrooms* (6th ed.). Upper Saddle River, NJ: Prentice-Hall.

Linneman, R. D. (2001). *Idiots: Stories about mindedness and mental retardation.* New York: Peter Lang.

Linton, S. (1998). *Claiming disability: Knowledge and identity.* New York: New York University Press.

Martin, B. (2002). Review of "Disciplined minds: A critical look at salaried professionals and the soul-battering system that shapes their lives." *Radical Teacher, 62,* 40–43.

*Mastropieri, M. A., & Scruggs, T. E. (2003). *The inclusive classroom: Strategies for effective instruction.* Upper Saddle River, NJ: Prentice-Hall.

McDermott, R. P., & Varenne, H. (1996). Culture, development, disability. In R. Jessor, A. Colby, & R. A. Shweder (Eds.), *Ethnography and human development: Context and meaning in social inquiry* (pp. 101–126). Chicago and London: University of Chicago.

McNeil, L. (2000a). The educational costs of standardization. *Rethinking Schools, 14,* 8–13.

McNeil, L. (2000b). *Contradictions of school reform: Educational costs of standardized testing.* New York: Routledge.

Mercer, J. R. (1973). *Labeling the mentally retarded.* Berkeley: University of California Press.

Merriam, S. (1998). *Qualitative research and case study applications in education.* San Francisco: Jossey-Bass.

Metcalf, S. (2002, January 28). Reading between the lines: The new education law is a victory for Bush and his corporate allies. *The Nation, 274*(21), 18–22.

*Miller, S. P. (2002). *Validated practice for teaching students with diverse needs and abilities.* Boston: Allyn & Bacon.

Miner, B. (2003). For-profits target education. In A. Kohn & P. Shannon (Eds.), *Education, Inc.: Turning learning into a business* (pp. 131–139). Portsmouth, NH: Heinemann.

Mitchell, D. (1997). Modernist freaks and postmodernist geeks. In L. J. Davis (Ed.), *The disabilities study reader* (pp. 348–365). New York: Routledge.

Mohanty, C. T. (1994). On race and voice: Challenges for liberal education in the 1990s. In H. A. Giroux & P. McLaren (Eds.), *Between borders: Pedagogy and the politics of cultural studies* (pp. 145–166). New York and London: Routledge.

Nagel, T. (1986). *The view from nowhere.* New York: Oxford University Press.

Oliver, M. (1990). *The politics of disablement.* New York: St. Martin's Press.

Orfield, G., Eaton, S. E., & the Harvard Project on Desegregation. (1996). *Dismantling desegregation: The quiet removal of Brown versus Board of Education.* New York: New Press.

Patton, J. M. (1998). The disproportionate representation of African Americans in special education: Looking behind the curtain for understanding and solutions. *The Journal of Special Education, 32*(1), 25–31.

*Peterson, J. M., & Hittie, M. M. (2003). *Inclusive teaching: Creating effective schools for all learners.* Boston: Allyn & Bacon.

Pinar, W. F. (1997). The reconceptualization of curriculum studies. In D. J. Flinders & S. J. Thornton (Eds.), *The curriculum studies reader* (pp. 121–129). New York: Routledge.

Richardson, V., Casanova, U., Placier, P., & Guilfoyle, K. (1989). *School children at-risk.* London: Falmer.

Rodis, P., Garrod, A., & Boscardin, M. L. (2001). *Learning disabilities and life stories.* Boston: Allyn & Bacon.

Rogers, L., & Swadener, B. B. (2001) *Semiotics & dis/ability.* Albany, NY: State University of New York Press.

Ryan, W. (1971). *Blaming the victim.* New York: Random House.

*Salend, S. J. (2001). *Creating inclusive classrooms: Effective and reflective practices* (4th ed.). Upper Saddle River, NJ: Prentice-Hall.

Sapon-Shevin, M. (1999). *Because we can change the world: A practical guide to building cooperative, inclusive classroom communities.* Boston: Allyn & Bacon.

Sarason, S. (1990). *The predictable failure of school reform.* San Francisco, CA: Jossey-Bass.

Schmidt, J. (2000). *Disciplined minds: A critical look at salaried professionals and the soul-battering system that shapes their lives.* New York: Rowman & Littlefield.

Skrtic, T. M. (1995a). The functionalist view of special education and disability: Deconstructing the conventional knowledge tradition. In T. M. Skrtic (Ed.), *Disability and democracy: Reconstructing [special] education for postmodernity* (pp. 65–103). New York: Teachers College Press.

Skrtic, T. M. (1995b). Power/knowledge and pragmatism: A postmodern view of the professions. In T. M. Skrtic (Ed.), *Disability and democracy: Reconstructing [special] education for postmodernity* (pp. 25–62). New York: Teachers College Press.

Skrtic, T. M. (1995c). Theory/practice and objectivism: The modern view of the professions. In T. M. Skrtic (Ed.), *Disability and democracy: Reconstructing [special] education for postmodernity* (pp. 3–24). New York: Teachers College Press.

Slee, R. (1993). The politics of integration: New sites for old practices? *Disability, Handicap, and Society, 8*(4), 351–360.

Slee, R. (1996). Disability, class and poverty: School structures and policing identities. In C. Christensen & F. Rizvi (Eds.), *Disability and the dilemmas of education and justice* (pp. 96–118). Buckingham/Philadelphia: Open University Press.

Slee, R. (1998). The politics of theorising special education. In C. Clark, A. Dyson, & A. Millward (Eds.), *Theorizing special education* (pp. 30–41). London: Routledge.

Sleeter, C. (1986). Learning disabilities: The social construction of a special education category. *Exceptional Children, 53,* 46–64.

*Smith, D. D. (1989). *Teaching students with learning and behavior problems* (2nd ed.). Englewood Cliffs, NJ: Prentice-Hall.

*Smith, D. D. (2004). *Introduction to special education: Teaching in an age of opportunity* (5th ed.). Boston: Pearson.

*Smith, T. E. C., Polloway, E. A., Patton, J. R., & Dowdy, C. A. (2001). *Teaching students with special needs in inclusive settings* (3rd ed.). Boston, MA: Allyn & Bacon.

*Smith, T. E. C., Polloway, E. A., Patton, J. R., & Dowdy, C. A. (2004). *Teaching students with special needs in inclusive settings* (4th ed.). Boston, MA: Allyn & Bacon.

Stoughton, E. A. (2003). *"I wish I could tell them how I feel": Sharing the stories of young people labeled emotionally disturbed and their families.* Doctoral dissertation, Indiana University, Bloomington.

Taylor, S. J. (1988). Caught in the continuum: A critical analysis of the principle of the least restrictive environment. *Journal of the Association for Persons With Severe Handicaps, 13,* 41–53.

Thompson, J. B. (1990). *Ideology and modern culture: Critical social theory in the era of mass communication.* Stanford, CA: Stanford University Press.

Tomlinson, S. (1982). *A sociology of special education.* London: Routledge & Kegan Paul.

Tomlinson, S. (1995). The radical structuralist view of special education and disability: Unpopular perspectives on their origins and development. In T. M. Skrtic (Ed.), *Disability and democracy: Reconstructing [special] education for postmodernity* (pp. 122–134). New York: Teachers College Press.

Trent, J. W., Jr. (1994). *Inventing the feeble mind: A history of mental retardation in the United States.* Berkeley: University of California Press.

Troyna, B., & Vincent, C. (1996). The ideology of expertism: The framing of spceial education and racial equality policies in the local state. In C. Christensen & F. Rizvi (Eds.), *Disability and the dilemmas of education and justice* (pp. 131–144). Philadelphia: Open University Press.

*Turnbull, R., Turnbull, A., Shank, M., & Smith, S. J. (2004). *Exceptional lives: Special education in today's schools* (4th ed.). Upper Saddle River, NJ: Prentice-Hall.

Tyack, D., & Tobin, W. (1994). The "grammar" of schooling: Why has it been so hard to change? *American Educational Research Journal, 31,* 453–479.

Valencia, R. R. (Ed.). (1997). *The evolution of deficit thinking: Educational thought and practice.* London and Washington, DC: Falmer.

Varenne, H., & McDermott, R. (1998). *Successful failure: The school America builds.* Boulder, CO: Westview.

Walker, H. M., Forness, S. R., Kauffman, J. M., Epstein, M. H., Gresham, F. M., Nelson, C. M., & Strain, P. S. (1998). Macro-social validation: Referencing problems in behavioral disorders to societal issues and problems. *Behavior Disorders, 24*(1), 7–18.

Ware, L. (2001). Writing, identity, and the other: Dare we do disability studies? *Journal of Teacher Education, 52*(2), 107–123.

Wright, S. E. (1993). Blaming the victim, blaming society, or blaming the discipline: Fixing responsibility for poverty and homelessness. *The Sociology Quarterly, 34*(1), 1–16.

Zizek, S. (1994). Introduction: The spectre of ideology. In S. Zizek (Ed.), *Mapping ideology* (pp. 1–33). London and New York: Verso.

Chapter 4

How Does It Feel to Be a Problem? Race, Disability, and Exclusion in Educational Policy

Nirmala Erevelles
Anne Kanga
The University of Alabama

Renee Middleton
Auburn University

When describing the historical construction of the African American as denigrated other in U.S. society, American sociologist W. E. B. DuBois (1999/1903) wrote, "Between me and the other world there is ever an unasked question: . . . How does it feel to be a problem?" (p. 164). A century later, this argument still holds true not only for people of color, but also for persons with disabilities. For example, public schools, especially in economically deprived urban and rural areas, continue as segregated institutions that undereducate the disproportionately large number of students of color using antiquated educational resources in run-down facilities (Kozol, 1991). In a similar fashion, special education programs across the country serve more than 6.1 million students with disabilities in educational contexts that are both separate and unequal (Horn & Tynan, 2001). In both cases, educational policymakers, rather than addressing the persistent structural inequalities reproduced in educational settings, continue to blame the failure of inclusive strategies on the teachers, administrators, and students (Shanker, 1994; Sleeter, 1993).

Unfortunately, with a few exceptions, scholars in both the areas of critical race theory and disability studies have rarely explored the critical connections between these two historically disenfranchised groups within educational contexts. Critical race theorists, burdened by the debates associated with the Bell Curve and its assertion of racial intellectual inferiority, have actively attempted to distance themselves from students with disabilities (especially students with mental retardation). The Disability Rights

Movement, in an effort to claim for itself a political and cultural identity as a minority group with civil rights, has sometimes overlooked the critical aspect that persons with disabilities are also separated along the axes of race, class, gender, and sexuality. Although some scholars (Begum, 1992; Fine & Asch, 1988; Morris, 1991) have attempted to address these political and conceptual tensions between different minority groups by claiming that the collective experience of marginality can be construed as the common thread linking these axes of difference, others have argued that it is more important to move beyond this obvious commonality and treat disability as a critical theoretical category—one that can also effectively account for the theorizing of difference along the axes of race, class, gender, and sexuality (Erevelles, 2000; Middleton, Rollins, & Harley, 1999). We subscribe to the latter position. Therefore, in this chapter, we examine the history of education policies of exclusion and inclusion in U.S. society, and we explore its current implications for both persons with disabilities and persons of color in U.S. public schools within the specific and interlocking contexts of disability studies and critical race theory.

RACE AND DISABILITY: A PROVOCATIVE RELATIONSHIP

As mentioned in the introduction, this analysis that maps a critical relationship between race and disability is potentially controversial because both these categories of social difference have proved to be uneasy bedfellows, especially in educational contexts. Despite the critical intervention of Disability Studies in educational and other contexts, disability continues to be theorized via a deficit model that associates disability with deviance and disorder. This is especially true with regard to cognitive/learning disabilities because, in educational contexts, the social construct of intelligence is valorized more than anything else. It is this association of disability with "deviance" and "the lack of intelligence" that has caused several race scholars to distance themselves from any critical analysis of the category of disability as is evidenced in the critiques leveled against Herrnstein and Murray's (1994) controversial book, *The Bell Curve: Intelligence and Class Structure in American Life*. For example, in response to this text, distinguished intellectuals like Stephen J. Gould (1995), Henry Louis Gates (1995), Howard Gardner (1995), and Jacqueline Jones (1995), among others, have argued against making any linkages between disability and race because such linkages erroneously demonstrate the "collective *stupidity* of the group" (Jones, 1995, p. 81; italics added). Stated simply, critical race theorists have actively sought to distance race from any associations with disability because they have recognized that this association has been used to justify the brutality of slavery, colonialism, neocolonialism, and the continued exploitation of people of color (Erevelles, 2000; Gould, 1981; Sarason & Doris, 1979).

Interestingly enough, some scholars in the area of special education have also sought to distance themselves from analyses that link race and disability together. For example, one such scholar, Kauffman (1989), critiqued proponents of the Regular Education Initiative (REI) for comparing special education with racial discrimination. Kauffman claimed that equating race with disability, when discussing equal educational opportunity, is demeaning to racial groups experiencing discrimination because their differences (i.e., differences in skin color) are trivial compared with those of students with disabilities who need complex accommodations to meet their educational needs. Accusing REI supporters of making emotional claims that the segregation of students with disabilities is similar to apartheid, Kauffman distinguished between the civil rights claims of racial and ethnic minorities and those of students with disabilities. According to Kauffman, although racial and ethnic minorities have argued for equal access to educational opportunity regardless of their differences, people with disabilities have described equal opportunity as the access to a differentiated education designed specifically to meet their unique needs. In making these claims, Kauffman sought to demonstrate that, whereas race (i.e., skin color) is irrelevant to teaching and learning outcomes, disability is not, and so any relationship between these two categories is problematic to say the least.

In this chapter, we critique both these positions on the grounds that they draw on narrow definitions of race and disability that are rooted in biological determinism. For example, in the first position, race theorists have invoked the biological definition of *disability* as an immutable and pathological abnormality rooted in the "the medical language of symptoms and diagnostic categories" (Linton, 1998, p. 8). By doing this, they have ignored critical theoretical interventions from scholars in the area of Disability Studies, who have argued for a social model of disability (Linton, 1998; Oliver, 1990; Thomson, 1997). The social model offers a sociopolitical analysis that describes disability as an ideological construction used to justify not only the oppressive binary cultural constructions of normal/pathological, autonomous/dependent, and competent citizen/ward of the state, but also the social and racial divisions of labor (Erevelles, 2000; Linton, 1998; Russell, 1998). In other words, Disability Studies scholars have described disability as a socially constructed category that has historical, cultural, political, and economic implications for social life.

In a similar fashion, Kauffman showed his commitment to biological determinism when he described race solely in terms of skin color. This narrow definition of *race* as wholly determined by physical characteristics has been rejected by scholars in the area of critical race theory. Arguing for the significance of race in almost all aspects of American life, novelist Toni Morrison pointed out that, "Race has become metaphorical—a way of referring to and disguising forces, events, classes, and expressions of social decay and economic divisions far more threatening to the body politic than biological 'race' ever was" (cited in Ladson-Billings & Tate, 1995, p. 49). Expanding on this definition, critical race theorist Lopez (2000) argued that race is "neither an essence nor an illusion, but rather an on-going contradictory, self-reinforcing plastic process subject to the macro forces of social and political struggle and the micro-effects of daily decisions" (p. 165).

Clearly, the definitions of *race* and *disability* offered by both critical race theory and Disability Studies foreground one common theme—the rejection of biological criteria as the sole determinant of difference. At the same time, extrapolating from their respective definitions of race and disability, critical race theorists and Disability Studies scholars have also unwittingly collaborated to (re)theorize difference as a historical, social, and economic construct that is (re)constituted in complex ways by contesting ideological configurations. More important, as the following discussion demonstrates, advocates who have supported the inclusion of persons marked by race and/or disability in educational contexts have drawn on similar philosophical and constitutional arguments to frame educational policies that support this inclusion (e.g., *Brown v. Board of Education*, 1954; *Education of All Handicapped Children's Act* [*EAHCA*], 1975, renamed *Individuals With Disabilities Education Act* [*IDEA*] in 1990). Additionally, in recent years, race and disability have once again reappeared together on the educational stage in a recent court case (e.g., *Lee v. Lee County Board of Education*, 1997), where critiques have been made regarding the overrepresentation of minority students in special education classes. In light of all these intersections, we explore the philosophical, historical, and social connections between race and disability in the specific context of educational policy.

COMMON ORIGINS, COMMON OUTCOMES: THE RACIST AND ABLEIST POLITICS OF THE COMMON SCHOOL MOVEMENT

The intimate relationship between race and disability in educational contexts has existed since the inception of the common school movement. The common school, as originally envisioned by Horace Mann in the mid-19th century, was to become the "vanguard of societal redemption and renewal" (Gerber, 1996, p. 161)—an institution that would be able to solve all the social, economic, and political problems of society by placing all its members in a common context and by teaching them a common set of political and economic beliefs (Spring, 2001). In a historical context, where the immigration of poor illiterate peasants from Ireland, southern and eastern Europe, and Asia was at an all-time high, there was an urgency to support educational institutions that would protect class privilege and, at the same time, win consensus for the democratic ideals and republican virtues articulated by the Anglo Saxon ruling elite (Sarason & Doris, 1979; Spring, 2001). Moreover, the critical task of creating homogeneity from among this heterogeneous population required the deculturalization of these immigrants—a process Spring (2001) described as "the strange mixture of democratic thought and intolerance . . . [that] combines education for democracy and political equality with cultural genocide—the attempt to destroy [Other] cultures" (p. 168). Additionally, it was this same historical context that witnessed the ruthless colonization of Native American peoples, the annexation of their territories, as well as the brutal enslavement of Africans by the New Republic. In each of these examples, the violence embedded in these acts of deculturalization, exploitation, colonialism, and slavery was justified by linking racial and ethnic difference from Anglo Saxon norms with biological inferiority—thereby invoking the ideological construct of disability.

Disability Studies scholars have argued that linking the social construct of disability with biological inferiority is a modern myth that has derived from a number of social practices, such as "the desire to help and the need to control, infatuation with science and technique and professional status responses to social change and economic stability" (Trent, 1994, p. 6). Because disability does, in fact, represent radical physical and/or cognitive differences from the mythical norm, it has challenged the contradictory impulse of Western society to regulate difference and preserve homogeneity despite the celebration of liberal individualism espoused by Enlightenment thought. Unable to effectively regulate difference, Western society has sought to expunge it or, at least, distance itself from it, participating in what philosopher Etienne Balibar called *prophylaxis.* Prophylaxis, according to Balibar, describes the need to purify the social body—"to preserve 'one's own' or 'our' identity from all forms of mixing, interbreeding, or invasion . . . [and is based upon] the stigmata of 'otherness' [e.g., language, race, disability] . . . creating the icon of the 'other' body" (cited in Davis, 1995, p. 80) that has to necessarily be excluded from normal life.

In the historical context of common schooling, where nation building was a critical priority, the ruling elites supported ideologies that married disability with race in the constitution of nationalistic discourses. One symbolic manifestation of such ideologies was the Freak Show—a popular pastime in the mid-19th and early 20th centuries where obviously disabled people as well as nondisabled, non-Western people were exhibited in local fairs under the dubious category of *freak* (Bogdan, 1988). In one such exhibit, William Henry Johnson, a microcephalic African American, was described in these freak shows by his keeper as the "*connecting link between the wild na-*

tive African and the brute creation" (*Life of the Living Aztec Children*; cited in Bogdan, 1988, p. 137; italics added). Such depictions foregrounded how the physical differences of non-Western as well as disabled people were collectively designated as biological anomalies and used to justify their social and political exclusion from democratic life. Additionally, such representations that associated the "inalienable otherness" of "foreign peoples" with "natural inferiority" were also utilized to justify the colonialist and imperialistic practices of the New Republic while still maintaining national pride in its much celebrated democratic principles.

It was these same ideologies that interpenetrated the educational discourses of the early 20th century, when the enforcement of compulsory education laws disrupted the social context of the common school (Sarason & Doris, 1979). Now schools were compelled to deal with the new immigrant children (e.g., Italians and Irish) who were not so easily socialized into accepting the homogeneity expected of them. Rather than explaining these difficulties as societal (e.g., poverty, illiteracy, etc.), the schools located these difficulties in the child, who was now described as either physically, morally, or intellectually defective—characteristics that were seen as interfering with the development of physical, moral, and intellectual traits in schools (Trent, 1994). In an effort to meet the needs of such students without disrupting the normal functioning of the school system, the first special education classes were constructed that now contained "over-age children, so-called naughty children, and the dull and stupid children" for whom school "had little or nothing to offer them" (Farrell; cited in Sarason & Doris, 1979, p. 297). The introduction of special education classes now constructed a bifurcated school system—one for special students that was overwhelmingly represented by racial minorities and one for normal students. This overrepresentation of minority students (in this case, Italian American children) in special education classes was explained in a 1926 study by Florence Goodengough as follows:

> It is unquestionably true that the home surroundings of certain racial groups, notably the Italians and the Negroes, are, as a rule, far less favorable than those of the average American children. . . . "Social pressure" or "racial prejudice" is often urged as a reason for the segregation of certain racial groups within the poorer neighborhoods. In this connection it must be remembered that while racial prejudice may bring about segregation, the character of the neighborhoods thus set off is primarily dependent upon the people living within them. It is doubtful whether the Southern Negro has more to contend with in the way of this prejudice than the Chinese or Japanese in California: yet the contrast between the typical Oriental neighborhood and the Italian or Negro district is marked. . . . *It seems probable, upon the whole that the inferior environment is an effect at least as much as it is a cause of inferior ability, as the latter is indicated by intelligence tests.* (cited in Sarason & Doris, 1979, pp. 345–346; italics added)

Thus, rather than taking measures to ameliorate the social conditions within which the working poor among the immigrant and African-American population lived, dominant ideologies utilized the intersection of oppressive biological discourses of race and disability to support the exclusion of certain populations from the mainstream.

THE POLITICAL ECONOMY OF EDUCATIONAL ACCESS: REPRODUCING THE STATUS QUO

Although in later years, Italian Americans (as well as others of European origin) were culturally absorbed into the dominant populations and moved out of the ambit of cultural minority status to form a new racial category of *Whiteness* (Pinar, 1993), African Americans continued to remain the denigrated racialized other in U.S. society. In the North, prior to the Civil War and as early as 1803, freed slaves in the Boston area won the right to educate their children in segregated public schools (Spring, 2001). In the southern states before the Civil War, slaves were categorically denied an education for fear that this would inspire them to revolt against the peculiar institution of slavery (Anderson, 1988). However, after the Civil War, Southerners were forced to face the dilemma of how best to educate the newly freed slaves to fit into an increasingly industrialized economy. It is here again that the logic of disability can be seen to intersect with race and class in the formulation of educational policy.

Much of the discussion about education for African Americans in the southern states was located in attempts to support a segregated and stable South (Watkins, 2001). Simply put, if African Americans were to be educated, this education was not to disturb the racial and social class traditions of the South. Thus, what was suggested was a "special kind of education for southern blacks"—one that would teach African Americans to adjust themselves to the racial and class structure of the South. Southern planters, however, resisted all attempts to expand educational opportunities for African-American children, although some White southern industrialists backed by northern philanthropists collaborated to support segregated educational institutions that would provide manual or industrial education for African Americans. Such educational policies provoked debates within the African-American community, most notable being the debate between Booker T. Washington and W. E. B. DuBois. Washington favored the Hampton–Tuskegee model of manual education, whereas DuBois maintained that African Americans should receive the same educational opportunities afforded their Euro-American counterparts. In the end, the education made available to African Americans—an education that was both separate and unequal—served as an "ideological force that would provide instruction suit-

able *for adjusting blacks to a subordinate social role in the emergent New South*"
(Anderson, 1988, p. 36; italics added).

The prior arguments clearly link educational policy to the exploitative
interests of U.S. capitalism, especially in the maintenance of an unequal division of labor that was racially based. Similar arguments were also utilized
to justify the rapid proliferation of special education classes and large state
institutions for disabled people. One of the central purposes of public education was to upgrade the labor force so that it could efficiently support the
expanding capitalist industry and its profit-making interests (Gerber,
1996). In school systems that were to be necessarily organized on a large
scale in an effort to supply the economy with a constant supply of productive workers, schools needed to become efficient institutions that could
manage and control its diverse population of students (Gerber, 1996;
Sarason & Doris, 1979). Gerber reported that, at the turn of the century,
teaching was primarily conceived of as the "oral presentation and recitation
of subject matter and an array of drill and practice for acquiring basic academic skills" (p. 160). For students who appeared to be disruptive and/or
unresponsive to this mechanized routine (i.e., the nearly 2% of "imbeciles"
and almost 9% of the "mentally dull"), separate special education classes
were seen as the new panacea (Gerber, 1996; Trent, 1994).

Although some may argue that the provision of special education classes
for students labeled disabled did, in fact, support the "social work function of
the school," other arguments point to the development of such programs as
a thinly disguised way to preserve the status quo. Economic considerations always haunted these discussions as exemplified in a 1908–1909 article by the
then superintendent of the Baltimore Public Schools, James Van Sickle:

> If it were not for the fact that the presence of mentally defective [sic] children
> in a school room interfered with the proper training of the capable children,
> their education would appeal less powerfully to boards of education and the
> tax paying public. . . . [T]he presence in a class of one or two mentally or mor-
> ally defective [sic] children so absorbs the energies of the teacher and makes
> so imperative a claim upon her attention that she cannot under these circum-
> stances properly instruct the number commonly enrolled in the class. School
> authorities must therefore greatly reduce this number, employ many more
> teachers, and build many more school rooms to accommodate a given num-
> ber of pupils, or else they must withdraw into small classes these unfortunates
> *who impede the regular progress of normal children.* (cited in Sarason & Doris, 1979,
> p. 263; italics added)

Although clearly the interests of the normal children claimed higher priority than the mentally or morally defective children, we do not wish to suggest here that special education classes were not also simultaneously committed to transforming these students into productive and self-supporting

citizens. At the same time, there was a fear that the failure to realize productivity from these populations would also deprive society of the productive capabilities of those who cared for them (Trent, 1994). Thus, special education was viewed as a means of social control that could effect the rational socialization of students labeled mentally retarded into the smoothly functioning communities and the well-ordered fabric of American life (Trent, 1994).

However, because the dominant assumptions of productivity were narrowly defined in terms of assisting in the efficient extraction of surplus (Erevelles, 2000), special education classes often met with failure in terms of these requirements. As a result, for those individuals who were unable to effectively transform themselves into productive citizens, institutionalization became the next option, and this resulted in large numbers of people with disabilities being segregated from almost all aspects of mainstream life in large state-run institutions (Trent, 1994). However, these institutions did not abandon education. Rather, Trent pointed to an interesting shift in the purpose of education from being a means to an end to now becoming an end itself. As a result, these institutions became completely isolated and served as warehouses for people with mental and severe disabilities, living on bleak, self-sustaining campuses that utilized the unpaid labor of their inmates for their continued existence (Trent, 1994; Wolfensberger, 1975).

This discussion suggests that the political, economic concerns of schooling to produce a productive, efficient, and malleable citizenry were instrumental in supporting a separate and unequal education for both African Americans and people with disabilities, although in radically different ways. On the one hand, the education of African Americans was designed to transform them into more productive workers while preventing them from recognizing their own productive capacity as a valuable, marketable resource for fear that this realization would be damaging to the status quo. On the other hand, the resistance of people with disabilities to adhere to the narrow definitions of productivity for the sole purpose of extracting the maximum profit was described as morally degenerative behavior; as a result, they were first educationally segregated and then institutionalized. In both cases, segregation was supported by invoking intersecting ideologies of race and disability that were tied to issues of political economy, biological inferiority, and moral and mental degeneracy.

IDEOLOGIES OF EXCLUSION: THE POLITICS AND PROBLEMS OF RACE AND DISABILITY POLICY IN EDUCATION

By the early 1950s, racial segregation in public schools was the norm across America, especially because *Plessy v. Ferguson* (1896) formally legalized segregation by allowing what they termed *separate but equal school systems* for African Americans and Whites. In 1954, however, the landmark U.S. Supreme Court decision in *Brown v. Board of Education, Topeka* promised some changes in education for African Americans. In the *Brown* decision, the U.S. Supreme Court declared state-imposed racially segregated schools to be unconstitutional under the Fourteenth Amendment's equal protection clause. Thus, the *Brown* decision became the basis for school desegregation efforts that have spanned nearly four decades. The principal focus of these efforts was to achieve racially balanced schools. More specifically, efforts were made to ensure that the racial makeup in schools reflected the racial makeup of the populations located in specific school districts or within the state. Thus, for example, in some instances, busing and magnet schools were adopted as principal strategies to accomplish this racial balance.

Although most of these policies took effect soon after the *Brown* decision in the northern states, the southern response continued to be widespread resistance. Thus, 7 years after the *Brown* decision, there were still no desegregated school districts in Alabama, Mississippi, and South Carolina. Furthermore, fewer than 0.5% of the African-American students attending southern schools were doing so with Euro-American students. Southern resistance to desegregation efforts resulted in a proliferation of litigation designed to force school districts to comply with the *Brown* decision. In litigation beginning as early as 1963, several southern states were cited for operating a "racially dual school system," and, as a result, the courts ordered the respective State Superintendents of Education to require that all school districts in the named states dismantle racially segregated schooling. Some important cases cited by the Civil Rights Division of the U.S. Department of Justice included *Anderson and United States v. Madison County School Dist. et al.* (S.D. Miss.), *Lee and United States v. Macon et al.* (M.D. Ala), and *Monroe & U.S. v. Jackson Madison County School Sys. Board of Education* (W.D. Tenn). These court orders required school districts in these states to submit strategic plans " 'for complete disestablishment of [their] dual school system' " (U.S. Department of Justice–Civil Rights Division, 1998, p. 2) and to "resolve the outstanding issues" (U.S. Department of Justice–Civil Rights Division, 1998, p. 5) in an effort to attain unitary status. Recent reports from the U.S. Department of Justice–Civil Rights Division (1998) have described their ongoing involvement with more than 400 school districts still covered by similar desegregation orders. For example, *Lee and United States v. Macon et al.* (M.D. Alabama) describes some of these struggles. Many in the White community in Tuskegee, Alabama, called on the then Governor George Wallace to support their resistance to racial integration in schools and universities (Parrott, 2002). In support of this stance, Wallace stood at the door of the University of Alabama and responded to intervention from the Kennedy Administration by saying: "In the name of the greatest people that ever trod this earth, I draw the line in the dust and toss the gauntlet before the feet of tyranny, and I say, segregation now! Segregation tomorrow! Segregation forever!" (cited in Parrott, 2002). Kennedy federalized the Alabama National Guard and used their services along with other federal marshals to allow the first African-American students to enroll at the University of Alabama. With desegregation seeming to be an inevitable reality, White communities like the one in Tuskegee chose to find an alternative legal method to remain segregated by constructing a private school, Macon Academy. Macon Academy, instituted in direct opposition to the integration of the public school system, continues to house a primarily White student body (Parrott, 2002). Similar private schools, like the one in Tuskegee, were instituted in the South in an effort to maintain racial segregation.

The relationship between race and disability is clearly evident in the legislation pertaining to disabled students in U.S. public schools. Both philosophically and strategically, the movement toward reform in the education of persons with disabilities followed hard on the heels of the *Brown* decision and the 1960s civil rights legislation. Both landmark legislative reforms brought a heightened awareness to disabled people, their families, and their advocates of the injustice of exclusion based solely on physiological and cognitive differences. Prior to 1975, nearly 1.7 million children with disabilities were not receiving any educational services, and more than 3 million children with disabilities were not receiving an education appropriate to their needs (Katsiyannis, Yell, & Bradley, 2001). Education for students with disabilities appeared to be a privilege rather than a right. The *Brown* decision, which viewed racial segregation as the denial of equal educational opportunity, was now utilized by advocates of students with disabilities to demonstrate that educational segregation on the basis of disability was also an unconstitutional practice. Similar to *Brown,* two landmark cases of 1972, *Pennsylvania Association for Retarded Citizens (PARC) v. Commonwealth of Pennsylvania* and *Mills v. Board of Education,* were instrumental in the passing of the Education of All Handicapped Children Act (EAHCA) in 1975— also known as PL 94-142. The passing of the EAHCA was to ensure that (a) students with disabilities would receive a free and appropriate education, (b) the rights of these students and their parents would be protected by ensuring due process in all educational placement decisions, and (c) states and local agencies would be assisted in their efforts to provide such services. In 1990, PL 94-142 was reauthorized as the *Individuals with Disabilities Education Act (IDEA)*—a more comprehensive law that not only provides supportive funding to the states, but also governs how students with disabilities will be educated.

Twenty-five years after the passing of EAHCA, discontent continues to be voiced regarding the effectiveness of special education programs for students with disabilities. Those critical of the current implementation of special education programs cite the following reasons to support their critique: the unprecedented growth in special education programs as a result of inadequate diagnostic criteria and funding legalities; the rising costs ($79.3 million) that amount to $41.5 million more than that paid to regular education; the inadequate financial support from the federal government that places the burden on local school districts to produce the monies lest they be sued; and the accommodationist model of instruction that critics believe train low- and underachieving students for a lifetime of entitlement (Horn & Tynan, 2001).

The reason for this discontent, according to Gerber (1996), is because the education of students with disabilities has not yet been completely accepted as the stated mission of schooling. Gerber claimed that traditional schooling only sought to provide students with instructional opportunity. On the other hand, special education policy imposes on schools the obligation to seek out and instruct all students notwithstanding their difference— an obligation that schools do not feel compelled to meet and do so only grudgingly. Additionally, in a social context that requires measurable results regarding the effectivity of special education programs, critics of special education policy have asked: "[W]hat, indeed does it mean to provide equality of educational opportunity for children with disabilities if these children will always be at a competitive disadvantage when compared to their more normally achieving peers?" (Gerber, 1996, p. 65).

Questions regarding the equality of educational opportunity continue to also haunt racial minorities. Nearly 50 years after the *Brown* decision, African Americans continue to have access to educational opportunity in separate and unequal contexts—special education programs. As early as 1968, educational researcher Lloyd Dunn pointed out that nearly 60% to 80% of students labeled *mildly mentally retarded* were from low-status backgrounds and included African-American, Latino, and Native American children. In this chapter, we argue that there is something wrong with a society where people are segregated on the basis of race. Similarly, we argue that there is also something wrong with a society that continues to maintain classrooms segregated on the basis of disability. This phenomenon is most evident in our schools, where further segregation continues through misguided policies such as tracking: where Whiteness is equated with competence/ableism and Blackness with incompetence/disability.

Statistics revealed are a real cause for concern. Nearly 25 years later, in the Woodstock Report (1993), F. D. McKenzie, a former superintendent of schools in the District of Columbia, observed that, although African-American students made up approximately 16% of the school population, they made up 35% of the students assigned in special education classes. In K to 12 schools, 70% of students attended predominantly minority schools during the 1998–1999 school year, compared with 66% in 1991–1992 and

63% in 1980–1981. Latinos were even more likely to attend predominantly minority schools, with 76% attending such schools in 1998–1999, up from 73% in 1991–1992 (Zehr, 2001). Additionally, Artiles and Trent (1994) reported that there are distinct correlations between specific racial/ethnic groups and their disabling conditions in the overrepresentation data that point to the organization of special education programs along a specific racial hierarchy. Artiles and Trent also reported that:

> . . . Asian Pacific students are generally underrepresented in disability categories and overrepresented in gifted and talented (G&T) programs. . . . White students are consistently overrepresented in G&T and specific learning disabilities (SLD). . . . In contrast, although we have witnessed in recent years a steady decline in the overall enrollment in programs for students with mental retardation and a sharp increase in the enrollment in programs for individuals with learning disabilities, black students continue to be overrepresented in classrooms for students with mild mental retardation while there is a disproportionate number of Latinos in programs for students with learning disabilities and speech and language requirements. (pp. 414–415)

It is for these reasons that the *Lee and United States v. Macon et al.* (M.D. Alabama) was revisited again in 1997 as the *Lee v. Lee County Board of Education 963F.* Supp. 1122, 1124 (M.D. Ala. 1997) to respond to the overrepresentation of minority students in special education classes in Alabama.

One response to these correlations is to seek an explanation for why they exist. To explore this question, Artiles (1998) suggested that we shift our focus from the individual child to the "individual in action within special contexts" (p. 3). Artiles then went on to suggest two critical questions that interestingly echo the positions of Disability Studies scholars who have also suggested that all discussions of disability have to focus on the social context in which disability is situated. The two questions are as follows: When does difference count, under what conditions, in what ways, and for what reasons? Is the disproportionality in representation in special education programs due to structural factors (e.g., institutional discrimination) or to minority shortcomings produced by poverty?

Disability Studies scholars have already wrestled with the first question regarding difference that Artiles raised. Disability Studies scholars, in concert with the Disability Rights Movement, have steadfastly supported inclusive policies and have argued that the perceived problems in special education have more to do with how the concepts of *disability* and *inclusion* have been interpreted than with anything else (Danforth & Rhodes, 1997; Lipsky & Gartner, 1996; Taylor, 1988). Danforth and Rhodes (1997), for example, argued that failing to question and deconstruct the category of disability even by inclusion advocates has resulted in these same advocates working against their own integrationist and civil rights practices because they continue to support

the devaluation and stigmatization of students with disabilities. Lipsky and
Gartner (1996) claimed that most special education programs operate from
a deficit model, where the consumer (i.e., the student with a disability) is perceived as "having some inadequacy, shortcoming, failure or disease" (p.
153)—a position that already limits the possibilities for students with disabilities. Taylor (1988) described how even a progressive concept like the least restrictive environment (LRE) does, in fact, legitimize restrictive environments, sanctions infringements of the rights of people with disabilities, and
directs attention to physical settings rather than to the services and supports
people need to be integrated into the community. In each of these examples,
these scholars have been critical of the deficit model of disability used to justify the continued segregation of not only students with disability, but now
also racial minorities. Additionally, their arguments support the other contention that a "free appropriate public education" has served as an efficient
sorting tool to track students into special programs according to specific racial hierarchies that relate to the deficit model of disability.

In response to the second question Artiles posed, the statistics stack up
in favor of explaining this overrepresentation in the context of social and
structural factors. In current U.S. society, African-American families tend to
live in urban areas where the tax bases have shrunk in correspondence to
White flight in these same areas. As a result, both the urban public schools
and the child welfare agencies in the area are hopelessly underfunded
(Agbenyega & Jiggetts, 1999). Further, according to the 1993 Woodstock
Report, one third of African-American citizens live in poverty, and adult African-American males have not had an unemployment rate less than 10%
since the 1970s (Woodstock Report, 1993).

Statistics like these indicate that, despite progressive legislation, current
discussions regarding racial inequalities in public education cite problems
resulting from ongoing segregation caused by the residential isolation of
inner-city and poor rural communities from the more affluent suburbs
(Kozol, 1991). Juxtaposed are the challenges associated with the physical
integration of racially and ethnically diverse populations into predominantly White schools settings (Delpit, 1995). It is in this context that Kozol
(1991) described the economic disadvantages African-American children
face as savage inequalities in segregated inner-city and rural schools that
are underfunded, isolated, and deprived of even the most basic resources.
The net result, for the most part, is that African-American children continue to be deprived of equal opportunity in educational contexts, thereby
affecting their employment opportunities in their adult years. Consequently, if employed they will fill jobs that are at the lower ranks of the social division of labor. Thus, what becomes poignantly apparent is that, even
in today's so-called *liberal and inclusive climate*, ideological and structural
forces of institutional racism continue to provide educational opportunities

for African-American children that may not be different from the repressive and segregational educational policies of the late 19th and early 20th century described in earlier sections (Anderson, 1988).

Although most scholars have explained the overrepresentation of racial minorities in special education through the critical perspective of institutionalized racism, there have been few who have explored this issue from the critical perspective of Disability Studies. Treating both disability and special education as social and political constructs would require that we explore "the beliefs, assumptions, worldviews, ways of knowing, and cultural inclinations of those writing the special education scripts, rather than perseverating our focus on those acting out various roles" (Patton, 1998, p. 26). Additionally, Artiles (1998) and Patton (1998) suggested that revisiting the debate on special education requires that we bring to the table philosophical and ethical perspectives to bear on the discussion. It is to these perspectives that we turn to in the next section.

CRITICAL RACE THEORY MEETS DISABILITY STUDIES: SOME CRITICAL PERSPECTIVES

In this section of the chapter, we examine the central issues regarding the overrepresentation of African-American students in special education programs from the perspective of critical race theory in education as well as Disability Studies. Critical race theory in education focuses on the issues of social inequity in general and school inequity in particular, and it is based on the following three propositions: (a) Race continues to be a significant factor in determining inequity in the United States, (b) U.S. society is based on property rights, and (c) the intersection of race and property creates an analytical tool through which one can examine social and school inequity (Ladson-Billings & Tate, 1995). Critical race theory in education draws from critical race legal scholarship of the late 1970s, which challenged the traditional claims of legal neutrality, objectivity, color-blindness, and meritocracy in the U.S. legal system and called for a reinterpretation of civil rights law in light of its ineffectuality by demonstrating that most legislative reforms which sought to remedy racial injustices were often undermined before they could fulfill their promise. In making these arguments, critical race theorists draw on the perspective of racial realism, which requires that one views the law—and by extension the courts—as instruments for preserving the status quo and only periodically and unpredictably serving as a refuge of oppressed people (Bell, 1995b). It is only through this legal and social mechanism of racial realism, critical race theorists argue, that African Americans can rely on having their voice and outrage heard as they foreground the historical patterns, contemporary statistics, and oppressive practices that continue to maintain their social and economic marginalization in U.S. society.

According to Derrick Bell (1992), one of the most prolific scholars in this area, racial discrimination is hidden under "an atmosphere of racial neutrality that helps convince people that racism is a thing of the past" (p. 6). Yet Bell pointed out that when the progress of race relations has been examined from the point of view of racial minorities:

> [t]he fact is that, despite what we designate as progress wrought through struggle over many generations we remain where we were in the beginning: a dark and foreign presence, always the designated "other." Tolerated in good times, despised when things go wrong, as a people we are scapegoated and sacrificed as distraction or catalyst for compromise to facilitate resolution of political differences or relative economic adversity. (p. 10)

It is for these reasons, Bell asserted, that African-American people will never gain full equality in this country—a fact they must acknowledge "not as a sign of submission, but as an act of ultimate defiance" (p. 12).

In the specific context of education policy, Bell (1995a) argued that *Brown v. Board of Education* mandated equal educational opportunities through school desegregation plans aimed at achieving racial balance regardless of whether it was beneficial to students. In other words, Bell described school desegregation as requiring the actual presence of White children in schools with African-American children because it was assumed that only this sort of integration would ensure that African-American children would receive the same education as White children. However, as described earlier, what one observes in racially segregated schools is the low academic performance and large number of disciplinary and expulsion cases of African-American students. In other words, Bell pointed out that, notwithstanding these realities, the reason for persisting with the legal mandate for racial desegregation as articulated in the *Brown* decision has been primarily symbolic in marking the nation's presumed commitment to equal opportunity for African Americans. It is for this reason that Bell urged policymakers committed to social change to "make clear that the major social and economic obstacles are not easily amenable to the legal process and the vigilance and continued activity by the disadvantaged are the crucial elements in social change" (Leroy Clark; cited in Bell, 1995a, p. 18).

Part of the problem with liberal education policy is that it is committed to social reform rather than social transformation. For example, critical race theorist Kimberle Crenshaw (1995) argued that in antidiscrimination legislation a tension exists between conceiving of equality as a process and equality as a result. Crenshaw described the former as a restrictive view, where the focus is on preventing future wrongdoings that are comprised of only certain kinds of subordinating acts that occur in contexts where other interests are not overburdened. The more expansive view of equality as a result calls for the eradication of the substantive conditions of oppression on the basis of race and (in this context) disability. Such a position goes beyond the removal of formal barriers to advocate for the transformation of the normative structures that continue in an unspoken form the stereotypes used to legitimate both White supremacist and ablest society. In other words, Crenshaw's critique points to the limits of liberal educational policy that respond solely to the symbolic subordination of oppressed groups (formal denial of social and political equality through segregation) while paying scant attention to their material subordination. This point is clearly evidenced in the continued oppression of African Americans in educational contexts notwithstanding the landmark *Brown* decision and is also reflective of the experiences of students with disabilities notwithstanding IDEA.

Additionally, engaging the dialectics of ideology and economics, another critical race theorist Cheryl Harris (1995) offered an important argument that demonstrates how rights in property are "contingent on, intertwined, and conflated with race" (p. 107). Property rights, Harris argued, are not natural, but are in fact created by the law. More important, the notion of individual rights that emerged during the founding period of the new republic was rooted in the protection of one's property, where property as described by James Madison "embraces every thing to which a man may attach a value and have a right" (cited in Harris, 1995, p. 279).

According to Harris, the origins of property rights were instituted in racist institutional structures that only validated White possession and occupation of land and permitted as an extension of these rights the hyperexploitation of Black people and the claiming of Native American land. It is in this context that Whiteness as property became significant because it provided the ideological justification to exclude people of color from the privileges of owning property. Harris further pointed out that, because liberal legal institutions were constituted in a context that enforced and reproduced a property interest in Whiteness, they contributed to the reproduction of Black subordination. In this context, owning White identity as property affirmed the self-identity of Whites, especially the dirt poor White working class who reveled in their privilege of racial superiority despite their exploitation at the hands of fellow Whites.

We argue here that Whiteness as property was an intrinsic part of the ensemble of discourses that has been used to justify the racial superiority of White people over people of color by using the logic of disability (e.g., inferior genes, low IQ) to decide who has the rights and benefits to citizenship to fully experience equal educational opportunity (Erevelles, 2002). In other words, we argue here that Whiteness as property justified and (re)iterated the centrality of the nondisabled White heterosexual male body as the most productive and profitable citizen for the burgeoning capitalist society. As such it became critical that, in addition to Whiteness, ability (both cognitive and physical) was also an important property right that had to be safeguarded, protected, and defended in the attempt to decide who could or could not have access to public education.

One of the principal contexts that has enforced and reproduced a property interest in ability is education. Just as in a market economy where property can be bartered for economic gain, in educational institutions, ability as property is bartered for socioeconomic status in the capitalist economy. Moreover, although dominant ideologies represent the market as ostensibly a space where free exchange takes places, in both economic and educational contexts, it has become increasingly evident that all exchanges of property have historically always benefited the ruling class. In the specific context of public education, cognitive ability is constituted and validated by central practices of schooling: the national curriculum that supports the cultural capital of the White ruling class (Bourdieu, 1977), the evaluation strategies that include standardized tests that are biased against children of color and children living in poverty (Brantlinger, 2001), and the educational resources that are unequally distributed between the suburban and the "ghetto" schools (Anyon, 1997; Kozol, 1991). In each of these contexts, (cognitive) ability as property has provided the justification for segregating not only students with severe/cognitive disabilities, but also a disproportionate number of children living in poverty, children of color, and immigrant children with limited English proficiency—a segregation that has contributed to socioeconomic destitution of these populations (Brantlinger, 2001).

Referring to similar practices, multicultural scholar Sonia Nieto (2000) also described how policies and practices such as tracking and other traditional pedagogical practices such as compartmentalization of knowledge have all served to alienate certain categories of students while privileging others. For example, the latest policy of President George W. Bush, the *No Child Left Behind Act of 2001*, is based on the model of White American normalcy or White supremacy— a policy that supports the continued segregation of both disabled and minority students. For example, the four principles on which the *No Child Left Behind Act* is based (e.g., stronger accountability of results, increased flexibility and local control, expanded options for parents, and an emphasis on teaching methods that have proved to work) may sound positive, but are antagonistic to what equal access to education is all about. This is an example of how a policy that purports to be democratic is not.

The insistence on stronger accountability for results is a real drive to ensure that those children labeled *disabled* and other minorities who are presumed to have language deficiencies will of necessity be segregated to ensure that schools exhibit high scores in the high-stakes tests. Similarly, the enthusiastic support of the voucher system ignores the reality that children with disabilities could be excluded from private schools who boast about their high test scores and who are more intent on marketing themselves as conforming to the four basic principles in the *No Child Left Behind Act*. Additionally, the increased proliferation of *alternative schools* and the increased use of other *legal methods* have continued to contribute to the increased segregation of both disabled and minority students. Under the guise of expanding parents' options, the segregation of racial and disabled populations is maintained because economically advantaged students and a few economically disadvantaged gifted minority students will be admitted into both private schools and public schools with good teaching and learning resources. Yet what will happen to those children who are *pathologized* (Mutua, 2001)—children who are not academically gifted, economically disadvantaged, and/or labeled *disabled*? Further, the fourth principle of the Bush plan, which emphasizes proven teaching methods, is also misleading. Methods that have proved to work are likely to be alienating to the denigrated other because these are the methods constructed by the mainstream culture, which support the notion of ability and Whiteness as property, thereby benefiting the ruling class while segregating the constructed other.

CONCLUSION

In this chapter, we argued that it is becoming increasingly critical to discuss issues of race and disability as interrelated concepts, especially in the context of educational policy. We supported this claim by demonstrating how racial segregation has been historically justified by referring to the ideological construct of disability assumed to epitomize biological inferiority. Critiquing the biological determinism of this argument from the theoretical perspectives of critical race theory and Disability Studies, we have demonstrated how the concepts of *Whiteness as property* and *ability as property* have been used to segregate students on the basis of race and disability. This continued segregation of students, notwithstanding the landmark legislation in the areas of both race and disability, marks the continued failure of educational policy to support democratic principles of equal opportunity and social justice in U.S. schools.

Therefore, we argue that educational policymakers have to view the dismantling of racial oppression in conjunction with the dismantling of disability oppression. This requires that we institute education policies that are not based on a deficit model situated within the individual (e.g., remedial classes, special education, alternative school), but rather policies that support positive rights for all children (i.e., ensuring that social, economic, and political conditions are improved for effective education to take place). As noted in the Woodstock Report (1993), raising test scores, instituting competency tests, and increasing teacher standards without addressing the root cause of the problems has hurt more than it has helped. More specifically, education policy needs to be more focused on the continuing struggle to liberate schools from the shackles of Plessy's "separate but equal" dictum— a liberation that can only be achieved if education policy is able to creatively respond to the provocative relationship between race and disability.

If education policymakers are committed to the principles of equal opportunity and social justice for all students, especially those marked oppressively by race and disability, they will have to:

1. Support a concerted effort to sustain the commitment to public education. This will require that education policymakers challenge the increasing proliferation of alternative schools, private schools, and charter schools in an effort to prevent further segregation and the continued exclusion of students on the basis of race and disability.

2. Reduce class sizes and increase the number of highly qualified teachers in each public school classroom—teachers who are trained to meet the needs of the diverse student population notwithstanding their race and their disability.

3. Ensure that teacher training programs prepare educators for teaching in more inclusive settings. This would entail that all teachers attain dual certification in both regular and special education.

4. Support the radical transformation of classroom organization and planning that is geared toward a curriculum that is not based on conformity or homogeneity, but on heterogeneity and difference.

5. Support school practices that work toward the dismantling of institutionalized racism and institutionalized ableism.

6. Reorganize schools so that *Whiteness as property* and *ability as property* do not become the only currency used in schools to achieve academic success.

If these steps are followed, only then will children marked oppressively by race and disability not be perceived as the problem. Only then will public education be truly democratic.

REFERENCES

Agbenyega, S., & Jiggetts, J. (1999). Minority children and their over-representation in special education. *Education, 119*, 619–633.

Anderson, J. D. (1988). *The education of Blacks in the south, 1860–1935*. Chapel Hill, NC: University of North Carolina Press.

Anyon, J. (1997). *Ghetto schooling: A political economy of urban educational reform*. New York: Teachers College Press.

Artiles, A. J. (1998). The dilemma of difference: Enriching the disproportionality discourse with theory and content. *Journal of Special Education, 32*(1), 32–37.

Artiles, A. J., & Trent, S. J. (1994). Overrepresentation of minority students in special education: A continuing debate. *Journal of Special Education, 27*, 410–438.

Begum, N. (1992). Disabled women and the feminist agenda. *Feminist Review, 40*, 70–84.

Bell, D. (1992). *Faces at the bottom of the well: The permanence of racism.* New York: Basic Books.

Bell, D. (1995a). Serving two masters: Integration ideals and client interests in school desegregation litigation. In K. Crenshaw, N. Gotanda, G. Peller, & K. Thomas (Eds.), *Critical race theory: The key writings that formed the movement* (pp. 5–19). New York: New Press.

Bell, D. (1995b). Racial realism. In K. Crenshaw, N. Gotanda, G. Peller, & K. Thomas (Eds.), *Critical race theory: The key writings that formed the movement* (pp. 303–312). New York: New Press.

Bogdan, R. (1988). *Freak show: Presenting human oddities for amusement and profit.* Chicago: University of Chicago Press.

Bourdieu, P. (1977). *Outline of a theory of practice.* Cambridge, England: Cambridge University Press.

Brantlinger, E. (2001). Poverty, class, and disability: A historical, social, and political perspective. *Focus on Exceptional Children, 33*(7), 1–19.

Crenshaw, K. (1995). Race reform and retrenchment: Transformation and legitimation and anti-discrimination law. In K. Crenshaw, N. Gotanda, G. Peller, & K. Thomas (Eds.), *Critical race theory: The key writings that formed the movement* (pp. 103–122). New York: New Press.

Danforth, S., & Rhodes, W. C. (1997). Deconstructing disability: A philosophy for inclusion. *Remedial and Special Education, 18*, 357–367.

Davis, L. (1995). *Enforcing normalcy: Disability, deafness, and the body.* New York: Verso.

Delpit, L. D. (1995). *Other people's children: Cultural conflict in the classroom.* New York: New Press.

DuBois, W. E. B. (1999). Double-consciousness and the veil. In C. Lemert (Ed.), *Social theory: The multicultural and classic readings* (pp. 163–168). Colorado: Westview. (Original work published 1903)

Erevelles, N. (2000). Educating unruly bodies: Critical pedagogy, disability studies, and the politics of schooling. *Educational Theory, 50*(1), 25–47.

Erevelles, N. (2002). (Im)material citizens: Cognitive disability, critical race theory, and the politics of citizenship education. *Disability, Culture, and Education, 1*(1), 5–26.

Fine, M., & Asch, A. (Eds.). (1988). *Women with disabilities: Essays in psychology, culture, and politics.* Philadelphia: Temple University Press.

Gardner, H. (1995). Cracking open the IQ box. In S. Fraser (Ed.), *The bell curve wars: Race, intelligence, and the future of America* (pp. 23–35). New York: Basic Books.

Gates, H. L., Jr. (1995). Why now? In S. Fraser (Ed.), *The bell curve wars: Race, intelligence, and the future of America* (pp. 94–96). New York: Basic Books.

Gerber, M. (1996). Reforming special education: Beyond inclusion. In C. Christensen & F. Rizvi (Eds.), *Disability and the dilemmas of education and justice* (pp. 156–174). Philadelphia: Open University Press.

Gould, S. J. (1981). *The mismeasure of man.* New York: Norton.

Gould, S. J. (1995). Curveball. In S. Fraser (Ed.), *The bell curve wars: Race, intelligence, and the future of America* (pp. 11–22) New York: Basic Books.

Harris, C. I. (1995). Whiteness as property. In K. Crenshaw, N. Gotanda, G. Peller, & K. Thomas (Eds.), *Critical race theory: The key writings that formed the movement* (pp. 276–291). New York: New Press.

Herrnstein, R. J., & Murray, C. (1994). *The bell curve: Intelligence and class structure in American life.* New York: The Free Press.

Horn, W. F., & Tynan, D. (2001). Revamping special education. *Public Interest, 144*, 36–54.

Jones, J. (1995). Back to the future with the bell curve: Jim Crow, slavery, and G. In S. Fraser (Ed.), *The bell curve wars: Race, intelligence, and the future of America* (pp. 80–93). New York: Basic Books.

Katsiyannis, A., Yell, M. L., & Bradley, R. (2001). Reflections on the 21st anniversary of the Individuals with Disabilities Act. *Remedial & Special Education, 22,* 324–335.

Kauffman, J. M. (1989). The regular education initiative as Reagan–Bush education policy: A trickle down theory of education of the hard-to-teach. *Journal of Special Education, 23,* 256–278.

Kozol, J. (1991). *Savage inequalities.* New York: Random House.

Ladson-Billings, G., & Tate, W. F., IV. (1995). Toward a critical race theory of education. *Teachers College Record, 97*(1), 47–67.

Linton, S. (1998). *Claiming disability: Knowledge and identity.* New York: New York University Press.

Lipsky, D., & Gartner, A. (1996). Equality requires inclusion: The future for all students with disabilities. In C. Christensen & F. Rizvi (Eds.), *Disability and the dilemmas of education and justice* (pp. 145–155). Philadelphia: Open University Press.

Lopez, I. F. H. (2000). The social construction of race. In R. Delgado & J. Stefancic (Eds.), *Critical race theory: The cutting edge* (pp. 163–175). Philadelphia, PA: Temple University Press.

Middleton, R. A., Rollins, C. W., & Harley, D. A. (1999). The historical and political context of the civil rights of persons with disabilities: A multicultural perspective for counselors. *Journal of Multicultural Counseling and Development, 27*(2), 105–121.

Morris, J. (1991). *Pride against prejudice: Transforming attitudes to disability.* Philadelphia: New Society Publishers.

Mutua, N. A. (2001). Policed identities: Children with disabilities. *Educational Studies: A Journal of the Educational Studies Association, 32*(3), 289–300.

Nieto, S. (2000). *Affirming diversity: The sociopolitical context of multicultural education.* New York: Longman.

Oliver, M. (1990). *The politics of disablement.* Basingstoke: Macmillan.

Parrott, S. (2001). School segregation still alive. *Expression.* Retrieved on February 25, 2005 from http://www.auburn.edu/academic/classes/jml/4480001/index.html

Patton, J. M. (1998). The disproportional representation of African Americans in special education: Looking behind the curtain for understanding and solutions. *Journal of Special Education, 32*(1), 25–32.

Pinar, W. (1993). Notes on understanding curriculum as racial text. In C. McCarthy & W. Critchlow (Eds.), *Race, identity, and representation in education* (pp. 60–70). New York: Routledge.

Russell, M. (1998). *Beyond ramps: Disability at the end of the social contract.* Maine: Common Courage Press.

Sarason, S., & Doris, J. (1979). *Educational handicap, public policy, and social history: A broadened perspective on mental retardation.* New York: The Free Press.

Shanker, A. (1994, February 6). Inclusion and ideology. *New York Times.*

Sleeter, C. (1993). How White teachers construct race. In C. McCarthy & W. Critchlow (Eds.), *Race, identity and representation in education* (pp. 157–171). New York: Routledge.

Spring, J. (2001). *The American school, 1642–1996.* New York: McGraw-Hill.

Taylor, S. J. (1988). Caught in the continuum: A critical analysis of the principle of the least restrictive environment. *Journal of the Association for Persons With Severe Handicaps, 13*(1), 41–53.

Thomson, R. (1997). *Extraordinary bodies: Figuring physical disability in American culture and literature.* New York: Columbia University Press.

Trent, J. W., Jr. (1994). *Inventing the feeble mind: A history of mental retardation in the United States.* Berkeley: University of California Press.

U.S. Department of Justice–Civil Rights Division. (1998, February). Civil Rights Division Activities and programs.

Watkins, W. H. (2001). Blacks and the curriculum: From accommodation to contestation to beyond. In W. H. Watkins, J. H. Lewis, & V. Chou (Eds.), *Roles of history and society in educating African American students* (pp. 40–46). Needham Heights, MA: Allyn & Bacon.

Wolfensberger, W. (1975). *The origin and nature of our institutional models.* Syracuse: Human Policy Press.

Woodstock Report. (1993). *Brown v. Board of Education of Topeka 40 years later.* Retrieved on February 25, 2005 from http://www.georgetown.edu/centers/woodstock/report/r-fea34. htm

Zehr, M. A. (2001). Schools grew more segregated in 1990s, report says. *Educational Week, 20*(3), 16–17.

Multicultural Education:
Not Needed in the Suburbs!

Ashley de Waal-Lucas
Ball State University

A collection of papers about disciplinary knowledge and quality education was published in the August/September 2004 edition of *Educational Researcher*. Writing from a critical social theory perspective (which combines aspects of critical theory and social theory), Zeus Leonardo argued that "quality education is proportional to the depth of criticism available for students" (p. 3). He went on to clarify:

> Insofar as critical social theory provides the analytical tools for a more complete understanding of social oppression and educational inequality and how to counteract their effects, the students' learning experience approaches quality education. (p. 3)

Leonardo further elaborated that critical social theory accomplishes the quality educational goal by problematizing social relations that reinforce oppression, interrogating the nature and extent of students' complicity with domination, and helping students plan for alternative worlds. Leonardo's recommendations are consistent with those typically made by the imminent multicultural scholars James Banks (1993) and Geneva Gay (1994, 2000).

According to Lipman (1997), a misconception held particularly by Euro-Americans is that multicultural education is specifically for minority students, hence only necessary or valuable in classrooms with an ethnically/racially diverse student body. This view accentuates the idea that multicultural education's fundamental purpose is to raise the self-esteem of students from African-American, Latino, or other minority ethnic backgrounds. This view is in sharp disagreement with the criteria for quality education put forth by Leonardo (2004). Indeed his definition implies that multicultural education is of most value to students who might be "complicit with domination" or are involved in actions that might "reinforce oppression."

Ideally, American public schools should be integrated along as many sociocultural dimensions as possible. Social isolation is a serious problem for a multiethnic society that has hopes of preserving its democratic social life. As early as 1954, Allport espoused the theory that substantive contact among social equals of various races (such as might happen among students in integrated schools) was necessary to reduce prejudice and social inequality. Harvey (1996) addressed the deleterious impact of social isolation on interpersonal perceptions. He hypothesized about the "geographical imaginary" of people who lack contact with each other. Harvey claimed that groups project negative characteristics onto their unknown others. They are also inclined to believe that those in other groups are substantially and significantly different from themselves—that they do not share a common humanity. Unfortunately, the social contact necessary to dispel such social myths are not likely to happen in the near future. With the expansion of the suburbs, socially inclusive schools are rarely the case, and schools with a homogeneously affluent and Euro-American student body are extremely common (Knapp & Woolverton, 1995). As the income gap between rich and poor increases, the rich can afford to live in exclusive suburbs while the poor are left in urban areas with decaying homes and schools. Due to the history of racism in America, there is a high correlation between social class and racial affiliation: African Americans, Hispanics, and Native Americans remain financially disadvantaged in the United States, and most cannot afford to live in areas known for having good schools. Orfield and Eaton (1996) documented that, since *Brown v. Board of Education* (1954) was litigated, many school districts have become more, rather than less, racially segregated.

THE STUDY

I supervised student teachers in a town I call New Canaan. While I worked, I noticed the homogeneously Euro-American nature of the student body as well as the lack of multicultural curriculum in evidence. Based on these observations, I decided to do my dissertation study at the local middle school. I was particularly interested in how middle-school teachers addressed race/ethnicity, social class, and gender in their classrooms. Four of the five New

Canaan Middle School (NCMS) social studies teachers agreed to take part in the study. Nathan, Jacob, and Catherine only held teaching positions in the New Canaan school district. Both in their 50s, Nathan had 33 years of teaching experience, whereas Catherine had only taught for 2 years. Both taught eighth-grade U.S. history. Jacob, in his 30s, had taught 6 years. He currently taught U.S. history and World Cultures. Sarah, who is in her 30s, had taught in several districts during her 7-year teaching career. At NCMS, Sarah taught seventh-grade World Cultures. All the participants were Euro-American, as were all the NCMS teachers.

The study included multiple interviews with the four teachers and a series of observations of their teaching. It also included document (test, textbook, teaching materials) inspection. To ensure authenticity, participants were not informed that multicultural education was the primary focus of the inquiry. Instead they were told that the study was designed to examine the connection between what is taught in university social studies methods courses and what actually is covered in classrooms.

NEW CANAAN MIDDLE SCHOOL

On first impression, NCMS might be seen as a model school. It enjoys the distinction of being a four-star school (on a four-point ranking scale). The community is proud of the school district's recent standardized test scores. In 2003, the local newspaper categorized the seventh and eighth grades as placing first and second, respectively, in the region. Indeed the Department of Education Web site indicates that for the 2002–2003 academic year, 91.1% of NCMS students passed these exams, compared with the state average of 67.7% passing the test.

New Canaan is considered one of the wealthiest of a ring of suburbs that surround a large midwestern city. In 2000, the median home value was listed at $246,300. The wealth of New Canaan is reflected in its beautiful, clean middle school. The modern two-story building is full of windows that let in plenty of natural light. The level of technology at NCMS is impressive. There are seven computer labs plus two-classroom sets of 20 wireless laptops that teachers can borrow for group projects in classrooms. The walls in the classrooms and in halls are covered with student work. Overall the school is a welcoming place, with a relatively calm atmosphere. Although the noise of preteen chatting fills the halls during passing periods, for the most part students appear to be respectful and surprisingly polite for middle-school students. During my time at NCMS as a researcher, and at other New Canaan schools as a university supervisor for six student teachers, I never saw a discipline situation erupt. One thing that is readily apparent at New Canaan schools is that they are White schools. The ethnic breakdown for students for the 2002–2003 school year include: 0% Native American, 0% Black, 1% multiracial, 1% Hispanic, 2% Asian, and 96% White.

Despite high standardized test scores and four-star status, it turns out that NCMS students are missing out on cross-cultural contact. Furthermore, at least according to Leonardo's (2004) idea of a quality education, NCMS students are missing out on an essential component of their education: multicultural education. Before I started my study, I suspected that teachers did not do much with multicultural themes. In the end, I was surprised both at the extent of its exclusion from the social studies curriculum and also at the hints of hostility expressed by teachers about the idea of including multicultural education. In this chapter, I report on what four middle-school teachers directly said about multicultural education and what I saw in their classrooms. I also focus on the multicultural coverage in the social studies textbooks that were adopted while I was conducting my study. Finally, I discuss the exclusion of women's issues and the silencing of girls in one teacher's class. I hope to illustrate how White privilege and, to some extent, male domination are endorsed and perpetuated in one suburban middle school, and how teachers are still insensitive to cultural, social class, and gender issues.

TEACHERS' IDEAS ABOUT THE (NON)IMPORTANCE OF MULTICULTURAL EDUCATION FOR NCMS STUDENTS

The purposes of multicultural education and for whom it is important are often debated. There is general agreement that multicultural education covers: (a) learning about people of different ethnicities, races, cultures, social classes, religious affiliations, genders, and sexual orientations; (b) studying the similarities and differences in people's cultures and perspectives; (c) understanding how diverse students learn best; (d) learning to think critically about the nature of domination and oppression as it relates to humans; and (e) understanding the nature of social justice and equity.

When teachers were asked to discuss multicultural education in individual interviews, their answers proved disappointing. With what appeared to be antipathy, Sarah and Jacob circumvented the question and failed to provide clear definitions. Sarah replied, "I don't know if there is a definition of it. I mean you can pull out a dictionary and get a definition, but I think it depends on the teacher and assessing the needs of the students and how much they are willing to do" (Interview #2, May 20, 2003). Sarah's "depends on the teacher" implied that she thought multicultural education was optional and should be left solely to the discretion of teachers. Although how much multicultural content teachers incorporate into their curriculum may, to some extent, depend on the needs of the students, this teaching flexibility is not really related to the meaning of *multiculturalism*. It is also questionable that what is taught should necessarily be left up to particular teachers. Sarah's statement, "how much they [the students] are willing to do" revealed a stand on multicultural content that would probably be quite different than her stand on, say, mathematics. It is unlikely that a teacher would feel how much math is taught should depend on students' willingness to learn the material.

Similar to Sarah's fuzzy perception of multicultural education, Jacob replied: "What is it supposed to mean? Boy, I don't know. I pretty much just try to stick with the curriculum" (Interview #2, May 15, 2003). Jacob's flippant response revealed a dismissive attitude toward multicultural education. He did not even attempt to define the term. The rest of his response ("try to stick with the curriculum") seemed to reject multicultural education on the grounds that it was not legitimate curriculum. His response might mean that he did not want to deal with controversial issues in his classroom. This interpretation of his incentive for avoiding multicultural education is consistent with what I observed in his classroom.

Both Sarah and Jacob referred to the need to maintain a traditional Western European oriented curriculum. Sarah observed:

> We went into this whole thing about multicultural education in social studies textbooks and we stopped talking about the major White figures. There were more pages devoted to Harriet Tubman than George Washington. It has to be a balance in multicultural education. It is what you eat and where you go. (Interview #2, May 20, 2003)

Sarah was distinctly negative when speaking about the inclusion of multicultural content in textbooks, indicating her sense that the focus on non-Whites or lower status historical figures had gone overboard and takes too much time away from the traditional curriculum. She also alluded to the idea that perhaps multicultural education was not something to be learned from textbooks. She conveyed that students needed to be formally *taught* about Washington, but could pick up knowledge of multicultural issues incidentally—for instance, by going to an ethnic restaurant.

Like Sarah, Jacob also emphasized the need to teach Western-based social studies: "A lot of the curriculum for U.S. History is the dead White guys. It is kind of necessary to learn about our government and our system so you study the dead White guys" (Interview #2, May 15, 2003). Jacob's comment on the importance of teaching the traditional historical figures indicated a conformist orientation to social studies, which would result in including certain traditional topics and people and excluding others. When asked to comment further, Jacob markedly rejected the entire rationale for multi-cultural education:

> I really don't know what multicultural means, I guess. I have friends from other countries and Black friends who grew up differently than I did, and we became buddies in college because we ran track together. I don't know how I would teach or talk differently to a Black person from inner city St. Louis. They talk slightly different from me. But when it comes to school, it is all the same. They are learning the same things as I am. (Interview #2, May 15, 2003)

Here Jacob vacillated. First, he acknowledged that he had international and African-American acquaintances who did come from different cultural milieus. Then he stressed that curriculum should be independent of the student body of the school ("But when it comes to school it is all the same. They are learning the same things as I am"). The question that then arises is what kind of curriculum was Jacob talking about? Was it a traditional Western European curriculum or was he alluding to something more inclusive? Jacob later commented on the value of global education because it taught students about other cultures. When it came to multicultural education, however, Jacob seemed confused. Apparently he did not realize the impact of cultural differences within the United States and how ethnicity contributes to its sociocultural fabric.

However, when he was asked to comment more generally about whether it might be important to incorporate more multicultural content into school curriculum, Jacob responded decisively:

> Oh yeah, definitely. Kids that are Black tend to have Black friends and kids that are White have White friends, and kids that are Asian have Asian friends and they are more similar because they are alike. Everyone needs heroes that are like them. (Interview #2, May 15, 2003)

This statement makes it clear that Jacob equated multicultural education with instruction for racial and ethnic minority students. His glib endorsement of multicultural education for other people's children reconfirms that he also felt it was of little relevance to his own teaching of upper class, White children at NCMS.

The notion that a diverse or predominantly African-American school needs a different curriculum than an all-White school was directly counter to Jacob's initial point that all children should be taught the same. It was only when he was directly asked whether it was important for Euro-American students to know more than dead White men did he concede and say:

> Yeah, and I think it is getting easier again with the president's cabinet. It really bothered me when I was younger and hearing these White kids say "n- this"

and use these other bad words. It was just the redneck. I hated it. I don't hear it here. I have heard it at other schools, but not here. It probably has a lot to do with the parents and I think with most kids here they are not afraid of Black people. They don't think, "That guy is Black." It is kind of like "Colin Powell, yeah, he is Black." It is really nice here because I honestly have not heard one racial comment against Black people in my six years here. That astounded me because I thought I was going to hear it, but I never did. (Interview #2, May 15, 2003)

Jacob's assumption that his students were not racist was a theme that surfaced several times in his interviews. Perhaps it is true that he did not hear the blatant racism that he heard as a student in a different community. This does not mean, however, that racism was not present when students talked among themselves (as they did during some of my observations). There is also a difference between making openly racist remarks and being influenced by racist perceptions—the latter is less visible to outsiders, but nevertheless has an important impact on students' lives. In addition, certainly evidence of racism and situations of racial and social class conflict would not be obvious when the students live isolated from other ethnic groups and social classes. Last, Jacob's responses implied that he was employing race blindness as a pedagogical strategy. His sense of race did not make a difference to his students, and he believed teachers should not draw attention to race by bringing it up or officially including racial topics in his classes.

When asked whether he worried about his students being isolated, Jacob replied, "Some are, but isolated from what?" (Interview #1, April 24, 2003). When asked to comment further, he added:

I think a difference between here and some other schools is it is upper-middle class. Yeah, most are Christian. There are some Jewish kids in here, a couple of Black kids, a couple if kids who are Muslim. There is some of that, but the parents are educated and a lot have BAs, MAs, and PhDs, and I do think they have a decent understanding of the world and I think they give that to their kids. So are our kids isolated? Yes, in a way, but I don't see the name-calling and racism and stuff like when I was growing up. I grew up in the sticks and I didn't like it. I did not like that. The racist thing doesn't exist. I haven't seen it, which has kind of been amazing. It was kind of shocking to me in this all White community. They have their biases like everyone. I think the parents are more educated than in some other places and pass that onto their kids. (Interview #1, April 24, 2003)

Here Jacob reasserted his conviction that NCMS students were not racist. He also equated advanced education levels with antiracist or tolerant sentiments. It was curious that at the start of his narrative he responded, "isolated from what?" It seems plausible that Jacob had not considered or did not believe that students being educated in social class and racial/ethnically homogeneous situations was a problem. Additionally, he did not question whether there might not have been some latent racism behind the parents' choice to live and educate their children in this isolated community and for teachers to teach in schools in these communities. For Jacob, everything was swell in New Canaan.

The idea that it is students of color, not Euro-American students, who need multicultural content was a theme that repeatedly came up in one form or another in all four teachers' interviews. For example, Sarah admitted, "We chuckle about getting Martin Luther King, Jr. Day off. I mean for the fact that we have one African-American student" (Interview #2, May 20, 2003). Sarah communicated her belief that Martin Luther King, Jr. Day was a holiday specifically for African Americans, so it made little sense to celebrate it in a school with few African-American students. Apparently for Sarah, the milestones of African-American history did not really belong to what she felt to be *"our* history." It appeared that even when she directly covered African Americans' history, she felt their place as "a minority" relegated them to a fringe phenomenon.

The other two interviewed teachers—Catherine and Nathan—had a better understanding of multicultural education. Perhaps because of this, they had fewer misgivings about it. Catherine responded:

> I am thinking of two different things. If I were teaching it then I would want students to understand different cultures and learn about everything from their religion, their beliefs, and their traditions. But if I am talking about the classroom then I would want others to understand that people in our class have different cultures and we are not all Christian, White people and that we have different beliefs and backgrounds. (Interview #2, May 15, 2003)

Catherine distinguished multicultural education (learning about differences within America's own culture) from global education (learning about other national cultures). However, her qualification ("if I was teaching it") suggests she viewed multicultural education as something separate from the regular curriculum. It also implied she did not teach it because she did not need to. Although this seemed as dismissive as Sarah's and Jacob's replies, Catherine's definition came closer to what is found in the multicultural education literature.

According to Nathan, multicultural education pertained to American culture. Nathan initially focused on cultures and ethnicities when he said:

> I think it would be a type of learning that approaches the curriculum from different backgrounds. Not only approaches it from the students' own backgrounds, but discusses different cultural and ethnic groups. I think it is important that you emphasize in our society the blending of those cultures. (Interview #2, May 21, 2003)

Nathan indicated that it was important in American society to teach students about different cultural and ethnic groups. Nevertheless, Nathan's focus on the *blending* of cultures may be problematic. Blending has a positive connotation regarding racial integration. However, multicultural education scholars worry that the potential danger in the idea of blending is that it can deemphasize the richness of ethnic differences and the importance of retaining and celebrating cultural distinctions. To make an even stronger point, blending can mean wanting others to become part of Euro-American, middle-class culture that is so dominant and widespread it is almost an invisible ingredient. Talking about multicultural education as blending makes it a temporary thing—a precursor and facilitator to the abolishment of cultural diversity.

Nathan, Sarah, and Catherine concentrated their discussion of multicultural education on ethnicity and culture. Sarah underscored that multicultural education should be about people, culture, geography, and values. Only Catherine and Nathan mentioned religion. None of the teachers mentioned that social class could be a component of multicultural education. Nathan was the only one to include gender in his definition.

TRACKING AND TEXTBOOKS

Tracking, although no one seemed to want to call it that, was a prominent arrangement for social studies classes at NCMS. This seems somewhat unusual because in many schools social studies is one of the few subjects for which students are not divided into academic tracks. At NCMS, for the 2002–2003 academic year, social studies classes were divided into three levels: traditional (lower achieving students), regular, and academically talented (AT). For the 2003–2004 school year, however, the principal eliminated the traditional tracks. Social studies classes were divided into 24 regular classes and 6 AT classes. Not all the teachers were pleased with the tracking policy. Sarah and Catherine thought it was unnecessary to track for social studies, whereas Jacob thought it was a mistake to get rid of the traditional classes. As he said:

> I liked it. I know plenty of people who like inclusion, but I think it is really difficult for teacher. When I taught traditional [the lowest of the three tracks] I would say to the kids, "you are obviously here because there is a problem" and we worked on their confidence. We had smaller classes and I could work individually with them. So throwing them in a class with 29 students who are much brighter and faster is a mistake. I am not smart enough to challenge the kid who really needs a challenge and slow down for the other student. This heterogeneous grouping sounds great, but I can't do it that well. Someone loses. (Interview #3, October 31, 2003)

One outcome of tracking was that students were exposed to different multicultural experiences due to differing amounts of attention to multicultural content in the regular and AT textbooks. The textbook for the regular track, *Creating America: A History of the United States* (Garcia et al., 2002), provided an altogether different approach to history than the AT track's Boorstin and Kelley (2002) textbook, *A History of the United States*. Although there was some concentration on military history and nation building in *Creating America,* social history played an important role as well. Multicultural content was not only in an ethnic mix of pictures, instead it was integrated into the main text. For example, in a section about improving education, discussions about women and African Americans in education were not isolated by separate headings, but were integral to the text.

In contrast, the AT textbook, which was a re-adoption, was a throwback to textbooks of a decade ago. Boorstin and Kelley (2002) was a high school textbook with an 11th-grade reading level. The dense book's focus was on military history and nation building. There was little social history, hence no thorough examination of the lives of people of color or women. What was most striking was how it was dominated by pictures of Euro-Americans. A quick perusal of the images selected show only 2 of people of Middle Eastern descent, 14 of Asians (most of these were photos of people living in Asia, not Asian Americans), and 4 Latinos. Native Americans fare somewhat better, with 6 individual pictures and 11 group images. There were 36 individual pictures of Euro-American women and 6 more with one male and one female. There were only 11 individual images and 24 group images of African Americans. In contrast, there were 95 individual images and 165 group images of Euro-American men (some included a few women). The large discrepancy was exacerbated by the fact that many of the same images of people of color were repeated in the textbook. The AT text emphasized a traditional Western curriculum, and hence offered AT students little substantive multicultural content.

This difference in the amount of focus on multicultural content in textbooks did not seem to be intentional on the part of teachers. During the time of my study, social studies was going through textbook adoption. When asked what they looked for in a new text, none of the teachers claimed to want a change in the amount of multicultural content, although the current regular and AT textbooks had little coverage. The teachers were concerned about getting textbooks with the higher reading levels that they felt were more appropriate for NCMS students. The teachers did not seem aware that the selected books had quite different levels of multicultural content. When asked if he liked the new textbook, Nathan responded, "Well, it really doesn't matter to me which textbook we use. I had as much input as I wanted. I was in agreement pretty much with the choice. It is all American History, and I only use it as a base anyway" (Interview #1, April

30, 2003). Nathan's statement ("it is all American history") is troubling because it showed he viewed history as static and uniform. Yet history textbooks are not all the same, and their variety stretches beyond innovations in supplementary features. Some textbooks concentrate more on traditional history of important politicians and military leaders, whereas others include social history with a comprehensive coverage of ordinary lives of diverse people. Some are better at examining the lives of such forgotten society members as women and people of color.

When asked directly, Sarah and Jacob hesitantly granted that the new textbook for the regular tracks was an improvement in terms of multicultural content. Jacob evaluated:

> I think there is only so much you can do. There has been an improvement and they do mention some things like David Farragut was Hispanic or they speak a lot about Frederick Douglass or various people in history. They are there and they exist and are important to history. I don't know, I haven't been teaching long enough to know if things have really changed. Shoot, my seventh grade is all Asia and Africa; my eighth grade has been about slavery ever since the revolution. That is the one question we always talk about. We do talk a lot about women's rights—or the lack of it—because half the class wants to know that. (Interview #2, May 15, 2003)

Jacob's opening showed his antipathy toward multicultural education. In this respect, Jacob resembled Sarah, who defined *multicultural education* as "going too far." Jacob acknowledged the importance of multicultural content, but added that it was almost a side note. Because people of other ethnicities do exist, they cannot really be ignored. Diversity was an accident of history that teachers could not really avoid talking about, however briefly. Jacob gave the impression that he felt the text forced him to recognize peoples he might otherwise choose to ignore. Jacob stressed how much of his coverage of American history was overshadowed by discussions about slavery: "My eighth grade has been, ever since the revolution, about slavery." His final comment provided some insight into his own perspective on gender equity ("We do talk a lot about women's rights—or the lack of it—because half the class wants to know that"). Obviously, "half the class" referred to girls. Perhaps women's rights would not have been taught were Jacob to teach an all-boy class.

This attitude that textbook or course content should match student ethnicity or gender reflects other studies, which found that teachers' ideas of how much multicultural content should be offered depended on how many students had multicultural backgrounds. Thus, the relevance of multicultural content is measured not by its role in American history, but on the ethnicity of the local student body. To be fair, Jacob must be commended for including women in his discussion about the Cultural Revolution in

China. Before his lesson, he had written on the board, "Women equal to men" in an outline of notes on China (Interview #2, May 15).

There was some disagreement about readopting the Boorstin and Kelley book. The conflict was not, however, over the limited inclusion of multicultural content. Sarah and Catherine felt the 11th-grade reading level was too high for their 8th-grade AT students. In contrast, Jacob "loved it" (Interview #3, October 31, 2003). When asked why, he simply said, "Because it has more history. It is at a higher level. There are better descriptions and more explanations" (Interview #3, October 31, 2003). Although it is certainly true that the AT book had much more lengthy descriptions, it is curious that Jacob claimed it had "more history." Jacob's implication seemed to be that social history, which was emphasized in the regular textbook, was not quite history. Therefore, social history, which typically includes more multicultural content, was deemed not as important as traditional history.

SOCIAL STUDIES: PRESIDENTS AND GENERALS

Although Nathan was the only one of the four teachers to include gender in his description of multicultural education, a look in his classroom and observations of his teaching revealed he did not actually address gender. Indeed his sole focus was on nation building and military history, which are not topics that typically cover women's issues. Although Nathan denied having a passion for military history, it dominated his classroom decorations. Pictorial depictions of the American Revolution and the Civil War, the majority of these having to do with battles, covered one classroom wall. There were 10 photos of navy ships. Four model ships were placed on shelves around the classroom. Individual portraits of the first 23 presidents lined the top of the front bulletin board. Five pictures of eagles and one of the White House hung on other walls. The only pictures of people other than White men were a group of photos of five Native American tribal leaders. Of all the 80 pictures in his fully decorated room, it was disappointing not to see a single African American, Latino, or Asian American. The only women represented were in a drawing of Bull Run, which showed a picnic with White women in antebellum gowns and parasols.

The most noticeable classroom decorations were eight flags that hung in the back of the classroom. Nathan said that he changed the flags three times during the school year to coordinate them with the Revolutionary period, the period between the wars, and the Civil War. When I first entered his classroom in the spring, he had six historic variations of the American flag, an Irish Brigade flag, and, most surprising, a Confederate flag. When asked whether anyone had asked him about it, he said, "no." He went on to say he brought it up and led a class discussion about the controversy surrounding the South Carolina state flag. Nathan commented, "I am not from South Carolina or Georgia. I am not making a political statement. I am just offering it as a historical artifact" (Interview #3, October 31, 2003). One could argue that the Confederate flag is part of American history and therefore belongs with the decoration scheme, especially given the attention to the Civil War. However, it seemed a questionable choice for a middle-school classroom. The fact that it hung there unchallenged provided a revealing picture of the school community. One could assume that if the school had any African-American staff or more African-American students, it would not have been allowed to hang in his classroom.

Of the four teachers, Nathan had the most traditional teaching style. Nathan lectured and students busily took notes. Like the pictures in his classroom, most of his lectures encompassed some part of military history. In the spring, he talked about Civil War battles; in the fall, it was the French and Indian War. The lectures always made their way to some aspect of the military. For example, during one class, he spent 15 minutes giving a detailed description of the Battle of Quebec. He drew diagrams on the board to show how the battle played out. As part of this lecture, Nathan also passed around an artifact of a bullet maker from the revolutionary period. During some classes, he included short video clips from documentaries to emphasize points in his lectures. I saw a video clip from Ken Burns' Civil War documentary on ironclad ships, a short biography of Ulysses S. Grant, and a 5-minute description of the Boston Massacre.

One of his lectures on military reconstruction and Ulysses S. Grant took an interesting turn in an AT class. It demonstrated how students can feel excluded in the classroom. What was of most concern about this class period was not the lecture, but the tense dynamics between some of the boys and girls. One girl got quite frustrated and voiced her annoyance about how everyone laughed at her when she asked questions. She continued by exclaiming that she was "not some dumb girl" and that "this class is getting to me." Nathan basically ignored this comment. Throughout the class, he allowed one rather arrogant boy to do most of the talking. This boy later upset another girl when he offhandedly dismissed her comment. The girl felt her comment deserved to be heard. She was obviously upset by being ignored and told the boy that "she hates it when he does that." The first girl piped in again and said, "That is so rude!" Nathan's only response to this conflict was to tell the boy that he can "rebut, but to do so in a gentleman-like manner."

The dynamics between the boys and girls was also apparent in some of Nathan's other classes. For the most part, girls tended to be silent and raised their hands only to verify a point in the lecture for their note taking. In one regular class, there were only 4 girls and 17 boys. Not one girl spoke the entire class period, whereas the boys were quite vocal. To Nathan's credit, after this class session, he said, "How did you like my all-boy class?" His question seemed to indicate that Nathan acknowledged that gender imbalance in participation was an issue. When directly asked whether he felt that the girls were not participating as much, his response was that he never noticed it. He explained that he was especially sensitive to gender issues because of his background in sociology. On one occasion, he did correct a boy when the student described a woman in a picture as a "chick" (Observation #5, October 8, 2003). Given that he never noticed the discrepancy of class participation, nor had any substantial images of women, one wonders how sensitive he really is to gender disparity issues. He seemed unaware that what he chose to focus on in his classes might have exacerbated the girls' exclusion from discussions.

In connection to the issue of Nathan's sensitivity, I was surprised to hear the jokes he told in class, including: "Why doesn't a blind person like to skydive? It scares the dog." "What do a Texas tornado and a Tennessee divorce have in common? Someone is going to lose a trailer" (Observation #6, October 9, 2003). It was unclear why his one class had such a gender imbalance (17 boys, 4 girls). He felt it was "just how the classes worked out." I was unable to find out if boys' parents had requested him and girls' parents had asked not to have their daughters in his class because of his reputation. The observation scenarios illustrate how groups of students—in this case, boys and girls—find different things important and easily feel alienated if their interests and comments are systematically ignored or shoved aside. As a former history student, I understand all too well the frustration of being in a male-dominated field in which women's ideas are not valued. To include female students in social studies content, it seems there is a need to move away from a military-based history program that is centered solely around nation building toward social history, which focuses on how people in the past coped with their daily lives not only in the political domain, but also in terms of social, economical, moral, religious, and environmental issues. From a multicultural perspective, it is important for students to be aware of the nature of class, gender, and ethnic issues in social life.

IMPLICATIONS OF THE STUDY FOR OTHER PEOPLE AND THEIR CHILDREN

This chapter explored how four suburban middle-school social studies teachers gauged the need for multicultural education for their predominately White, high-income students. Although the teachers maintained that they somewhat appreciated its importance generally, they all expressed some form of the belief that there was no need to incorporate multicultural education beyond a rudimentary level at their school on the grounds that it had limited diversity. They indicated that multicultural education mainly applied to students who did not connect to the regular White curriculum. Because it was perceived as largely irrelevant to their White, upper class students, they did not take multicultural education seriously. Furthermore, they communicated that multicultural education was a distraction that took time away from traditional social studies content. Their views reflected an attitude that Western culture is superior and only traditional Western European subject matter is necessary unless diversity among the students requires the inclusion of nontraditional subjects. In short, they believed that teaching about other cultures prevalent elsewhere within the United States had no redeeming value that would merit its full inclusion in the curriculum in their schools. Although these teachers had recently gone through a social studies textbook adoption process, none mentioned that solid multicultural education content had been a criterion in their selection.

These four teachers gave limited and confusing definitions of *multicultural education*, focusing primarily on race/ethnicity and, to a lesser extent, on culture. Because they were unaware of racism in their students, they did not see the point of covering racial issues. None of them mentioned that social class would be included. Indeed they did not appear to be sensitive to problematic aspects of social class, seeing it mainly as something that advantaged their students. Only one teacher brought up that gender would be part of multicultural content. It was interesting that he was also the one teacher among the four who almost totally excluded gender as a topic in his American history classes. He was also the one who had highly disparate amounts of participation for boys and girls in his classroom. Girls were relatively silent. When some girls expressed resentment about their exclusion, he promptly dismissed their complaints and moved back to the formal curriculum.

A consequence of this growth of the suburbs is that students are mostly isolated from people of color and lower social classes. If the four teachers at NCMS are representative of suburban teachers more generally, then White middle- and upper class students are not being exposed to the kind of education that Leonardo (2004) called "quality education." Leonardo equated quality education with students being able to think critically about social problems and learning to appreciate transformative ways of bringing about equity in America's democracy. Not only did the teachers not problematize the White privilege and class advantage of their suburban students, they seemed mostly unconscious that social class and race status had an impact on them. This is an unfortunate development because these students are most likely to become leaders in government and business. They will carry their sense of superiority as well as the legitimacy of their advantage into their powerful adult roles. Because they live in segregated neighborhoods and attend segregated schools, it is especially important that suburban students' education give them opportunities to gain knowledge about those not in their same ethnic or social group.

Gay (1994, 1997, 2000) wrote how it is the duty of all teachers and administrators to promote multicultural education regardless of the makeup of the student body. Informed scholars, such as Banks (1993), also argued that multicultural education needs to be of equal focus in all schools, not only in those with diverse student bodies. In fact, as my study revealed, the challenge of restructuring the curriculum to fully integrate multicultural education is perhaps greatest in schools that are predominately affluent and Euro-American. Because of the evidence that an increasing percentage of Euro-American students are being educated in predominantly Euro-American and upper income suburbs, this study is relevant in documenting the extent to which students are not being exposed to an appropriate multicultural curriculum. Including courses such as *Teaching in a Pluralistic Society* or *Multicultural Education* in teacher education will not have much impact if teachers continue to believe its content and messages are only relevant to teachers who teach in urban schools or schools with a certain amount of diversity. How suburban teachers view their role in including multicultural curriculum, and whether they actually teach it, should be of vital concern to teacher educators and educational policymakers. Suburban schools are often seen as model schools because of their high test scores. Test scores, however, do not measure student knowledge of issues related to race/ethnicity, social class, sexual orientation, and gender. Students such as those in NCMS have little contact with people outside their same ethnic or social group, therefore they are likely to hold stereotyped and biased views of these others. Perhaps before school success is determined by test scores that measure primarily math and reading skills, one should first delve deeper to see what students are missing.

REFERENCES

Allport, G. (1954). *The nature of prejudice.* Cambridge, MA: Addison-Wesley.

Banks, J. A. (1993). Multicultural education; Development, dimensions and challenges. *Phi Delta Kappan, 75*, 22–28.

Boorstin, D., & Kelley, B. M. (2002). *A history of the United States.* Needham, MA: Prentice-Hall.

Garcia, J., Ogle, D. M., Risinger, C. F., Stevos, J., & Jordan, W. D. (2002). *Creating America: A history of the United States.* Evanston, IL: McDougal Littell.

Gay, G. (1994). *At the essence of learning; Multicultural education.* West Lafayette, IN: Kappa Delta Pi.

Gay, G. (1997). The relationship between multicultural and democratic education. *The Social Studies, 88*, 5–9.

Gay, G. (2000). *Culturally responsive teaching: Theory, research, and practice.* New York: Teachers College Press.

Harvey, D. (1996). *Justice, nature and the geography of difference.* Cambridge, MA: Blackwell.

Knapp, M. S., & Woolverton, S. (1995). Social class and schooling. In J. A. Banks & C. A. M. Banks (Eds.), *Handbook of research on multicultural education* (pp. 548–569). New York: Macmillan.

Leonardo, A. (2004). Theme issue: Part II of introduction to disciplinary knowledge and quality education. *Educational Researcher, 33*(6), 3.

Lipman, P. (1997). Restructuring in context: A case study of teacher participation and the dynamics of ideology, race, and power. *American Educational Research Journal, 34*(1), 3–37.

Orfield, G., & Eaton, S. (1996). *Dismantling desegregation: The quiet reversal of* Brown v. Board of Education. New York: New Press.

Chapter 6

The Impact of Reform
on Students With Disabilities

Sally Harvey-Koelpin
Indiana University, Bloomington

Representative George Miller of California and Senator Christopher Dodd of Connecticut introduced the *No Child Left Behind Act* (*NCLB*) to Congress in May 2001. It became Public Law 107-110 in January 2002. The passage of this 670-page bill was essentially a reenactment of *The Elementary and Secondary Education Act of 1965* (*Title I*), with the addition of a few new twists and turns. The updated legislation requires the evaluation of public schools based solely on scores derived from standardized testing. Under this requirement of *NCLB*, many low-income schools were targeted for school improvement in March 2002 based on low standardized testing scores.

Mamlin (1999) argued that, in the past, "Most school reform efforts . . . have not considered special education issues" (p. 227). Billed as "an act to close the achievement gap with accountability, flexibility, and choice, so that no child is left behind" (*NCLB*, 2001, p. 1), the supposed purpose of the *NCLB* legislation "is to ensure that all children have a fair, equal, and significant opportunity to obtain a high quality education and reach, at a minimum, proficiency on challenging State academic achievement standards and state academic assessments" (p. 1). Success or failure is singularly determined by high-stakes testing. Proponents of the bill claim that requiring *all* students to achieve mastery of state-mandated proficiencies by the 2013–2014 school year will result in a better quality of education for students with disabilities. Their rationale for accepting this idealistic and seemingly unrealistic goal is that "students with disabilities seem to respond well to higher expectations" (Buntin, 2002, p. 46).

119

Supporters of *NCLB* also indicate that school districts must exert more effort to raise the achievement levels of students with disabilities. For example, Buntin enthusiastically proclaimed that this legislation will be particularly beneficial for students with disabilities:

> Thanks to the *Leave No Child Behind Act*, the sweeping education reform bill signed into law earlier this year by President George W. Bush, schools are under unprecedented pressure to improve the educational achievements of all students, including students with disabilities. Under the measure, school districts must disaggregate test results for students with disabilities and demonstrate yearly progress in their achievement or face "interventions" that can culminate with staff dismissals and a state takeover. (p. 45)

The singular use of high-stakes test scores to determine success or failure appears to raise a number of concerns, rather than provide assurances for improving the quality of education students with disabilities receive. How will the 100% mastery requirement of *NCLB* impact students with disabilities? How will *NCLB* influence teachers' attitudes toward students with disabilities if scores are to be disaggregated and teachers held accountable for students' test scores? How might the requirements of *NCLB* impact a low-income urban school's ability to effectively respond to the needs of students with disabilities? In summary, the concerned public must evaluate whether *NCLB* will help or hurt students with disabilities. Although the stated goals of this legislation certainly appear worthy, it is imperative to look beyond the promises to the reality of how this reform initiative impacts students with disabilities in a low-income school labeled as failing at the time this study was conducted.

METHODOLOGY

The research design of this study falls under the definition of a bounded case study. It is bounded in that it investigated a school placed on school improvement status as a result of *NCLB*. It is a case study in that it entails only one school site.

Site Selection

To begin to explore the focus questions of this research study, a low-income urban public school identified as a failing school under *NCLB* for the 2002–2003 school year was selected for the study site. As one of the two identified failing schools out of a large midwestern city's 49 elementaries,

Creekside was chosen because it was familiar to the researcher and hence accessible.

Study Participants

In the quest to discover the impact of reform on students with disabilities, it was important to explore the focus questions of this research study from perspectives of faculty and staff members involved in the implementation process. To accomplish this goal, purposeful sampling was used to include the voices of the administrator, general education teachers, a paraprofessional, and inclusion faculty to provide a more holistic portrait of the impact of *NCLB* from "the experiences and perceptions of people having different associations with the program" (Merriam, 2001, p. 83). Therefore, participants were selected based on "the potential of each person to contribute to the development of insight and understanding of the phenomenon" (p. 83). Consequently, participants became co-constructors in the research process.

Thirteen Creekside faculty and staff members participated in this study. Thus, throughout the discussion section, you will hear the voices of the principal, a special area teacher, the Title I reading teacher, the magnet facilitator, a paraprofessional who works with classified students, the school psychologist, three inclusion teachers, and four general education classroom teachers.

All of the participants were White females because neither the two African-American teachers nor the one male teacher were available to participate in this study. Participants' teaching experience in an urban environment ranged from 3 to 43 years. Most have been associated with the school for over 10 years.

Data Collection

Merriam (2001) argued that, "Understanding the case in its totality, as well as the intensive, holistic description and analysis characteristic of a case study, mandates both breadth and depth of data collection" (p. 134). As such, a multilayer research design using qualitative research methods was chosen to provide for thick data collection, as well as for flexibility in data-collection techniques to allow for the unanticipated. Qualitative methods such as surveys, informal and semistructured interviews, and document analysis were selected to align with the purpose of this study to uncover the voices of participants.

Qualitative methods were used in conjunction with participant observation because participatory research is "best suited to describing the realities of schools and schooling" (Rist, 2002, p. 24). Data were collected during the 2002–2003 school year from observations and interviews, helping in classrooms, conducting document analysis, and meeting with participants in social settings. In addition, the researcher attended staff meetings, professional development workshops, evening and weekend school-related activities, and system-wide multicultural events and conferences.

Merriam (2001) explained, "in the real world of case study research, interviewing, observing, and examining documents merge in the process of understanding and describing the phenomenon of interest" (p. 149). Therefore, a variety of qualitative research techniques were employed to provide multiple perspectives, offer a greater understanding of the issues, and increase the credibility of the study's findings.

Establishing Trustworthiness and Credibility

The credibility and trustworthiness of this study was established through the use of a broad range of literature regarding urban education issues, as well as a variety of data-collection techniques. Member checks occurred continuously throughout the research process. Participants were provided with a copy of their interview transcript to edit for accuracy. Triangulation of the data was accomplished by comparing and contrasting the findings to the researcher's own urban teaching experience and the experience of other urban educators.

Researcher's Positionality and Bias

As a 16-year teaching veteran of Creekside, this research study was in many ways a personal journey back to a place that played a central role in my life for many years. Throughout the years, the staff members formed strong bonds with each other, which were strengthened continually as we helped each other navigate through the joys and struggles of a uniquely urban school environment. Thus, many of the participants in this endeavor were and continue to be personal friends.

Returning to Creekside as a researcher had its advantages. As an insider, I encountered no resistance in gaining access to the site. All of the staff members were extremely helpful in providing answers to the multitude of questions I posed to them. One of the most important aspects of being an insider was that, throughout the process, I was able to complete member checks by calling on various participants to clarify information, fill in missing details, recall memories, or help with interpretations. As a result of knowing where to look and with whom to speak, I had access to information an outsider might not have been able to gain.

Research conducted as an insider presented its own unique challenges and pitfalls as well. The flip side of possessing an advantageous insider's position was that I was engaged in a constant struggle to define the boundaries between being a researcher and being a friend. The line between the two became fuzzy at times. This was particularly true in social settings in which many times it was necessary to make a decision as to whether a conversation was on or off the record.

Another drawback of being an insider was that it was extremely difficult to be critical of my participants. I was continually making conscious efforts to differentiate between the friend and the professional. In creating this separation, I believe I was able to portray the participants in a more realistic light while consoling myself with the understanding that the perfect educator does not exist.

It is hoped that the advantages of engaging participants as co-constructors of knowledge far outweighed the disadvantages. In making the participant/researcher relationship explicit and with the disclosure of a pro-teacher stance, I believe the reader will find the authentic and often silenced voices of urban educators as they struggle to triumph over a label that has essentially branded them and their students as failures.

CONTEXTUAL INFORMATION

Worn out by years of urban decay, the neighborhood surrounding Creekside is plagued by violent crime, vandalism, and drugs. Most houses are in various degrees of disrepair, and trash litters yards and front porches. Although not zoned for livestock, several families keep chickens and goats in their yards, and at times the stench of animal waste permeates the air. The neighborhood creek that runs in front of the school, and in which all students play at one time or another, is frequently found to contain increased levels of e-coli bacteria. A major utility plant is located a few blocks east. The plant periodically emits irritating vapors and ash, causing everything to quickly become covered with particles of black soot.

Creekside is bordered on all sides by streets. It appears much like an island, with boundaries that clearly separate it from the rest of the community. The physical structure has changed little in 60 years, and the building is in various states of disrepair. The approximately 15 concrete stairs leading to the front doors are crumbling. Estimates for an adequate repair job exceed tens of thousands of dollars, so the district continues to ineffectively patch them each year. A valiant effort at landscaping has been sabotaged by theft, and several holes remain where expensive shrubbery had once been planted. An incident of vandalism early in the year of the study left gang graffiti sprayed across large areas of the building, which need to be sand blasted off. The culprits were apprehended and found to be former Creekside students.

Most conspicuous is the lack of a playground. No brightly colored equipment—characteristic of an elementary school play area—exists. The children have recess on an asphalt parking lot. Thus, students play in and around the teachers' cars that are parked on the lot. A basketball goal is the only play equipment provided. Due to vandalism, the hoop must be taken down each evening and weekend.

For the most part, the building is clean. Positive messages regarding learning and school attendance adorn hallway bulletin boards, and a variety of student work is on display. Banners with motivational messages such as "Read and Succeed" are located above door jambs. However, the building does bear the scars of urban life. A bullet hole remains visible in a wall opposite a window in a first-floor classroom. Ceilings in a number of areas are crumbling bit by bit. One restroom for girls and one for boys serve the entire student population. Two classrooms were combined to create the media center, and the music room is located in a converted coal bin that floods several times a year due to sewer backups. In addition, the building is infested with cockroaches and mice.

Accurate up-to-date enrollment statistics were difficult to obtain due to the district's 69% student mobility rate. At the time the study began, the official enrollment for the 2002–2003 school year was 384 students. The ethnic breakdown was 72.1% White, 18% Black, 5% Hispanic, 1% Asian, 0.3% Native American, and 3.6% Multiracial. Seventy-five percent of the students received a free lunch, and 16% received a reduced lunch. Hence, 9% of students paid for their lunch. Based on the 91% free and reduced lunch rate, the school was designated as a full Title I site. Statistics compiled during the 2002–2003 school year indicated that 19% of the population was labeled as students with disabilities.

Creekside Elementary has had eight principals in the last 20 years. With the exception of the first during that time, all were first-year principals. The administrator at the time of the study was beginning her second year and essentially inherited many problems, including the failing label.

At the time of the study, the faculty was made up of both new and experienced teachers. There were 20 self-contained general education classrooms and two self-contained special education rooms. As a full inclusion school, three inclusion teachers were assigned to the building. Rounding out the licensed staff were three special area teachers for art, music, and gym; and there were two Title I reading teachers. Out of 29 full-time teachers, 7% were African American and 93% were White. Creekside's support staff included a part-time social worker, a part-time school psychologist, as well as a part-time speech and hearing therapist. A nurse was provided for 1 half day per week by the County Board of Health. Non-licensed personnel included three Title I classroom assistants. There was no school counselor.

Due to limited resources, an attempt was made to place all inclusion students in one classroom at each grade level—a clustering arrangement theoretically done to make collaboration and planning easier. As a result, general education classrooms were comprised of anywhere from 0% to 47% inclusion students.

Creekside Elementary was put on school improvement status for failure to make adequate yearly progress (AYP), according to the standards set by *NCLB*, for 2 consecutive years. Adequate yearly progress, as defined in the legislation, means that all students "must meet or exceed the objectives set by the state" (*NCLB*, 2001, p. 24). The state objectives, better known as *cutoff scores*, were determined by a select group of educators from districts around the state. It is important to note that few representatives from urban districts were included in the process.

As a result of being placed on school improvement status, the school was required to hold a meeting with parents to advise them of their option to transfer to another school. Although flyers were sent to all parents announcing this meeting, only seven parents attended in May 2002. Seventeen parents chose to transfer their children to another school in the district.

According to the requirements of *NCLB*, test scores for the 2002–2003 school year are to be disaggregated for race, class, gender, and disability status. Creekside Elementary will be evaluated based on the progress of the group representing the lowest score. The Fall 2002 third-grade USTEP scores will be used for the purpose of this evaluation. The State introduced a new third-grade USTEP test during the year of the study, which became the source of added anxiety because, in most cases, "When tests are first administered, the scores are distressingly lower" (Kohn, 2000, p. 25). Consequently, staff members wait with their fingers crossed for test results that will determine whether they remain on school improvement status.

As mandated by *NCLB*, if Creekside "fails to make adequate yearly progress . . . by the end of the second full year" after identification for school improvement it will be subject to "corrective action" (*NCLB*, 2001, p. 60). *Corrective action*, as defined by *NCLB*, include the following options:

1. Replace the school staff who are relevant to the failure to make adequate yearly progress.
2. Institute and fully implement a new curriculum, including providing appropriate professional development for all relevant staff, that is based on scientifically based research and offers substantial promise of improving educational achievement for low-achieving students and enabling the school to make adequate yearly progress.
3. Significantly decrease management authority at the school level.
4. Appoint an outside expert to advise the school on its progress toward making adequate yearly progress.

5. Extend the school year or school day for the school.
6. Restructure the internal organizational structure of the school. (*NCLB*, p. 60)

DISCUSSION OF FINDINGS

Much of the following discussion is presented in a conversational format using the voices of urban educators. Use of this format symbolizes the entering of the previously silenced voices of urban educators to the dialogue on school reform. Ultimately, it is left up to the reader to decide whether this case is similar to the multitude of other failing schools, and whether *NCLB* is indeed effective in fulfilling its promises.

Teachers Could Be Doing a Better Job

Inherent in the philosophy of pro-accountability and high-stakes testing is the implication that "teachers could be doing a better job but have for some reason chosen not to do so and need only be bribed or threatened into improvement" (Kohn, 2000, p. 39). Furthermore, as Brantlinger (2003) explained, "the standards and accountability movement is based on the complementary premises that some teachers and/or students are inadequate and either/both must improve" (p. 6). In fact *NCLB* specifically aims at "significantly elevating the quality of instruction" (*NCLB*, p. 16) low-income students receive in schools performing poorly on standardized tests. In effect this act holds teachers and administrators solely responsible for seeing that adequate yearly progress is made to ensure that "*all* students will meet or exceed the State's proficient level of academic achievement on the State's assessment" (*NCLB*, 2001, p. 24; italics added). By villainizing teachers and blaming schools for student failure, politicians appear heroic in their concern for a noble cause, diverting responsibility away from their own lack of action in equalizing school expenditures or even making sure all adults in our society receive adequate pay to support their families. Today, and historically, it appears that school reform in the United States is promoted by politicians "as a painless substitution for the redistribution of wealth" (Katz, 2001, p. xxix). However, policymakers need to be held accountable for the legislation they enact. One way to accomplish this is to explore how implementing the requirements of *NCLB* has impacted an urban school and students with disabilities from the perspective of urban educators engaged in the process to determine whether this legislation can deliver its promise to enhance the quality of education for *all* students.

Labeled as Failures

If current political rhetoric revolving around *NCLB* is believed, it might lead some to place sole blame for the academic failure of students in low-income areas on the poor quality of the teachers. This rhetoric paints a picture in our minds that urban schools contain substandard, ineffective, and uncaring teachers. The following selected professional biographies of Creekside teachers are offered in an attempt to deconstruct this myth. They challenge this rhetoric as they illustrate that there are, in fact, a number of accomplished educators who are committed to serving students in poverty.

Special Area Teacher: *I have a bachelor's and two master's degrees, one in music education and one in music therapy. In addition to my normal teaching load, I have organized a choir consisting of 60 fourth- and fifth-grade students, which is rather large. Although it is an audition choir, I look for the children who are dedicated, rather than those who can match pitch. They have sung for a statewide honors dinner for Habitat for Humanity, the National Reading Conference, and various other local community events. They sent an audition tape to the National Music Educators' Association for the World's Largest Concert and were selected to participate. Their videotape was made though our local PBS station. The tape was viewed in the United States and around the world by children in all different countries. It was quite an honor to have been selected because they only chose about 16 video clips.*

In addition, I serve on the school's Multicultural Cadre and have previously been the team leader. We participate in the district's Multicultural Fair and the Children's Folk Dance Festival. Thirty or more schools participate, and about 1,500 students attend the festival held on a Saturday in the spring.

In the past, I have received several music grants, including a variety of instruments to use for a year. Recently I received a VH1 "Save the Music Foundation Grant" and with that received 16 student keyboards, a teacher's station, and the software for teaching piano skills for kindergarten through grade five. In 2001–2002, I received the award for the Elementary Music Educator of the Year from The Music Educators Association of the State. I was nominated by friends and colleagues.

* * *

Classroom Teacher: *I have bachelor's and master's degrees in Early Elementary Education. I have been teaching for 27 years and have been with this district for 10. About 5 years ago, I took a leave of absence and taught first grade in an American International School in Kuala Lumpur, Malaysia. The children in my classroom were from 14 different countries. All of them spoke some English. However, I* *had taken Bahasa Malay before I went over. I was there 14 months. It was a wonderful experience.*

* * *

Classroom Teacher: *I have both bachelor's and master's degrees. This is my 43rd year of teaching at Creekside Elementary. I cannot believe I have taught this long. I am still learning and trying new things and want to continue to do that as long as I teach. I love to teach children. I figure that each year I'm learning more than they are. I have been a member of the site-based decision-making committee for several years, as well as the grade-level team leader. In the past, I have been nominated several times for Teacher of the Year.*

* * *

Classroom Teacher: *I earned my bachelor's degree in education with distinction. This is my 18th year with the district. Last summer I became a Globe Science teacher, which enabled me to interact with the Globe program worldwide. My class recorded data and entered it for use by scientists at NASA. We have a weather station and hope to test the water in the creek in front of the school. That's our goal by the end of the year. At school I am on the school committee for site-based decision-making, the Honor Roll Committee, and the Professional Development Committee.*

In addition to being experienced and accomplished, most teachers work long hours in the evenings and on weekends to provide their students with a quality education. This is despite the fact that they are not paid for the extra time they work. As one classroom teacher explained:

We all care about the kids. We put pressure on ourselves. The staff here works late and takes work home. They even come in on Saturdays and Sundays.

Indeed it is typical to find many teachers working late into the evening every night as another participant indicated:

My usual day is a 10-hour day. Sometimes I have worked later, but I know a lot of people put in as many hours as I do, if not more.

In higher socioeconomic districts, parents are able to provide extracurricular lessons and activities for their children. These lessons and activities are often financially out of reach for lower socioeconomic parents. In an effort to level the playing field somewhat, teachers at Creekside provide students with enrichment lessons and tutoring before and after school. For example, the special area teacher explained:

Before and after school, l teach the children folk dances from approximately 14 different countries. Also before and after school, I provide piano lessons for selected students free of charge.

These biographies demonstrate that many Creekside staff members bring something unique to the table and work hard to provide their students with a quality education. They are a testament to the fact that we do have accomplished, talented, experienced, and dedicated teachers serving children in poverty. They are people who espouse no rhetoric, yet they speak with their actions and quietly make significant differences in the lives of their students on a daily basis. It became evident by observing and speaking with these urban educators that:

> Elementary school teachers do the heavy lifting of American education. Yet few rewards go their way. The best have courage and inner resilience the rest of us can only imagine. (McCarthy, 2002, pp. 2–3)

By focusing blame on the teachers, politicians draw attention away from the social, political, and economic policies they legislate, which effectively create and maintain the conditions of poverty in our society.

It Is Always on Our Minds

In the past, research studies have investigated the debilitating effects of negatively labeling students (Rosenthal & Jacobsen, 1968). In 1968, Rosenthal and Jacobsen concluded, "Teachers' expectations of their pupils' performance may serve as self-fulfilling prophecies" (p. 182). In other words, the expectations teachers hold for students greatly influence their academic achievement. The findings of Rosenthal and Jacobsen's study have resulted in a positive transformation in pedagogical practice for many educators.

However, rarely have researchers explored the effects of labeling schools and teachers. Furthermore, politicians, policymakers, and educational reformers are currently labeling schools as *failing* without fully comprehending the implications of doing so. To begin to understand how schools and teachers are impacted by this categorization, it is important to explore teachers' perceptions and feelings regarding the failing label. One participant expressed a great deal of shame regarding being labeled as failures—in need of improvement.

> *There is a stigma that goes along with being told you are failing, that you are not doing what you need to do to meet the needs of the child.*

Another agreed and added:

> *It is very demeaning, disheartening, and demoralizing to be placed on that status.*

One participant contended that the stress and shame related to the failing status had taken a toll on her emotionally:

I wake up each morning and do not want to go to work. I used to love my job and was always eager to go to school. I am now taking Prozac just to make it through the day.

McCarthy (2002) argued that elementary school teachers are:

Expected to discipline, entertain, correct, nurse, motivate, grade, call parents, fill out attendance sheets, do lunchroom duty, tell kids not to run in the hall, and tell them again the next day, and the next, find lost raincoats and boots, put chairs back in place, order books, hustle for book shelves, and then go home to turn on the evening news to behold still another politician blasting the schools for failing. (p. 3)

Not only do teachers at Creekside feel personal pressure to do well, they are often faced with brutal criticism from the media. As Brantlinger (2003) explained, "One message that has dominated the media is the supposed decline of schools" (p. 17). As such one teacher expressed how she struggles daily to keep a positive perspective in dealing with the frustration and pressure of being labeled a failure despite constant media reminders:

When we read about it (the label) in the newspaper, or hear about it on the radio, or see it on the television it would be easy to think we are failing. I try and keep things in perspective and just do a good job every day. That is something that I have a battle with because the pressure is there. I keep thinking what else can we do? What can we change? Do we even need change? If we do, what should those changes be?

The media are not the only ones perpetually reminding staff members of the failing status. As one participant suggested, teachers are confronted with the label and messages of failure are ubiquitous within the parameters of the school district where Creekside is located:

At the workshop I recently went to on how to help children do better on standardized tests, there was a list of schools at the top of the sign-in sheet. The sheet stated that it was highly recommended that the schools listed attend as they were failing schools. Creekside was one of them. It was embarrassing!

Furthermore, as a result of these constant reminders, staff members have in many ways become obsessed with the label. Rather than focusing on what they believe is the best way to instruct students, one Creekside teacher described how this legislation and the accompanying monitoring dramatically altered her teaching style:

> *The label is always in the back of my mind. I feel like our students have to learn at a fast pace, which takes all the fun out of teaching and learning. The label has stifled me quite a bit. I like to joke around with my children and be in a classroom where we are active and integrate the curriculum with student projects. We don't get to do that now. I feel like we always have to read the text and be on task. When you are done with one scripted program then you move on to the next. There are always people coming in from downtown to check on what lesson you are on, which to me is absolutely ridiculous.*

Due to the failing label, teachers at Creekside had no choice but to concentrate on test-driven instruction to avoid punitive consequences. They were required to do so despite what they believed was best for their students, which greatly increased their level of stress. Compounding the anxiety they felt was the fact that use of these mandated test-driven strategies and scripted programs resulted in a form of deprofessionalization. Consequently, as Hargreaves (1994) explained, teachers' work becomes:

> ... more routinized and deskilled, more like the degraded work of manual workers and less like that of autonomous professionals trusted to exercise the power and expertise of discretionary judgment in the classrooms they understand best. (pp. 117–118)

Compelled to raise test scores to be removed from school improvement status and avoid punitive consequences, teachers asked, What else could we do? Yet another source of stress was expressed by a novice teacher who voiced a concern for the future of her teaching career. She feared that the stigma of the failing label would follow her in the future, making her essentially not hireable in more *desirable* teaching environments:

> *It worries me that if I ever want to move out of the district or state, other schools would be able to look back and say "Oh! Well, she was part of a failing school, we don't want her. She's not a good teacher." That does concern me. It always is in the back of my mind if I ever decided to switch schools. What would they say about the failing label?*

If, as Rosenthal and Jacobsen (1968) concluded, "People, more often than not, do what is expected of them" (p. vii), then labeling schools as failures or in need of school improvement might prove to be damaging in the long run. Disheartened by the label, good teachers may give up on schools serving low-income students and students with disabilities altogether.

Worse yet, new teachers will avoid taking positions in schools where a majority of the students live in poverty. This might ultimately prove to be devastating to low-income students, rather than improve the quality of their education, and higher income students will continue to receive the best teachers. If it is in fact true that "the teacher's expectation . . . can come to serve as an educational self-fulfilling prophecy" (p. viii), it may also be true that failing schools will eventually live up to the label placed on them by policymakers.

The Reality of Special Education at Creekside

Of the 19% special education population of the school, 8% were students with emotional handicaps, 36% were students identified as learning disabled, 24% were students classified as mildly mentally handicapped, 18% were identified as students with communications disabilities, and 14% were students who were identified as having multiple disabilities. The almost 20% identified students was 5% higher than either the state or district averages.

Curiously, none of the teachers interviewed or surveyed was aware that a high percentage of Creekside students were labeled as special education, although many were not surprised when I told them the figure. Participants were asked why they believed Creekside had such a high percentage of students with disabilities. They speculated about a variety of reasons. Based on her own experiences at Creekside, one member of the inclusion staff indicated it might be generational or hereditary:

> Sometimes we have several children within the same family who are identified as special education. Many times when the parents come in and talk with you, you become aware that they too were special ed students. Some (parents) will tell us outright "I was a special ed student myself." I think special ed can be generational and run in families.

Due to a lack of health insurance and access to medical care, the general health of the majority of Creekside parents and students is visibly poor. Thus, the issue of poor prenatal care was offered by one participant as an explanation for the high rate of identification of students with disabilities at Creekside:

> We suspect that maybe prenatal care was poor and the normal development of the brain just didn't happen. Sometimes physically or mentally they do not have the ability. It is not there.

Various forms of birth control are also quite expensive to acquire. As a result, low-income areas often experience a higher occurrence of teenage pregnancies. One participant observed that in many instances these young parents do not possess adequate parenting skills, which may result in developmental delays in their children:

> *I think it is environment. The majority of students that attend this school do not necessarily move out of this area. They stay here as adults, and now I have their children in my classes. They have a tendency to have children at a very young age. They become teenage parents. I think that the parenting skills are just not there. It's because they are so young and they haven't been children long enough themselves, and now they are forced to be an adult. They can't cope with that. They try. They love their children, but they don't know how to be the best parents. They are not able meet their children's needs.*

Low-income urban areas also suffer from a variety of social issues, all of which have the potential to directly contribute to the greater incidence of students with disabilities in these areas. One participant argued:

> *A lot of it is drug abuse. I have children who have been born addicted to cocaine. I have children who have been abused physically, sexually, and mentally. All of that affects their learning.*

In many low-income urban areas, children live in older homes that are in disrepair. One participant observed that not only are these homes highly susceptible to fire but they also contain toxins that have proved to be harmful to children, and may affect their mental and physical growth:

> *Most students live in older homes where the paint is chipping. Consequently, several of our special education students have suffered from lead poisoning, which has caused their learning disabilities.*

In summary, teachers indicated a variety of reasons for the high identification of students with disabilities at Creekside. It is disheartening to step back and realize that many of these causes, such as lack of health insurance and access to medical care, availability of drug rehabilitation programs, and adequate housing, could be prevented. Legislation that addresses these social issues is vital to improving the quality of life for students living in poverty.

Setup for Failure

All of the study's participants expressed concern regarding the impact of *NCLB* on students with disabilities. Namely, they were concerned with the specific requirement that "All students will meet or exceed the State's proficient level of academic achievement on the State's assessment" (*NCLB*,

2001, p. 24). One teacher viewed the 100% mastery requirement as unattainable:

> *It is an impossible goal that they have set before us. I really feel we are going to fail if that is how we are going to be evaluated.*

More significant, another participant not only felt hopeless about attaining the requirements mandated by *NCLB*, but viewed students with disabilities as a major barrier to the achievement of this goal:

> *We have ultimately been set up for failure especially with the number of special education students we have.*

In addition, one participant believed that students with disabilities would not benefit in the push to achieve 100% mastery because it would deprive them of an education that would be more relevant and meaningful to their lives:

> *I don't know that this legislation will be of any value to the special education child. We have an emotionally handicapped classroom. We have inclusion students who are learning disabled. We have students in self-contained special education classrooms that are mildly handicapped. We have two misplaced students that are moderately handicapped,[1] and these children need simple life surviving skills. And here we are trying to teach them something that their mental capacity is not able to even comprehend. We are dealing with students who have IQs of 50. And they (the politicians and policymakers) want these children to succeed and be on grade level with their peers? I just don't think it's possible. They don't have the mental capacity to do that.*

Moreover, the push to achieve 100% mastery may negatively impact students with disabilities by creating high levels of frustration. As one staff member concluded:

> *The students will be severely frustrated. It is unrealistic to impose higher and higher and higher standards on a child who cannot meet those standards. The child CAN improve and learn. The problem is they are not going to do (academically) what my top child can do.*

Another participant questioned whether students with disabilities would receive equitable treatment under the requirements of *NCLB* as some inclusion students at Creekside were tested without the adaptations specified in

---

[1]Creekside Elementary does not have a program for moderate or severe disabilities.

their Individual Education Plans (IEPs) in the general classroom settings. She explained that this occurred primarily because of the lack of available staff members to administer the test with individual adaptations:

> *Well, they (students with disabilities) will be treated unfairly. First we go and label them special ed. Telling them that they are not "normal." Yet we're going to tell them that they have to take and pass the "normal" test without adaptations.*

Ironically, legally these students must receive instruction based on the individual adaptations specified in these IEPs.

During the course of the study, many participants voiced the concern that *NCLB* was written by policymakers who were uninformed about education. This is reflected in one staff member's response:

> *Honestly, my opinion is that whoever wrote this legislation really knows nothing about education. If they did, they would never have required inclusion children to achieve 100% proficiency. If they came in here and sat for a day they would know why!*

It appears clear from these responses that there is an inherent danger in enacting educational legislation that assumes all students come to school on an even playing field. These policies, promoted by politicians who are misinformed, ultimately damage the most vulnerable of our students and effectively set low-income public schools up for failure.

On Our Own

General education teachers need a variety of resources and support to provide a quality education for students with disabilities in their classrooms. As an inclusion school, general education classrooms at Creekside Elementary are comprised of anywhere from 0% to 47% inclusion students. Classroom teachers who had included special needs students were asked whether they felt they received adequate resources and support to help them address the specific needs of students with disabilities in their classroom to help them meet requirements of *NCLB*. Their responses varied somewhat. One participant suggested:

> *Yes, I think we receive adequate resources and support. We have the classroom teacher and then one full-time inclusion teacher for each grade level. Inclusion students are pretty much housed within one classroom, which makes it easier for the inclusion teacher to be right there with them. Yet even with that there is a drawback. In first grade, one inclusion teacher is shared between first and second grades. That's a real stretch for her to be able to move between these children.*

Another explained:

> *We receive adequate resources and support. Just this week we started the Corrective Reading program. It is a pull-out program for 45 minutes 2 days a week. It is designed for fourth-grade students 2 years or more behind in reading. My children are the rock-bottom group.*

These positive and mixed responses were the exception. Most classroom teachers at Creekside did not feel they received adequate resources and support to meet the needs of students with disabilities. Classroom teachers overwhelmingly echoed the sentiment that they were primarily on their own with inclusion students, as one participant's response reflected:

> *I have been totally on my own this year as far as inclusion is concerned. The first 2 months of school, I received a half an hour of help per day from the inclusion teacher on a semiregular basis. That help just dissipated. There were a variety of excuses given, and I finally quit asking.*

Although the general classroom teachers were more than willing to collaborate with inclusion teachers, one respondent cited a lack of co-planning time during the day to help them effectively address the needs of students with disabilities:

> *As far as co-teaching and co-planning? Absolutely not! It does happen in some of the other grades. This year the special ed teachers have more of a pull-out program. But the thing is, we are not a pull-out school. We are an inclusion school. Some of the pull-outs are necessary because we are doing a new Corrective Reading program. Those kids have to be pulled out. When the teacher is not doing the Corrective Reading program, she should be in my room moving around from student to student helping them with their work. So I don't really feel I have the support that I should. I don't feel that the special ed kids' needs are being met. Last year in my room, because I had so many special ed kids, their needs were not being met and neither were the needs of my regular ed kids because I could not do it myself. I had to make a whole new curriculum for some students. We were doing fourth-grade math and they were doing first. We were doing fourth-grade reading and they were doing first. I did it all on my own for the most part.*

In addition, another pointed out that this lack of classroom support was a result of the large amount of paperwork that is required of inclusion teachers:

> *This was supposed to be a co-teaching classroom, but because the special ed teacher assigned to my room has so much paper work and testing to do, her time with me is very very limited. I hardly ever have a full day of her being in the room and able to*

help. It isn't necessarily her fault. It is because of a lack of special ed staff and school psychologists. Her workload has doubled. And when another inclusion teacher was out on maternity leave, her work was tripled. She was covering for all of those thing and *was responsible for being in a room.*

One participant suggested that the inclusion teachers often worked with the general education students who were struggling to prepare them for spring testing:

I have an inclusion teacher who comes in twice a day. But she is still not meeting the needs of my inclusion child and neither am I because we are so busy pushing, pushing, pushing for everyone else to get their test scores up. There is not a lot of time to sit down and work with the inclusion child. Also, she is not always available. If someone is ill, she is pulled to do their job and sometimes they are at meetings.

In doing this, however, they ended up ignoring the needs of inclusion students altogether. The marginalization of students with disabilities within the general education setting suggests that, in light of the current high-stakes testing environment, perhaps it is time to rethink the value of inclusion in low-income schools because as one participant explained:

Most of our regular education students are as needy as our special education students. They require a great deal of time and effort also.

Even when teachers desperately reach out for help with inclusion students, they are often thwarted in their efforts. Perhaps one of the most poignant illustrations of the lack of support general education teachers at Creekside receive to help them meet the sometimes challenging needs of students with disabilities was provided by a classroom teacher who recounted a recent experience:

I received a new student from out of the district who came with an IEP (Individual Education Plan). The parent kept questioning me as to why her student was not receiving the necessary services so I brought it to the attention of the Support Services Team (SST). For weeks the IEP was ignored by the team, so I called an IEP meeting myself to discuss the fact that this particular IEP called for the inclusion of the student in the regular classroom provided the child has a full-time aide present at ALL times. I had to convene the meeting on my half-hour preparation time. The SST members and special education representatives from downtown were 15 minutes late. By the time the meeting officially started, I had to return to my classroom. The meeting was held and decisions were made without my input. Instead of dealing with the provisions of the IEP, the student was moved to another regular classroom where the teacher (a second-year teacher) would be less likely to question the IEP.

This demonstrates that, despite the fact that general educators are held responsible for the academic achievement of students with disabilities, they have little or no say in major decisions that are made regarding the quality of education they receive.

It is important to note that inclusion teachers also expressed great concern with many of these issues as well. In addition, they voiced frustration about the fact that they are not seen as having to be in any one particular place during the day, and thus are viewed as floaters. Many substitute teachers are unwilling to work in urban schools. As a result, licensed staff members such as inclusion teachers may be pulled from their assignments to perform various duties and tasks, including filling in for absent staff members. As one inclusion teacher indicated:

> *It is very frustrating when you come to work to do the job you were hired for only to find out you will be used as a sub when a teacher or the secretary is absent. When you come into work, you never know what duties you will be expected to perform during the course of the day. Often these assignments are given at the last possible moment, often too late to notify the teachers I am working with in classrooms.*

Faculty and staff members at Creekside also felt that as part of an urban school they were at a financial disadvantage when it came to providing adequate resources and support for inclusion teachers and students with disabilities. As one participant explained:

> *We do not have an inclusion program like schools in the wealthier districts. Not only do they have inclusion teachers available on a regular basis, they also have an abundance of parent volunteers who help in the classroom. It is not like that here. We do not have adequate support, and we have many more challenging students. It takes more human hands than are available.*

Much of this they blame on the unequal funding of public schools. In fact according to school statistics posted on the State's Department of Education Web site, Creekside's district spends approximately $5,000 per student each year. In contrast, an adjacent and more affluent district's per-pupil expenditure was almost $9,000. Not only does the adjacent district spend almost twice as much money per student, but all of the schools have extremely active parent organizations involved in massive fundraising efforts. For example, an elementary school newsletter from the higher socioeconomic district boasted:

> Fall fundraising efforts are underway via catalog sales. Please ask your family and friends to help our school by purchasing products. Speaking of fund raising—ask your children about all the great new updates on the playground

that occurred over the summer! About $12,000 of fundraiser money was spent upgrading and adding equipment and resurfacing play areas. (School Newsletter, August 2003, p. 4)

The newsletter goes on to thank a long list of parent volunteers. Creekside, in contrast, has a parent group comprised of two volunteers, and fundraising efforts are minimal and unsuccessful at best. As a result, Creekside cannot provide the same level of resources and support for students with disabilities as higher socioeconomic districts.

In addition to these concerns, more than anything else, general education teachers voiced the belief that they felt unprepared to meet the needs of students with disabilities due to several factors. First, they believed they lacked a clear understanding of disabilities and cited that they had taken no coursework in teaching students with disabilities in undergraduate or graduate education programs. They also cited a significant lack of professional development opportunities at both the school and district levels. The few in-house workshops that were provided focused primarily on administrative tasks, such as how to fill out referral and intervention forms, and defining what is or is not in the inclusion teacher's job description. Finally, they indicated that there was a lack of time within the high-stakes testing environment to meet the individual needs of all students because Creekside teachers are required to use a scripted curriculum. This prepackaged curriculum leaves little time to deviate from one-size-fits-all lessons to address the specific adaptations contained in the IEPs of students with disabilities. All of this contributed to the pervasive view that there was a severe lack of resources and special education support staff.

Intrusion or Inclusion?

Under the requirements of *NCLB*, standardized test scores for each classroom and school are disaggregated according to race, gender, and students with disabilities. Teachers are then evaluated according to the lowest of these scores. Creekside teachers were asked whether this requirement would affect their willingness to accept special education students in their rooms. One teacher responded that *NCLB* would not affect her willingness to accept students with disabilities:

No, it does not because I believe we should accept ALL children and work with them.

Within the current high-stakes testing environment, teachers' willingness to accept students with disabilities became conditional based on the amount of time that would be required to address their particular needs. As one participant implied, she would be willing to accept inclusion students if they did not take up too much of her time and effort:

I'm OK with having special ed students in my classroom depending on the severity of their problems.

A more candid participant said that the requirement would affect teachers' willingness to accept special education students in their classrooms, especially if their own livelihood would be threatened by doing so:

Absolutely! Teachers don't want them. If my job depends on their test scores and they are reading at a first- or second-grade level and I am teaching fourth grade . . . I don't want those kids. I do because I am a teacher and went into teaching to help kids. But if my job depends on it . . . my car payments depend on it . . . my apartment payment depends on it . . . I don't want those kids.

In making the standardized test scores for students with disabilities a liability to general education teachers, *NCLB* effectively works to further their marginalization within the school setting. As one member of the inclusion staff concluded:

This legislation is a big concern to special education. Teachers will push kids out of their class if they are evaluated on special education students' test scores.

Consequently, one is left to ponder once again just how *NCLB* might benefit students with disabilities.

Referrals to Special Education

As a result of the Accountability Movement, from the mid-1990s to today, there has been an increasing emphasis placed on high-stakes testing as a means to evaluate the performance of teachers and schools. Until *NCLB*, the scores of identified special education students were not included in these evaluations. If a teacher had a slow learner or a severe behavior problem, the norm was to refer these students for individualized testing. Thus, the students who were identified as special needs would still be required to be tested, but their scores would not count against the aggregate school scores in any way. Naturally, during this period, there was a marked increase in the number of referrals for special education testing because teachers wanted certain low achievers to be out of their own and the school's test score pool. The year of the study, *NCLB* required special education scores to be used in the total school performance evaluations. Interestingly, the number of referrals to special education decreased the year of

the study at Creekside. A repercussion of the decreased referrals will probably mean fewer support services for inclusion children.

Teachers were asked whether they continued to refer students for testing. One replied that she did not:

> *I have a tendency to kind of hold off on that. I've always been hesitant to recom-*
> *mend a child and have that child labeled. I think labels can be so detrimental to*
> *the child's self-image.*

A teacher who continued to make these referrals was asked her reasons
for doing so. Her response indicates that teachers are beginning to place a
higher value on test-taking skills over creativity and critical thinking as a result of high-stakes testing:

> *Some of the reasons I recommend students are for lack of focus and no attention*
> *span. I have worked with a lot of special ed teachers in my background and in my*
> *field, and I tend to be able to spot them right away. If they can't stay on task, are*
> *very frustrated, or the child just cannot remember things, I will refer them.*

In addition to teacher referrals, several interesting identification phenomena were observed at Creekside. Some parents of students with disabilities worked proactively to have their children classified as disabled or
placed in special education. One reason for doing so was because they had
been in special education classes in school and felt they had passed their
disability on to their children. More perplexing is that some parents actively
sought to have their children identified to collect additional monies each
month in their government assistance check, which may have been the real
reason for all such parental lobbying.

Will *NCLB* Help or Hurt Students With Disabilities?

Overwhelmingly respondents believed the requirements of *NCLB* would actually inflict harm on students with disabilities. Some wondered out loud
whether it was so politically incorrect to believe that, "*Yes* all children can
learn, but *no* not all children can master required proficiency levels." One
staff member felt that *NCLB* did not treat students fairly:

> *NCLB does not recognize student exceptionality in testing. For example, we iden-*
> *tify exceptionalities at great expense in terms of time and effort, but fail to consider*
> *these exceptionalities in standardized testing. High-stakes testing treats all stu-*
> *dents EQUALLY, but not EQUITABLY.*

Indeed with its one-size-fits-all approach to school reform, *NCLB* fails to recognize that, "Equity in education means equal opportunities for all stu-

dents to reach their fullest potential. It must not be confused with equality or sameness of result, or even identical experiences" (Bennett, 2001, p. 174).

Ultimately, the requirements of *NCLB* have resulted in high levels of frustration for students with disabilities and have displaced a meaningful curriculum in favor of a less valuable test-driven one. As one teacher explained this resulted from the fact that there was a marked increase in instruction focused primarily on preparing students with disabilities for the standardized test at Creekside:

> *NCLB is not beneficial to special education students. I have noticed a high level of frustration on the part of special education students preparing for the test. They are frustrated because the kids want to do well, and they feel sad when they can't do well on a standardized test. These students need language experiences, not test-taking skills. They need to be journaling to develop language skills, not learning how to fill in circles on an answer sheet.*

This does not bode well for students with disabilities because, as Kohn (2000) explained, high-stakes testing has caused "a meaningful curriculum . . . (to be) elbowed out to make room for test-oriented instruction" (p. 30). Kohn added that:

> It is far more difficult for teachers to attend to children's social and moral development—holding class meetings, building a sense of community, allowing time for creative play, developing conflict-resolution skills, and so on—when the only thing that matters is scores on tests that . . . measure none of these things. (p. 30)

CONCLUSION

These collective voices of urban educators are clearly telling us that *NCLB* will not prove to be effective in providing a higher quality of education for students with disabilities. In fact they are telling us that this legislation may even be harmful to students with disabilities in the long run. An overwhelming consensus was that it was cruel to subject students with disabilities to the pressures of high-stakes testing because it causes unhealthy levels of frustration for all involved. Mamlin (1999) agreed, stating, "In general current reform movements that stress higher, and more inflexible, academic performance requirements do not bode well for students with mild to moderate disabilities, such as learning disabilities" (p. 227).

A reality that cannot be ignored is the fact that wealthier districts have a seemingly unlimited amount of resources and staff to address the needs of students with disabilities. In urban districts, where there are greater percentages of both students with disabilities and low-income students, there is a severe lack of financial support. Therefore, meeting the requirements of *NCLB* becomes much more challenging.

Urban educators believe that the legislation contains an inherent bias against urban schools. Although it privileges schools in higher socioeconomic districts, it marginalizes urban schools and, in effect, sets them up for further failure. In planning reforms with a higher likelihood of success, it is important to remember that:

> Results should always be evaluated in light of the special challenges faced by a given school or district: A large number of students with special needs, or a very low-income community, provides a necessary context in which to understand a set of results. (Kohn, 2000, p. 47)

The findings of this study ultimately suggest that, by not keeping context in mind when formulating reform initiatives, policymakers and education reformers may actually lower the quality of education students with disabilities receive in districts already struggling for survival.

REFERENCES

Bennett, C. (2001). Genres of research in multicultural education. *Review of Educational Research, 71,* 171–217.

Brantlinger, E. (2003). *Dividing classes: How the middle class negotiates and rationalizes school advantage.* New York: Routledge Falmer.

Buntin, J. (2002, October). Special ed's dark secret. *Governing,* pp. 44–46.

Hargreaves, A. (1994). *Changing teachers, changing times: Teachers' work and culture in the postmodern age.* New York: Teachers College Press.

Katz, M. B. (2001). *The irony of early school reform: Educational innovation in mid-nineteenth century Massachusetts.* New York: Teachers College Press.

Kohn, A. (2000). *The case against standardized testing: Raising the scores, ruining the schools.* Portsmouth, NH: Heinemann.

Mamlin, N. (1999). Despite best intentions: When inclusion fails. *The Journal of Special Education, 33,* 227–240.

McCarthy, C. (2002). *I'd rather teach peace.* Maryknoll, NY: Orbis Books.

Merriam, S. B. (2001). *Qualitative research and case study applications in education.* San Francisco, CA: Jossey-Bass.

No Child Left Behind Act of 2001, Public Law 107-110, 107th Congr., 1st Sess. (2002).

Rist, R. C. (2002). *The urban school: A factory for failure.* New Brunswick, NJ: Transaction.

Rosenthal, R., & Jacobsen, L. (1968). *Pygmalion in the classroom.* New York: Holt, Rinehart & Winston.

Chapter 7

Marcus and Harriet: Living on the Edge in School and Society

Edyth Stoughton
Teachers College, Columbia University

Emotionally disturbed students are inattentive, disruptive, obnoxious, and have a bad attitude. Sometimes they work, but more often it's total chaos. They don't care. There are "regular" kids in here who want to learn, but I pity them. They're being dragged down by them.

—8th-grade social studies teacher
in a large, urban middle school

I don't think anybody in the school gave a dang about me.

—10th-grade student labeled
emotionally handicapped

They won't sit by me, and they accuse people of being my friend like it's some kind of punishment.

—8th-grade student labeled *emotionally handicapped*
speaking of fellow students in his English class

I'll tell you what makes me mad: when the "good" kids stop learning because of "those" kids.

—Middle-school foreign language teacher

THE DILEMMA OF TEACHING ED STUDENTS

Although school personnel in educational institutions espouse inclusion and the acceptance of diverse learners in classrooms, from the voices cited here, it seems that a rejecting and excluding climate may be the norm. It

145

appears that students labeled *emotionally disturbed* (ED) and some of the teachers with whom they interact may have fundamentally different belief structures about the nature of school problems and ways of being in the classroom. As noted by Artiles (2003), the educational message generally is that difference is equated with deviance, creating a situation in which a prerequisite for equality is sameness. Although classified students' access to general education classrooms is mandated by law and is supported by professional principles, it may be true that "access does not guarantee meaningful participation, full membership, or more comparable outcomes" (Artiles, 2003, p. 170). Too frequently classrooms embody areas of cultural imperialism, where the "dominant cultures' stereotyped and inferiorized images" (Young, 1990, p. 59) are regularly played out to the detriment of students with emotional and behavioral difficulties.

Ayers (1997) could have been speaking of many school faculty and administrators as he described, in his study of the juvenile justice system, an inability or unwillingness "to see children as full and three-dimensional beings or to solve the problems they bring with them through the doors" (p. XVI). As I look back over my 19 years as a teacher of middle-school students who are considered too emotionally handicapped and behaviorally disordered to function in general education classes, I have become very aware that to be labeled ED is to be given an identity that causes one to be looked down on, feared, ridiculed, and avoided. I have become increasingly troubled by how little is known about the students I teach and, as a consequence, how little empathy they receive in the school environment. ED students generally comprise the group of special education students whose complex needs and troubling behaviors cause them to be seen as the most difficult to educate. This perception causes a growing number of concerned educators and researchers to believe that public education for young people who have been labeled severely emotionally disturbed is largely a failed enterprise. Discussions about inclusion frequently falter as teachers and parents come up against the perceived dangers and seemingly insurmountable problems inherent in including students with such troubling behaviors in the classroom. Statistical data present a bleak picture as they seem to show that educational outcomes for ED students are poor. According to the 1999 report of the Office of Special Education Programs, the graduation rates for these students are low, with only 40% to 50% of students labeled emotionally disturbed graduating. Similarly, according to the U.S. Department of Education's 23rd Annual Report to Congress (May 10, 2002), half of the students classified with emotional and behavioral disorders dropped out of school in 1998–1999. This dropout rate represents the highest rate for any special education disability category.

As educators seek solutions to the dilemma of how to do a better job of reaching and educating ED students, hard questions must be asked about existing perceptions and beliefs. According to Roman (1996), when students are called emotionally disturbed, they can become the focus of fear and moral concern, which ultimately leads to seeing them as culprits in need of official intervention. The way in which young people labeled ED are perceived causes them to be characterized as *hostile, rebellious, aggressive, threatening,* and *strange,* regardless of their actual traits. Caplan (1995) asked, "When terms like 'abnormal' or 'mentally ill' are spoken, what kinds of images come to mind? Usually images of difference and alienation" (p. 11). Students who bear these labels tend to be considered fundamentally different and possibly dangerous, hence they are positioned in such a way as to make it seem necessary to remove and control them. Removal inevitably means placement in a self-contained special education classroom. In this way, self-contained ED classes have frequently become the means for containing young people whom public educators feel they cannot teach in regular classes.

Students who have been labeled emotionally disturbed or behaviorally disordered represent a wide range of needs and problems. In some cases, ED classrooms are used as places where students who do not adjust to the expectations and requirements of the school environment are separated from the mainstream school environment. However, certain students do have severe emotional problems and have a substantial need for adult support. Whether one's child is full of rage and acting out or withdrawn and depressed, emotional problems can be frightening and debilitating for parents and family members. Families of students with emotional needs may have a difficult time coping with their child's problems. Parents look to schools to be supportive and to care about their children, thus reducing the impact of problematic differences. As Taylor (1991) pointed out, "We all need to value parents' right to expect that the school will be an advocate for the abilities of their children, especially if those children experience difficulties in school" (p. xiii).

This expectation is not always met, however. Indeed the competitive and conformist nature of schooling may actually exacerbate students' original problems. Schools increasingly must survive in a climate of emphasis on test scores and meeting statistical norms. Our currently underresourced educational system is not geared toward understanding and addressing the needs of its tremendously heterogeneous population. Therefore, as a number of authors observe, a situation frequently develops in which the needs of troubled children are at variance with the needs for stability of institutions (Casella, 2001; Cottle, 2001).

If the response to children's problems is punitive or condemning, parents of these students also feel rejected. If school personnel blame them and see them as part of the problem, rather than forming partnerships to resolve issues, parents may feel disconnected. As Harry (1992) noted, the discourse between parents and the professionals involved with their children tends to be structured by the assumptions that technical/theoretical knowledge is more valid than commonsense knowledge, and that the educational experts should have the power to structure communication and make decisions concerning the child's educational future with minimal input from parents who are left with the choice of passively cooperating or forcing a confrontation.

The question then becomes, how can we alter commonly held negative narratives that place these students and parents in a marginalized, alienated position? One necessary component in dealing with such hard questions is the need for scholars and other professionals to begin from the standpoint of the students and look at how these students experience their education. Students who are categorized as emotionally disturbed frequently are disempowered both by the nature of the school hierarchy and the technical practices of special education that reduce the child's life to "a series of common, professional theories which define the child's existence" (Danforth, 1995, p. 140). There has been a great deal of research in the area of special education, but little of it has drawn on the lived experiences of students. As Featherstone (1989) wrote:

> Our increasingly polyglot and multiracial society is sorely in need of teachers who know how to honor the stories of their students and to join them to wider narratives and larger meanings. We need to learn better how to build on these stories, and, when they clash with mainstream stories, how to explore the discrepancies, rather than assume pathology. (p. 378)

Listening to Students' Perspectives as a Tool to Understanding

Narratives, or the stories we tell ourselves and others, are how people make sense of their experiences. We order, select, and interpret events so that we create a coherent explanation of ourselves and our world that makes sense and justifies our beliefs and actions. Stories play a significant role in the ways individuals construct and express meaning and maintain a feeling of consistency and coherence in their lives (Clandinin & Connelly, 2000; Mishler, 1986; Polkinghorne, 1988).

If our schools are to become more inclusive, responsive, and just, it is important that we value the voices of students who have been labeled emotionally disturbed and provide them with opportunities to speak out about their opinions and feelings. Nieto (2000) wrote that, "The voices of students are rarely heard in the debates about school failure and success, and the perspectives of students from disempowered and dominated communities are even more invisible" (p. 358). She further indicated that, "It is only by first listening to students that we will be able to learn to talk with them" (p. 382). We need to hear people share the reality and complexity of their lives in their own voices and in their own ways. Contextualized and nuanced storytelling is frequently the only way to understand, and vicariously experience, the lives and realities of others who are situated differently and who have disparate worldviews (Barone, 2001; Newman & Benz, 1998). Disability categories are culturally constructed concepts that reflect how a society responds to differences, and there are perceived characteristics and behaviors that accompany all special education classifications. According to Gallagher (2001), "It is the meaning we collectively bring to difference and the social, physical, and organizational arrangements built on our interpretations that make a person's difference a disability" (p. 3). Because an emotional or behavioral disorder is a category that is largely considered to be a catch-all for the behaviors that authority figures consider intolerable, it is viewed by many teachers as a particularly troubling label for students in their classrooms.

I had been troubled for some time about the common misperceptions about the students in my ED class. I knew that, to a great extent, they were considered to be thugs and troublemakers. As a result of my concerns, and because I believe that it is through telling stories and sharing experiences that empathy for others is developed, I set out to conduct a research study with the intent of providing a space for students who have been labeled emotionally disturbed and their parents to tell their stories. Through personal interviews with ED students and their parents, I proposed to create compelling cases or personal portraits that would convey their perspectives and situations to readers. The story of one mother–son pair that I share here is part of the larger study, in which I conducted a series of in-depth interviews with six high school-age students who had attended special education classes for students labeled emotionally disturbed for several years and with 10 parents and a case manager of one of the students I interviewed. Four of these young people were former students from my self-contained EBD classes in an urban middle school of 1,200 students. In the case of these former students, I was able to supplement the interviews with autobiographical experiences, memories, and observations. The remaining two students were enrolled in a large state-supported residential psychiatric facility when I spoke with them. The parents and students I interviewed were family units with four exceptions; I interviewed four parents without also talking with their children. In one of those instances, I was unable to interview the daughter as planned because she had unexpectedly been placed in emergency respite care.

Participants

My respondents ranged in age from 14 to 20 years. Of the six students with whom I spoke, five were boys and one was a girl. Three of the homes were headed by single mothers, three participants lived in families with both parents, and one girl lived in a foster home.

My participants also covered a broad economic range, including the wife of a wealthy owner of an electrical firm; a major in the army; an African-American single mother who was a business executive; an owner of a small car repair shop; an unmarried mother who was a cafeteria worker; and a single mother who struggles to support herself and her son and daughter on disability benefits.

The conversations with the respondents lasted 60 to 90 minutes. On completion of a first round of interviews, I initiated a second round to allow participants to clarify and expand on issues discussed during the first conversations. These second conversations allowed me a chance to follow-up on matters that, on reflection, were unclear or were of enough interest that further elaboration would appear to be fruitful. Second conversations did not always take place because they depended on the willingness and interest of the respondents to continue with the conversation as well as whether it appeared to me that more information would be pertinent. The fact that I had conversations with members of the same family allowed for triangulation, providing diverse perspectives on the issues discussed.

THE MARGINALIZING EFFECT OF ED LABELS

In the course of my study, several themes emerged. Because the goal of narrative research is to conceptualize rather than generalize, the gestalt of each individual story should be accorded the utmost importance. No story is ever completely idiosyncratic. In making sense of our experiences, we are all shaped by our ideologies and beliefs, which in turn shape our reflections. Therefore, stories tell us not only about the narrator's life, but also about her culture, requiring that we locate the focus and meaning of the individual story within the cultural context in which personally meaningful events are lived out (Cottle, 2001).

It became clear in talking with both students and parents that there was a strong feeling of alienation and estrangement from school personnel. Although this finding was not altogether surprising, the depth of the home/school separation was extreme in all cases. The most pervasive commonality among the parent and student participants in the research study was the feeling they shared of being devalued by school personnel. They felt that their identities were constructed as inferior by others in the dominant school culture, and they believed they were frequently the objects of ostracism and/or contempt. A substantial body of literature is in agreement that marginalization is a significant aspect of the ED label. Young (1990) told us that many of these young people believe that the dominant culture sees them as "marked or inferior" (p. 60). Parents are frequently driven away from interaction with school officials by the attitude of blame they feel directed toward them and their ability to parent.

To foreground this theme of profound disconnection from the school community, I chose one of the families with whom I spoke. This mother and son talked at great length and with much sadness about how devalued they felt by school personnel and how uncomfortable dealings with the school's faculty and administration were for them. I have known these respondents for 8 years, and their story is a complex, multilayered one complicated by dysfunctional relationships, general isolation both within and outside school, rejection by extended family members, and paranoia. Regardless of the dysfunctional behavior both brought to school, it becomes clear that their relations with school personnel probably exacerbated their problems rather than relieving them. It is important to honor their voices and listen to their version of the situation as they share their experiences and perceptions. Their story reveals a facet of the complexity and humanity of the lives of children identified as emotionally disturbed and their parents.

Marcus

I first noticed Marcus when, as a silent, sixth-grade boy with a grimy, ragged T-shirt and dark, hurt-looking eyes, he stood every day in the hallway watching the rowdy group of boys as they entered my self-contained classroom for students labeled *severely emotionally handicapped* carrying their brimming lunch trays. My students were the only ones in the school who were allowed to eat lunch in a classroom instead of the cafeteria—a privilege that was inextricably linked not just to their preference, but to alleviating cafeteria problems for school personnel. As the first weeks of the school year passed, Marcus continued his daily routine of silently watching the boys pass him and enter my room before he slowly made his way to the cafeteria, where he ate alone huddled over his lunch tray at the end of a long wooden table.

Intrigued and disturbed by his daily presence, I began inquiring into what was happening with Marcus in school, only to find that he was failing all of his classes, he appeared to have no friends, and none of my colleagues seemed to know much about him or, in fact, to have any connection with him. Although I am not an advocate of removing children with handicapping labels from regular classes, I do believe in the healing power of safe places when they are needed. As I observed this lonely, envious observer of my students, I felt that Marcus probably needed connections and relationships that might be available in a space where he could feel safe and welcomed. So after completing the necessary paperwork, Marcus became a member of our class community. Gradually he relaxed his guard as he joined us for several of his classes throughout the day and became an integral member not only of the "lunch group," but of my class. He delighted in bringing little surprises to his classmates, his shy grin broadening when they seemed pleased. Soon we came to expect Marcus to come to school bearing treats such as a huge platter of homemade Cheez Whiz and cracker canapés or grimy, twisted paper napkins full of popcorn.

My special education room was a haven for this lonely youth. However, because Marcus was dealing with a range of emotional issues that were not totally responsive to the comfort of my classroom, there were times when he would become frightened or distraught, and then he would retreat into dark places filled with anxiety even within the safe space of my room. Sometimes when the world got to be too much, he barricaded himself under his desk, piling up books and notebooks and leaving only small holes through which he would dangle his shoes from his hands. If I sat quietly and calmly on the floor next to the barricade, he, acting as the ventriloquist, would talk to me using his shoes as spokesmen in expressing feelings he could not say face to face.

After leaving middle school and my class, Marcus struggled in high school. My initial inquiries about his high school adjustment indicated that things seemed to be starting out on a fairly positive note for Marcus. At least when I inquired of school personnel about him, the casual, vague response of, "Oh sure, he's doing fine," gave me no indication that all really was not well. However, it was not long before periodic phone calls began coming from Marcus. He had a decidedly different perspective from his teachers as he recounted that he hated school and that he was miserable. Official reports also began filtering down to me concerning the problems high school personnel were having dealing with a student with such severe difficulties. These reports were not consistent with the gentle, shy, eager-to-please boy I remembered Marcus to be when he was in middle school. Resentment that Marcus and his mother were unreasonable complainers who "just didn't get it and didn't even try to cooperate" was expressed by the high school staff. It appeared that, instead of the attachment and connectedness he had felt with me and his peers in the climate we had created in our ED class and that he still craved, Marcus was experiencing increased rejection and the terror that inevitably accompanies being ostracized by others.

At the time of the study, 5 years after he left my class, Marcus still called me several times a year to tell me the latest events in his life. High school remained a struggle for him. He was suspended numerous times and finally informed me with some embarrassment that, due to excessive absences and suspensions, he dropped out. Based on the attitudes toward him that I observed on the part of the high school personnel, I am sure his dropping out was with their blessing.

At age 20, Marcus pretty much hung around at home with his mother. He reported that he had no friends and never achieved the quality of relationships he had found in my self-contained classroom. He was not working, nor did he have feasible plans to find a job. His latest scheme was to enroll in a $200 class, which would entitle him not only to have a chance to try out to be a wrestler in the World Wrestling Federation, but would also provide him with a special stage name and costume. Yet even the temporary boost in spirits that this fantasy option provided had disappeared with time. His most recent phone calls had been somewhat joyless and dispirited. Having lost a sense of social connectedness and belonging to any community beyond his home life with his mother, Marcus seemed to be drifting aimlessly into a future truncated from productive work or social relationships.

Harriet

To begin to understand Marcus and his attitudes and behaviors, it is necessary to also come to know his mother, Harriet. Harriet was an older mother who worked sporadically because she says she is handicapped, although I have never seen evidence of a handicap nor has she informed me of the nature of her disability. Marcus and his younger sister, Mandy, were adopted as young toddlers by Harriet and her husband, who died when the children were quite young. She appears to have no friends or community support, and she is estranged from her family largely because she, a White woman from West Virginia, married an African-American man and adopted Marcus and Mandy, who are biracial.

Many of Harriet's behaviors can be described as eccentric and amusing. Early in our relationship, soon after Marcus had become my student, she arrived at my middle-school self-contained classroom announcing that she had come to have lunch with Marcus. She was wearing a cocktail dress, large rhinestone jewelry, and stiletto heels. Her hair was piled on top of her head in a large, jeweled bow. I was somewhat taken aback by her attire, but as she swept past me, she announced in a loud voice, "Marcus says I embarrass him cause I come to school dressed bad, so I decided to dress up so he wouldn't have to be embarrassed by me." Unfortunately, there were other times when her behaviors seemed harmful and even devastating to Marcus. I remember one occasion in particular when, on one of her frequent visits to school, Harriet, Marcus, and I were standing in the hallway talking, and she suddenly turned to me and said in a loud, clear voice, "You know I've been calling that Children's Bureau place trying to get them to take Marcus back. They gave me a defect." At first I thought, uneasily, that her statement was a very bad joke, particularly because Marcus was 14 years old at the time and had been adopted as a young toddler, but her tone of deadly seriousness and Marcus' stricken face convinced me she was not joking.

A lonely, isolated woman, Harriet desired friendships, but had little comprehension of how to establish them. She frequently came to my classroom and simply stood silently in the doorway waiting to be noticed. On one occasion, she swept into the room bearing her own McDonald's lunch, which she spread out in front of the students who hungrily watched her gulping down her hamburger and fries while she proclaimed loudly that she was glad that Marcus was in a class for "crazy kids" because he certainly needed all the help he could get. At the close of one after-school conference, still talking, she followed me to my car with Marcus trailing behind. On several occasions, Marcus tried to interrupt her monologue. She finally grabbed my arm in an exasperated manner and pulled me away from Marcus, saying, "I guess he just don't want us to be friends."

There is a close, complicated bond between Marcus and his mother. Sometimes it appears that Marcus acts as a parent to this volatile woman. Although Harriet often embarrasses Marcus and frequently says disparaging things about him, he knows that she will do her best to defend and protect him, and he is acutely aware that she is the only consistent support he has. Since Mandy dropped out of school and moved in with an older boyfriend, Marcus and Harriet seem to have only each other. Perhaps in their mutual social isolation and loneliness they need each other. Since Marcus has dropped out of school and neither he nor his mother have a job or a car, it seems that Harriet and Marcus spend the majority of their time together in the small, government-subsidized apartment they share.

Harriet's lack of effective communication skills has frequently created problems both for her and for Marcus. The blunt, exceptionally honest manner in which she expresses herself is humiliating to Marcus, and school personnel are inevitably annoyed by her intense, antagonistic form of speech. Her abrasive discursive manner with teachers may, to a certain extent, have been influenced by her belief that both of her children have been mistreated by the school system. Harriet has told me on several occasions that she has no one to depend on but herself, and she firmly believes that if she does not fight for her children, no one will. Although one might hypothesize that early complaints from teachers triggered her now consistently hostile tone, unfortunately, this attitude tends to work against her as her often aggressive and confrontational manner has caused school personnel to discount her as uncooperative and emotionally unstable.

The Most Important Thing Is—Someone Who Cares for the Kids

As Marcus spoke with me about his school experiences, the point about which he was most emphatic was that he felt uncared for and ostracized at school. An oft-repeated refrain in his conversations was, "They wouldn't listen to me." He explained to me that he and his mother had requested a meeting with school officials to address perceived unfairness in the way Marcus had been treated by school personnel. In reference to this meeting, Marcus said:

> They don't seem like they care at all. The teacher always heard about our complaints and stepped in to the meeting even though we didn't want her there. They would listen, but they just wouldn't believe us. Basically, they'd just tune people out and do what they usually do, just sit and stare.

Marcus also perceived that school personnel cared so little for his feelings that they embarrassed and humiliated him in front of his classmates. He recounted bitterly, "The teachers blurted out stuff in class that my Mom told them." He returned to this as an explanation for why he dropped out of school:

> I was so frustrated because of all that derogatory stuff that teacher kept saying about me out loud in front of everybody. She kept bugging me. That's why I dropped out of school.

Harriet also brought up this incident during one of our conversations, citing it as an example of the lack of professionalism and unkindness that she believed teachers exhibited toward her and her son. As she described it:

> I would talk to the teachers about Marcus' problems and I didn't know the teachers were turning around and saying all that stuff out loud. The teacher would say, "Your Mom says you do this and that," and all the kids were listening. I thought you were supposed to take your students into a quiet room and talk to them.

Marcus discussed other issues that contributed to his disaffection with school, several of which are, to a great extent, common to ED students. He became discouraged because, "I got accused of stuff all the time because of my reputation," and it angered him that they searched him on a regular basis. As he told me, "Every day when I came to school they would make me empty out my pockets. One time they suspended me for a week because I refused."

As my interview with Marcus drew to a close, he expressed his sense of the importance of relationships when I asked for his suggestions as to how schooling could be changed to make it better for kids. He responded:

> It was good most of the way. It was OK in middle school, not high school. Students should have a choice about what they should do and what they should

take. But the most important thing is somebody who really cares for the students.

In talking with Marcus, I was struck by the fact that, although several years had passed since he had found refuge and companionship in my classroom, Marcus was still a lonely boy who had desperately looked for someone in high school to connect with him and to care about him. To a large extent, he was unknown to those in his school environment. He believed that no one knew what he was thinking or feeling, what his goals and dreams were, or what could work to help him realize those goals and dreams. Students like Marcus are disempowered in a variety of ways. They diverge drastically from the pedagogic goals of the school community, and they find social acceptance to be elusively beyond their reach. Our identities are, to a great extent, context-dependent, and who we are in a given situation has a great deal to do with our social surroundings (Ferguson, Ferguson, & Taylor, 1992). If a child's environment gives him the information that he is damaged goods, he will be forced to struggle mightily to find either a positive sense of self or feelings of confidence. Marcus did not find that, and, lacking recognition and approval he lost a sense of future possibilities.

"They Didn't Respect Us At All"

Harriet's complaints against school personnel during our conversations were remarkably similar to those of Marcus. The same themes of being ignored, devalued, and shut out that were evident in speaking with Marcus surfaced repeatedly in Harriet's words. Her conversation was peppered with statements such as, "They [school authorities] didn't believe anything I said" and "I guess they have no feelings for their students." In addition, on several different occasions, Harriet indicated that she not only felt devalued, but that she had also lost trust in the benevolence and fairness of the school system. She expressed her perception of this breakdown in trust when she said:

> I used to think a lot of Leland Township [pseudonym] when my kids first went in there, but now I don't like them. They messed up. The Head of Special Ed. didn't do nothing for us all those years. He didn't listen to us. He'd just sit there and then leave. The teachers have a lot of education, and they are the teacher, so there's no way they aren't going to win. That's awful that the school always believes the teachers. They've made up their mind before they even hear your story.

This same sentiment was reiterated when Harriet said at a later point, "They try to find something wrong with all of the [ED] students so they can get rid of them," and still later, "It happens a lot that they kick kids with disabilities out of school." Her lack of trust in school personnel seemed to extend to a mistrust as to whether school personnel would abide by their own educational promises as she said:

> They weren't there for Marcus. They weren't there for Mandy. She was just sort of wandering around. They didn't do anything. Anything they said they were going to do, they didn't do it. They didn't do anything they said. They said, "We are going to call you every time her grades drop. If her grade drops to an 'F' we'll call you." They never did that. They waited until she flunked and until she got so discouraged she couldn't get back up. They didn't follow their paperwork. I think they must just throw it away. They blame the students for what they [educators] do wrong.

Harriet was quite bitter about the ways in which she believed school personnel disregarded students' feelings. In addition to her indignation over occasions when teachers shared confidential information with an entire classroom of Marcus' peers, she was deeply offended when she felt educational professionals spoke disparagingly about her children in other forums:

> Schools say all negative stuff. Mandy would just cry. They kept on saying, "Mandy can't learn," "Mandy can't do this." How do they know? They shouldn't talk awful about kids in front of them. I don't even believe they should have the student in there at the conference if they're going to talk about them in front of everybody. Teachers at a conference shouldn't be saying things like "Mandy is bad in this, and she can't learn, and she can't do this." I thought they weren't supposed to use those kind of words. The students already have low esteem, so why should they have to hear it? I think that's why she didn't make it, [Mandy dropped out of school.] She got her feelings hurt.

Not only was there a parallel in the words of Marcus and Harriet, but there was a remarkable similarity in their educational experiences. Harriet talked about her own struggles with disability as she said sadly:

> I have a learning disability. I've had it since grade school, but they didn't have any special ed. They laughed at me in school. They laughed at me and called me dumb and stupid. I wouldn't do the spelling bee because I couldn't pronounce my words. I had to go upstairs for reading class and math. I couldn't be a nurse. I tried to take the test in Chicago and I flunked it. So, I ended up being a housewife. Then later I tried to go to Ivy Tech and they said, "We don't think you can do this." That's when they put me in Vocational Rehab. I was upset.

Harriet's recurring references to the cruel treatment of her children hauntingly invoke images that Harriet used in her description of herself as a little girl; that is, poor, struggling in school, and laughed at because of her learning disability. She seemed to carry her own victimization experience into the perceptions of her children's treatment continuing them into the present day.

The way that Harriet viewed her relationship with educators can be examined through the lens of the power of personal narratives in providing explanations for life events. According to Polkinghorne (1988), things and events that happen to individuals become understandable when placed within the context of their lives. Polkinghorne (1988) further explained that people order their lives according to plots they construct in an ongoing process of making meaning of their experiences. The narrative that Harriet had constructed involved her perception of the callousness of school personnel and the mistreatment she and her children had suffered at their hands. This outlook determined how she positioned herself in relationship to school personnel and how she felt and acted in relation to them. Her behavior, in turn, provided a logical, internally consistent explanation about why she was treated in a certain way by those with whom she interacted. These behaviors and attitudes also appear to be reenacted by Marcus and render him ineffective as he struggles to relate to peers and seek acceptance from school personnel.

Intergenerational Influences

There are many questions that stand out in the story of Harriet and Marcus regarding the interaction between Marcus' disability and his mother's behavior. As the single mother of two children of a different race, Harriet had no support from her family, and it is likely she was not made to feel welcome in either the Black or White community. Although she clearly loved her children, they were also subjected to her verbal cruelty. She had much to be angry about—from her own school experiences to family difficulties—and her children bore the brunt of these unresolved mental health issues. Marcus has not felt emotionally able or willing to establish his independence. As a consequence, over time a pattern of remarkably similar maladjusted behaviors has developed between Harriet and Marcus. This appears largely to be a function of their being bonded and their isolation from other supports and relationships, which could potentially supply a correction to Harriet's often skewed thinking. Marcus' identification with Harriet's worldview has seemingly been enabled and magnified by their closeness. When Marcus became disconnected from the balancing influences of school and peers, his thinking increasingly mirrored that of his mother. In their longitudinal study of the developmental pathways of children, Cairns and Cairns (1994) wrote that, "We cannot hope to understand an individual's behaviors and beliefs independently of the social network in which they are embedded" (p. 248). Marcus, unlike most young adults his age, has an extremely limited social network. As a result of his emotional problems, which cause him to be socially awkward and fearful, his world is bounded to a great extent by his relationship with his mother. Therefore, he is extremely susceptible and vulnerable to her influence.

Alienated, Left Out, and Ignored

Harriet knew she was not accepted by school authorities. As we exited the restaurant and walked to my car after our interview, she said ruefully, "I guess they just don't like me over at that school." In one way or another, she has felt like an outcast all of her life. Perhaps Harriet's bluster and "touchi-ness" are stances she takes in an attempt to compensate for her feelings of inadequacy and inferiority, which have stuck with her from her childhood years, in which she describes herself as the "ugly duckling" in a large family growing up in poverty. It seems clear that Harriet and Marcus need connec-tion, attachment, and some form of constructive work. During the conver-sations we shared, a recurrent theme emerged. Harriet felt rejected and de-graded by school personnel, and she felt they had hurt her feelings and angered her. She translated these feelings into a fear that, because school personnel did not like her, they were taking advantage of her children.

Harriet's feelings are shared to a certain degree by other participants in my study who also feel demeaned by teachers and administrators. The words of another mother of a child labeled emotionally disturbed in de-scribing her dealings with school authorities parallel those of Harriet: "I feel like I don't fit in. I want to some day feel like I'm not an outcast. I feel that way because I think I let these people get to me. I always feel inade-quate" (cited in Perez, 1998, p. 156).

Pressing Questions With Few Clear-Cut Answers

We do not always find answers from listening and learning from the narra-tives that people tell us, but rather we are frequently faced with more in-triguing questions. This account raises many questions and does not pro-vide many easy answers. However, dealing with these questions reflectively and honestly is our only hope to have a chance to reach the many students and parents who are disengaged from our schools. I wonder how irrevoca-bly Marcus' school failures were bound up in the attitudes learned from his mother and to what extent we as educators could have changed the trajec-tory of Marcus' life with appropriate interventions. It appears that Harriet's emotional problems played a large part in Marcus' inability to function suc-cessfully in school and society. Social ineptitude, suspicion, and isolation are all contributory factors in Marcus' present circumstances. Yet there was a lack of response and intervention on the part of school personnel. Harriet offended faculty and administration with her demanding, often irrational interactional style, and so they dismissed her and refused to deal with her. Therefore, the frequent absences, increasing unhappiness, and lack of connectedness to school evidenced by Marcus went unnoticed and uncorrected. Instead of understanding the difficulties a mixed-race boy with an unstable single mother would undoubtedly have and seeking to remedy their situation with greater understanding and extensive support, Marcus appeared instead to be rejected as part of the strange mother/son pair.

There is a concern among a growing number of scholars that, in the current atmosphere of high-stakes accountability in schools, caring for student needs tends to be devalued. Rauner (2000) asserted that schools lack attentiveness, which she describes as "the investment in time and effort required to come to know a young person" (p. 21). Mickelson (2000) spoke about the essential nature of the "three C's of caring, concern, and connection" (p. 111). Yet Finders (1997) wrote that, "Constrained by limited contact time with students, teachers have few opportunities to learn of students' life experiences that might affect behaviors within the classroom" (p. 50).

One confounding question is: What are we, as educators, to do with someone like Harriet? Nagle (2001) affirmed that parents like Harriet who find themselves in the position of being excluded and marginalized by school personnel realize that the hierarchical power structure of school is much like that of the larger society, empowering some while disempowering others. Although much has been written about difficulties in communication across ethnic, racial, and socioeconomic differences, there is little said about the lack of tolerance for differences that are due to paranoia, eccentricity, or social ineptness. Conversations about ways to deal fairly and effectively with special education students and their families rarely talk about how to dialogue with parents who are difficult and frustrating because of their personalities or their way of looking at things.

One of the criteria related to whether one is heard is the manner in which one expresses oneself. Harriet had some important things to say, but unfortunately her manner of saying those things was offensive to school personnel, so it became easier to avoid and ridicule her than to listen and try to understand her. Perhaps if those in school were committed to getting past parents' eccentricities and really hearing them for the sake of their children, a cooperative relationship could take place between parents and school personnel. Such interactions certainly could have made a difference in Marcus' school career.

A second question that emerges from this story is: What can be done to connect with students like Marcus, who go through their school days feeling ostracized, marginalized, and disconnected, and who finally drop out of school because of their profound lack of a sense of belonging? It is certainly possible that the bitter severance in relations with school that Marcus and Helen experienced would not have occurred if someone in the high school had reached out to Marcus and shown concern and an interest in him. As Rauner (2000) wrote:

> We have tended to see schools and other important institutions as value-neutral product providers with no caregiving role or responsibility. . . . It is not enough to counsel kindness in face-to-face encounters. We must also think, quite radically about how we can organize the social, civic, and economic institutions in which we participate so that they are caring places as well. (p. 3)

Marcus drifted unhappily through his school experience until he finally just stopped participating. Unfortunately his failure and isolation in school transferred to his postschool life. He is certainly not alone. Possibly Rauner is correct and something as simple as being intentional about showing kindness and sensitivity to these *shadow students* could make the difference.

Finally, we wonder how effectively schools can intervene to disrupt the cycle of distorted thinking and maladaptive behavior that is passed on from parents to their children. The answer to this question may lie in the answers to the prior two questions. Effective and caring intervention in cycles of dysfunction in families may be found through sincerely and genuinely searching for answers to the questions of otherness and establishing connections.

It appears from the families with whom I spoke during the larger study of which Harriet and Marcus were a part that the reality of the relationships ED students and their parents have with schools is far different from the relationships they would like to have. In her narrative study, Perez (1998) found that the parents she interviewed wanted to feel included in the school community, to have a relationship with school personnel in which they were not blamed, and "to feel a genuine connection with educators and a sense of belonging" (p. 238). According to Young (1990), students desire recognition and a sense of belonging, hope, and possibility.

SUMMARY

The story of Marcus and Harriet points up the key role relationships play in human development and well-being. Disinvestment in families that are difficult and frustrating can lead to a bleak future for "throw away" young people. Lacking effective supports, this lonely mother and son continued to withdraw further into social isolation. There is a need for educators to continue to be involved in a dialogue about what it means to care for young people in an acknowledgment that "caring is the essential component of influential relationships" (Rauner, 2000, p. 1).

It is clear—both from the literature and the words of the respondents in this study—that if we are to have schools that are responsive and inclusive, we can no longer marginalize and alienate people who fail to fit our image of normalcy. Students are often held at arm's length as *other* by those in the school environment who stereotype them as deviant and discount their positive qualities. Their parents are driven away by the attitude of blame they feel directed toward them and their ability to parent. The challenge is to "change the terms of the conversation" (Cook-Sather, 2002, p. 11). I fully agree with the words of Maxine Greene (1993) as she wrote:

> It seems clear that the more continuous and authentic personal encounters can be, the less likely it will be that categorizing and distancing will take place. People are less likely to be treated instrumentally and to be made "other" by those around them. (p. 13)

REFERENCES

Artiles, A. J. (2003). Special education's changing identity: Paradoxes and dilemmas in views of culture and space. *Harvard Educational Review, 73*(2), 164–202.

Ayers, W. (1997). *A kind and just parent: The children of juvenile court.* Boston, MA: Beacon.

Barone, T. (2001). *Touching eternity: The enduring outcomes of teaching.* New York: Teachers College Press.

Cairns, R. B., & Cairns, B. C. (1994). *Lifelines and risks: Pathways of youth in our time.* Cambridge, England: Cambridge University Press.

Caplan, P. J. (1995). *They say you're crazy: How the world's most powerful psychiatrists decide who's normal.* Reading, MA: Perseus.

Casella, R. (2001). *Being down: Challenging violence in urban schools.* New York: Teachers College Press.

Clandinin, D. J., & Connelly, F. M. (2000). *Narrative inquiry: Experience and story in qualitative research.* San Francisco: Jossey-Bass.

Cook-Sather, A. (2002). Authorizing students' perspectives: Toward trust, dialogue, and change in education. *Educational Researcher, 31*(4), 3–13.

Cottle, T. J. (2001). *At peril: Stories of injustice.* Amherst, MA: University of Massachussetts Press.

Danforth, S. (1995). Toward a critical theory approach to lives considered emotionally disturbed. *Behavioral Disorders, 20*(2), 136–143.

Featherstone, J. (1989). To make the spirit whole. *Harvard Educational Review, 59*(3), 367–378.

Ferguson, P. M., Ferguson, D. L., & Taylor, S. J. (Eds.). (1992). *Interpreting disability: A qualitative reader.* New York: Teachers College Press.

Finders, M. J. (1997). *Just girls: Hidden literacies and life in junior high.* New York: Teachers College Press.

Gallagher, D. J. (2001, June). *How do we talk about teaching practices from a disability studies perspective?* Paper presented at the first annual Second City Conference on Disability Studies and Education, Chicago, IL.

Greene, M. (1993). The passions of pluralism: Multiculturalism and the expanding community. *Educational Researcher, 22*(1), 13–18.

Harry, B. (1992). Restructuring the participation of African-American parents in special education. *Exceptional Children, 59*(2), 123–131.

Mickelson, J. R. (2000). *Our sons were labeled behavior disordered: Here are the stories of our lives.* Troy, NY: Educator's International Press.

Mishler, E. G. (1986). *Research interviewing: Context and narrative.* Cambridge, MA: Harvard University Press.

Nagle, J. P. (2001). *Voices from the margins: The stories of vocational high school students.* New York: Peter Lang.

Newman, I., & Benz, C. R. (1998). *Qualitative-quantitative research methodology: Exploring the interactive continuum.* Carbondale, IL: University of Illinois Press.

Nieto, S. (2000). Lessons from students on creating a chance to dream. In B. M. Brizuela, J. P. Stewart, R. G. Carrillo, & J. G. Berger (Eds.), *Acts of inquiry in qualitative research* (pp. 355–388). Cambridge, MA: Harvard Review.

Perez, S. B. (1998). A narrative account of how three parents of students labeled severely emotionally disturbed talk about special education (Doctoral Dissertation, University of South Florida, 1998). *Dissertation Abstracts International, 59,* 07.

Polkinghorne, D. E. (1988). *Narrative knowing and the human sciences.* Albany, NY: State University of New York Press.

Rauner, D. M. (2000). *"They still pick me up when I fall": The role of caring in youth development and community life.* New York: Columbia University Press.

Roman, L. G. (1996). Spectacle in the dark: Youth as transgression, display, and repression. *Educational Theory, 46*(1), 1–22.

Taylor, C. (1991). *Learning denied.* Portsmouth: Heinemann.

U.S. Department of Education. (2002, May 10). *23rd annual report to Congress on the implementation of the Individuals with Disabilities Education Act.* Retrieved August 13, 2002 from http://www.edpubs.org/.

Young, I. M. (1990). *Justice and the politics of difference.* Princeton, NJ: Princeton University Press.

Chapter 8

No Place Like Home

Genell Lewis-Robertson
Indiana University, Bloomington

Those eyes.
If his sandy blonde hair was brushed back long enough, you could catch just a glimpse of those eyes.
Eyes troubled with anger. Confused by adults. Too knowing for a ten year old.
Those eyes.
Eyes that reflected a child's compassion for life, excitement, wonder, and awe for new things discovered.
Those eyes.
Eyes that rippled with muddled memories of fighting, drugs, abandonment.
Those eyes.

My first impressions were of Elijah's eyes. Others may have begun with his unkempt appearance—hair down to his chin, shorts so large that they met the ground, tattered shoes with untied shoestrings, and a holey, wrinkled shirt almost as long as his shorts. Others' first impressions of Elijah may have been based on the ebbing flow of opinions unwittingly escaping the mouths of frustrated teachers.

I was drawn to Elijah's eyes. Elijah's eyes were how he expressed his true feelings and where he wrote his untold story. Those eyes that sparkled and glowed with anticipation and happiness. Those eyes that burned with anger, like intense lasers hammering down along with his fists. Much like the eye in the center of a hurricane, even his calm was clouded with hurt and remorse. As a teacher I had seen many sets of 10-year-old eyes. Ten-year-old eyes hold innocence and trust. Elijah's eyes held neither.

WELCOME HOME

Anyone who has been a teacher or works with children knows that there are certain children whose presence never leaves their lives even after they have long been gone from their classroom. Long after the warm air of summer turns crisp and autumn's wind blows in the new menagerie of fresh faces, the spirits of students past echo from the walls. Elijah[1] is one of those spirits. I found myself checking in to see his progress after I left the classroom to pursue graduate school. Of course my pride as a teacher peaked my curiosity about his well-being after he left my nurturing side, but there was more. Throughout my year as his fifth-grade teacher, Elijah intrigued me and challenged me. I was kept awake nights worrying that the potential I saw in him would slip through the cracks of his difficult life. Elijah would glimmer with hope one day, then fade with discouragement the next. I think I followed Elijah into his sixth-grade year because I somehow felt responsible for his well-being, and I knew I couldn't stand the pain of the possibility that his glimmer could fall into total darkness.

My interest in Elijah was the initial reason I began this study. The understanding and insight I gained from learning about Elijah's life became a lesson about teaching that I felt propelled to share with others.[2] However, this lesson can only be taught through inclusion—inclusion of ideas about the feelings and experiences of family raising a child with oppositional defiance disorder (ODD), of a child living with addicts, breaking laws, and being an outsider in an educational system so hopefully designed for all learn-

---

[1]All people and places in this chapter are pseudonyms.

[2]Using a qualitative research method known as a *case study* (Merriam, 1998), interviews will be conducted with the mother of a 12-year-old male diagnosed with oppositional defiant disorder (ODD). ODD is a label given to children in which their behavior significantly impairs their ability to function within social and academic settings. The interviews will be focused on the issues and obstacles of raising a child with an emotional disability, under difficult living conditions, and will be taped knowingly by the participant for accurate transcriptions and analysis of data. On completion of the interviews, the researcher will observe the child for a day in his current home school environment to provide an accurate picture of the child's behaviors within his current academic setting. Interactions among the teacher, student, and other children will be written in field notes. Interviews will not be conducted during the home school visit. The other students in the classroom consist of three other boys who are the sons of the home school teacher, ages 6, 10, and 13.

In addition to the interviews and home school visit, observations made by the researcher about the child from his 2001–2002 school year will also be included. These existing data consist of teacher notes (the researcher was the student's fifth-grade classroom teacher) and observations made by the researcher to share and discuss with the mother patterns of behavior the child formed in the classroom. The notes will be used to generate an introduction for the research, and to develop a more thorough understanding of how the child's emotional disability affected him during the school day (data that the mother would not have first-hand knowledge of).

ers. I invite readers to search for the lessons and learn about Elijah by offering the same welcoming words of his mother who so openly shared her story with me, "I would be happy to help you."

HOME IS WHERE THE HEART IS

Flipping through the dusty stacks of "Parent Communication Journals" I had rubber-banded together according to school year in my basement filing cabinet, I finally discovered my scratchy writing in the notorious black Sharpie marker denoting the years 2001–2002. Thumbing through the stack of 28 students, I stopped at Elijah's journal. As I began to read through my comments, in an effort to provide the reader of this chapter with the most descriptive moments of Elijah's fifth-grade year, I became lost in nostalgia. Slowly the story of the school year replayed itself like video images in a movie within my mind: The first few weeks of school, when I began to uncover the many sides of Elijah's personality, attending camp together and watching Elijah's ecstatic smile as he danced in the glow of the bonfire with Indian war makeup under his eyes, and his obvious gratitude for the gift of a Chinese pen pal seen as he scribbled out a three-page letter, Elijah's excitement over the family-style dinner we ate together as a class, Elijah's charisma as he performed in the school's talent show, and my own wonderment at the adoring gaze Elijah cast on his father when this man finally made his first and only appearance in my classroom.

These accounts were memorable to me because they were all important benchmarks in my understanding of Elijah and in my development of a relationship that contained reciprocal trust, respect, and caring. My communication notes that were used to describe *school home* to Elijah's *living home* have appropriately become the springboard into the story of Elijah. I have chosen to share these accounts to introduce Elijah within the same setting that I was inducted as a teacher meant to care about students—a public school.

Hometown Elementary

Racing to the office, I bounded with the 30 other teachers in my building to receive our first copy of our class list. To a teacher, this list provides a wealth of valuable information the week before school starts: (a) How many students you have, (b) how many boys and how many girls, and (c) the names of your students. The latter is of utmost importance for it is with the names of these children that teachers can consult with the children's teachers from the previous year to find out about the students you will live with in the coming year. It is embarrassing to admit that you are one of the many teachers out there who participated in the "Teacher Grapevine" of gossip about students. Try as you might to not prejudge, when a colleague looks at your new list of students and gives you the, "Oh-I'm-so-sorry-look," it's hard not to feel a little discouraged. In 2001, however, I was pretty excited because I received fewer of those looks than ever before. My class looked pretty evenly balanced with boys and girls, and as an inclusion teacher, I had been given six *labeled* children who I already knew fairly well and had prepared for over the summer. In fact the only comment I received that year regarded student number 28 on my list. Looking through the names, my colleague and friend peered up to me smiling, "You have Elijah!"

"Who?" I questioned.

"Elijah, he was in my class last year. Wait 'til you see that smile. He's hard to resist. But keep in mind that all you would have to do is slap a green blazer on the kid and you have a used car salesman."

"A used car salesman?"

"He can argue and convince his way out of anything. Even when you know he is probably lying to you, you still feel inclined to believe him. You can't help but love him," she explained with a mischievous grin. I inquired more and she gave me a brief description of Elijah. He was a child who had attention deficit hyperactivity disorder (ADHD), was on Ritalin, and had basically raised himself. The only family history she could recall was that his parents had issues with drugs, but that his mom had turned her own life around, regained custody, and now had the task of attempting to raise a child who had experienced the freedoms of an adult for the first 8 years of his life. My curiosity was sparked as I looked forward to the first day of school and meeting my "used car salesman."

Enter Elijah (my notes on the first days of the semester):

Aug. 22—Elijah announced his entrance in the classroom, "Trouble is here!" Energy!!! I pulled him off of Garrett's back as he entered the classroom. Garrett and Elijah say they are best friends. I will have to monitor closely. Both were kicking each other in bus line and say they are practicing karate and Tai Chi.

Aug. 23—Moved Elijah's seat to the opposite side of the classroom and away from Garrett. Very argumentative. Refused to move at first, then refused to write, saying that, "Other people get to sit by their friends!" and that he doesn't work well next to his "enemies." I guess he means the other students? This concerns me.

Aug. 24—Elijah helped Traci today. Very impressed with his gentle, kind words and patience with Traci. Very calm, very different demeanor when helping her. Offered her some of his paper when she became upset about not finding her own.

I remember the chaos of that first week. If I had ever questioned before why the school calendar started in the middle of the week instead of on Monday, my query was no more. Twenty-nine faces, 29 abilities, 29 person-alities, all to work collaboratively for approximately 6 hours a day toward the goal of learning. I always started strong with my Parent Communication Journals, diligently writing a few sentences about every child every day. Yet every year my best intentions would fail me, and I would digress to writing in everyone's journal only about once a week. Parent Communication Jour-nals were my documentations, my thoughts. If parents called and asked how a child was doing, I was usually able to give them a brief synopsis by looking through their child's journal. Elijah's journal was unusually thick by the end of the year. Even within the first week, he had given me more to write about than any of the others. As I introduced myself to the new faces walking in, he burst in, shoving others to the side, and announced that he was proud to be the trouble-maker. Jumping on peers, slamming down books, kicking at friends, and flipping somersaults in the hallway. Offering hugs, sharing smiles, and a moment of compassion as he helped Traci, my student with Down syndrome, feel better about losing her paper. I couldn't believe that Elijah, an adorable child, could display such a range of behav-iors in such a short amount of time. Most students go through a honey-moon phase, or a week or two of impeccable behavior before they allow their true feelings to show. Elijah skipped this good behavior week com-pletely.

Elijah's self-professed "best buddy," Garrett, followed Elijah's every move and appeared to be fascinated by his actions. As a member of the fifth-grade class, Elijah's charisma made him a natural leader. However, it was appar-ent that the older sixth graders in my 5th/6th class did not appreciate Eli-jah's immature outbursts. Their initial negative approbations created the reaction of more attention-seeking from Elijah. In an attempt to hide his true feelings about the sixth graders' exclusion, he would act out in an ef-fort to keep from crying.

Sept. 3—Students chose friends to share a cabin with at camp.[3] Elijah very up-set that he may not be able to be in Garrett's cabin. Stated a list of reasons why they should be in the same cabin, the final one being, "I will do something bad if he's not in my cabin so I can be sent home! The camp is stupid anyways!" Had him help with collecting papers to calm him down.

Sept. 6—While making nametags for camp on wooden cookies,[4] Elijah threw his when it wasn't how he wanted—it shattered, almost hitting Claire. Ex-plained consequences for throwing things were a referral and time out of the

---

[3]All fifth-grade classes attend an outdoor, overnight camp for 1 week to study environmen-tal curriculum.

[4]"Wooden cookies" are small pieces of round, flat bark.

classroom. Elijah stated he didn't care and slammed door on his way to the office. I think he was sad because Trevor and John told him that he couldn't use the same design that they had drawn on theirs. I have requested to be in Elijah's cabin during camp.

Sept. 7—Asked Elijah to write a few sentences about what he looks forward to at camp. Refused. Stayed in with me at recess to work together. Pouted, threw head on his desk, sharpened pencil five times, and finally scrawled out, "Bein a way from here."[5] Tried to talk to him about this. He became tearful. Hugged me, then went outside for recess.

Having a multi-age classroom is a wonderful experience that starts approximately 1 month after the school year begins. Before then, younger children's insecurities and uncertainties about fitting in and finding their place within the classroom home that has already been occupied a year by the current sixth graders is always difficult. This transition to being a new student rather than a second-year old-timer (along with any transition I later found) was extremely difficult for Elijah. Unfortunately, his coping method for these uncomfortable situations was lashing out, which meant lashing out in anger toward, himself, his peers, and me. When he wrote about camp anticipations, this first real experience with writing in my class showed me that his spoken language was far more advanced than his ability to express himself with written words. This fact of inadequacy was a sensitive issue for a child who cared intensely about his competencies, but who pretended to be very tough-skinned.

Our school had the opportunity to take the entire fifth- and sixth-grade classes on a week-long trip to an overnight in the woods. The purpose of this cherished event was to explore outdoor recreation and nature curriculum. It was always a rewarding trip that resulted in the students bonding with each other and developing positive personal relationships with teachers. Our school's camp session was earlier than usual this year, so I did not yet know Elijah well. I viewed camp that year as an opportunity to learn more about Elijah when he was in a casual, nonthreatening environment. In the few weeks I had known him, it was clear that school was a threatening place for Elijah, and his behavior was erratic and troubling. However, my journal from camp reveals the same swift changes of mood and behavior.

Sept. 10—Elijah has picked on Tommy all day—making threats, kicking, and making fun of him. Already had to give him his first strike.[6] Seems he is trying to sabotage his stay. Finally calmed down after campfire. Enjoyed the songs and found enjoyment in attention received from farting during ghost story

---

[5]Text typed exactly as written by Elijah.

[6]Consequence system that resulted in students having to return home after receiving three "strikes" for inappropriate behaviors.

time. Stated he was going to stay awake all night and has plans to raid the girls' cabins.

Sept. 11—Elijah slept for 2 hours. Very hard to wake up—seemed excited about the all-day hike. During community circle about terrorist's attacks, commented, "It's because of our government." Yikes. Later, Elijah comforted Tommy who was frightened about the news. So difficult to figure out.

Sept. 13—Played a raisin in the cabin skit. Was wonderful! I have found Elijah's talent—acting! Great day—Elijah fished and played flag football. Unfortunately, yelled at Mrs. Marlene when she told him he had to stop playing with the bonfire. Screamed at her with fists clenched. Serious aggression, second strike.

Elijah made it through the full week. If he had received a third strike, he would have had to go home, and I really didn't want that to happen. The funny thing was, he knew I wanted him to stay. I suspect that was the reason he attempted to push the boundaries as far as possible. I felt that camp was the ideal place for Elijah to excel, and in so many ways he did. Every hour of that first night, I peeked out of my cabin room to observe him. Turns out that he had snuck dried beans from home; as soon as he thought everyone was asleep, he started to pitch them over onto the bunks of his classmates. I smiled and didn't say a word. The act was harmless, and he felt he was getting away with something. More than anything, I was beginning to realize how much his adult words and angry actions were just a façade. Elijah was still a child under all that pretense. On our last night at camp, he was the only camper to remind me (an hour after lights out) that I hadn't tucked everyone in. I zipped his sleeping bag completely up, and tousled his hair, "You're right and I'm sorry. Good night Elijah."

"Thanks. Good night Mrs. R."

The school year progressed, and I began to learn Elijah's games almost as quickly as he learned mine. Some weeks I saw amazing growth in his self-control. Other weeks made me feel as if I had been hit by a large bus. If he wasn't trying to talk me out of an assignment, he was fabricating a story about his weekend and why he hadn't been able to complete homework. Elijah became a regular at my after-school homework help club on Wednesdays. It wasn't Elijah's abilities that kept him from finishing assignments, it was the fact that he was dancing around the room, creating new Tai Chi moves, finding ways to cuss in Chinese, or showing peers how to disassemble a skateboard. Elijah found any distraction possible to keep from completing traditional class work. Most days I was patient because I saw though his veneer. He was so afraid of failing that he avoided all school work so that failing was exactly what he was doing.

The October 25th entry in Elijah's Parent Communication Journal was starred and highlighted. I remember the circumstances clearly. After repeatedly asking Elijah to write a final draft of an amazing story about "Ninja War" that he had already spent 2 weeks on, Elijah tore it to pieces. "What are you doing?" I asked in a strained tone.

"This story was crap!"

"It was creative!"

"You say that to everyone!" His voice rising, he continued, "And I don't give a crap about this stupid school or you!"

I had reached the point of total frustration and gave up my calm demeanor. Despite the fact that the remainder of my class looked on in stunned silence, I yelled, "If that is the way you feel, go sit in the hallway!"

"Go ahead! Yell at me! Everyone else does!" With that he began to storm out of the room knocking over desks.

"Keep on marching all the way to the office and fill out a referral for being disrespectful!" I added loudly as he slammed the door. I immediately grabbed my phone and explained to the office that Elijah should not return until he had filled out the referral. He did not return to my room for the remainder of the day, and I did not receive his referral form with its minimal admittance of disrespect until the next morning. I'm not sure why, but I didn't call his mom that afternoon, I just went home; I cried from frustration and hurt. The incident had reminded me of another time I was not so proud of: yelling at my 2-year-old for painting a closet full of clothes with oil pastels that I had left out. I felt remorseful about yelling. I was the one who had left the paints within her reach. But my daughter's words sat like a lump in my stomach. "It's okay mommy, you just forgot that I loved you."

Oct. 26—It's okay Elijah, you just forgot that I loved you.

I apologized for yelling, he apologized for yelling. I gave him a hug, and we went on with the school year, never mentioning the outburst ever again. And only now, as I write these words, it becomes very clear that this moment was a turning point for our relationship. I finally understood that Elijah was truly just a child, but a child with more insight than most adults I know. He knew where my breaking point was, and he never again attempted to reach it. However, that did not mean he completely gave up his usual mischievous antics.

Nov. 21—Elijah became very defensive when John made fun of our Thanksgiving Feast. Helped with arranging desks into long table. Played with burning candle wax, had to blow out candles. Really liked having lunch as a class.

Dec. 12—Gave class pen pals as presents. Elijah was so enthusiastic that he wrote a three-page letter to his Chinese pen pal. This was a great day for him! By far the most writing I have seen all semester. Call mom on positive note.

Jan. 8—Clothes filthy and smelly today. Very tired and nonresponsive.

Jan. 29—Hair greasy. Appears Elijah has not had a shower, and once again, very tired. Note: 4th week in a row he has started the week off filthy. Contact social worker and mom.

Feb. 8—Taking Elijah and Garrett to the science museum Saturday with my own young children. They are both looking forward to it. Elijah says his dad, Mark, is dropping him off. May get a chance to meet him.

Feb. 11—Mark left Elijah at the museum. Missed him again. Christy (mom) picked him up. Had a lot of fun. Elijah was wonderful with my children, and both boys were appropriate the entire time. Elijah showed me where he hangs out downtown during the weekends. Yikes!

Mar. 4—This was a pretty good Monday. Elijah is excited about Spring Break and getting to skateboard and go downtown to the local park. Had to take away two finger skateboards that he wouldn't stop playing with. Said his dad would come and get them back for him.

As the end of the year approached, Elijah developed an end-of-the-year pattern. Angry on Monday, depressed on Tuesday, brighter by Wednesday, model student on Thursday, and out of control on Friday. I wondered what was going on at home, but I asked very few questions. I wonder why I did not ask Elijah or Christy about possible reasons for this pattern of behavior.

Mar. 23—Christy says that Elijah is now labeled ODD instead of ADHD. States that he has been on a waiting list for a special counselor to talk through his issues. Note: Look up ODD tonight.

Christy had informed me that Elijah was being counseled and that he stayed with his father on the weekend. Despite numerous attempts by me to communicate with Mark, Elijah's father had never visited our classroom. He missed our poetry tea, parent–teacher conferences, and the conference concerning testing Elijah for a learning disability. I invented reasons to meet Mark. I wanted to learn why this evasive father was the same man that Elijah discussed with such enthusiasm and endearment. Yet each time I attempted to make contact, I was disappointed. I found it difficult to understand that Elijah would make excuses for Mark, yet still seemed to find every reason possible to condemn Christy, who as far as I could see was reliable. There were days when I would wait outside with Elijah when Christy was running late, and there were days when I could tell by her disgruntled demeanor that she was tired of arguing with Elijah and tired of being a single mom. However, most of the time she was there for Elijah. I was intrigued by why Elijah worked so hard to make her the evil one. It was as if he was trying to convince himself that she really was bad. Or maybe he was trying to find her breaking point; he was testing her love to find the point where she would give up and leave him. Was he staying angry at his mom to protect himself? Maybe he blamed his mother for leaving his father, or possibly he identified with Mark and wanted to test Christy to see whether she would abandon him like Elijah felt she had abandoned his father.

> Apr. 1—Tried many tricks. Very happy and mischievous today. Seems interested in inquiry project. Topic: Karate and Bruce Lee.

Elijah's choice of karate for our class inquiry project was not surprising. Since the first weeks of school, Elijah had indicated that karate was a passion. Nevertheless, his interest in the topic did not keep him on task. For most of the research time, he found ways to distract others. When I was able to devote time to him alone, Elijah worked very diligently. Most independent work time became a dance that we would perform:

"Where's your inquiry folder Elijah?"

"This project sucks!"

"Vacuum cleaners suck, you can be more creative than that."

"Whatever. I can't find it."

Two folders, two library books, two after-school help sessions, and 2 months later, Elijah had put together an actual poster presentation for our class "Inquiry Celebration!" Lined up with the other 28 projects, Elijah's posterboard sat leaning on his binder, with a two-page report about karate. It wasn't a true final draft, and the writing was fragmented facts that he had discovered, but the work was his. A carefully constructed Yen Yang was drawn on his title page, and written in pencil was his name with the words, "Karate and Bruce Lee the actor." I distinctly recall his comment as he colored in the black side of his Yen Yang: "This is just like me and my mom," and he pointed to the picture.

I wasn't sure what the turnout would be for our "Inquiry Celebration!" Many parents of children at my school worked during the days and evenings. However, I was pleasantly surprised when more than half of my students and their parents meandered into the classroom, looking over projects with pride. My greatest surprise, however, came with the addition of Elijah and his father. Walking with karate trophies in each hand, Mark walked through the door, guided by a giddy Elijah. Elijah quickly introduced me to his father and then led him over to his desk and report. Mark placed the karate trophies beside Elijah's poster, helping to prop it up. "These are my dad's trophies. He was really good at karate," Elijah presented to the group in attendance, "and my report is about Bruce Lee and how he and his son were both killed while making movies." Applause. I watched as Elijah pulled his dad from project to project, giving great details about each student in his class and speaking, as if he were a doting parent, about how proud he was of each of his peers. "Check this out dad! This is Trevor's and he put together a whole clay movie and everything! Oh, and here's Garrett. You remember Garrett, dad?" I'm sure I stared.

Bittersweet hours wrapped up the final days of school. My classroom had become a home to the 28 students it welcomed every day. And like a family, we loved each other, fought with each other, annoyed each other, and forgave each other. Working together, we created our yearbook page using a *Wizard of Oz Theme.*[7] Elijah made himself into a munchkin, hiding behind my "Glenda the Good Witch" dress.

We laughed together as several of my boys, including Elijah, dressed in wigs and skirts and floated across the stage to Abba's "Dancing Queen" at the end-of-year talent show. We cried together when I told them I was leaving to pursue my doctorate. "You're leaving us for a bunch of college students?" Elijah asked.

"I just have a great opportunity to grow as a person."

"Yeah, and make more money," he smirked. The entire class began to laugh. He continued this joke with me every time I stopped by the school the following semester, just to visit and check in. That was Elijah: endearing, unpredictable, wild, compassionate, independent, and confused. I guess that was why the news of his arrest didn't completely shock me.

Stealing Home

"You're probably not going to discover a whole lot more than what the books say because, a lot of it's true, you know, it's passed down." Over the clanking of silverware on plates, I strained to hear Christy's comments as I observed her shifting uncomfortably in her seat. Despite my best efforts to help her relax, clad in casual clothes and talking in a local restaurant, I felt her nervousness. Christy's hands anxiously moved as rapidly as the words pouring from her mouth. Nervous laughter accompanied by darting glances toward the minirecorder and its red eye glaring back were obvious indications that she was uneasy with what she was saying, yet, just the same, something told me she wanted to share.

I felt like a psychologist, poised with my notepad, listening to the hurt and frustration expressed by my patient. I wondered if no one had ever offered Christy the opportunity to talk before. In an embarrassed irony, I realized that, as Elijah's teacher just a year ago, I had never given her the opportunity to talk about her own life with her son. As Christy's story unfolded, I became enraged at myself at how little I truly knew about her past, her abilities, her experiences, and her expectations for herself and Elijah when I was Elijah's teacher.

---

[7]"Wizard of Oz" (1939) movie based on L. Frank Baum's *The Wonderful Wizard of Oz* (1900).

"Both of my parents were from the foothills of the Appalachian mountains," Christy remarked. Looking around as if searching for pieces of herself, Elijah's mother began her story from the life she knew as a child, the place where the person named Christy, not yet "Elijah's mom," took form:

> I have four older brothers and one younger sister so I have a really big huge family. I am the fifth kid in that line up so I am the first girl next to the youngest. Both of my parents were really hard workers. My mom worked at RCA for 25 years and my dad cut meat for a living; he had his own shop for a while. My dad died of alcoholism in 1997 and by the time I came along things were pretty bad in my family as far as the alcoholism goes. I pretty much lived in fear. He was abusive to my mother but he spanked me a total of two times and that was it, mostly because he was out getting drunk. I just remember things like him getting kicked out of a truck, crawling up the sidewalk in the rain, you know that kind of stuff. He would demand that my mother make him eggs, just a lot of chaos and verbal abuse. He didn't really beat my mom a lot, but I don't know what went on behind closed doors. They divorced when I was nine.

Without her husband, Christy's mom was forced to work long shifts to take care of her family. This left 9-year-old Christy alone frequently and placed her in the responsible position of taking care of her younger sister, despite that she was just a child herself:

> My mom worked for RCA so we moved up here, and I took care of my little sister which really wasn't a good idea because I was in a lot of pain and had a lot of anger so I in turn abused my sister. I mean I would hit her a lot, I would pull her hair. I was nine! I should not have been in charge but my mother was kinda like me; she made too much money for welfare to help her and she completely had to raise us on her own, up to that point. So through my teenage years it was really pretty bad.

Early on in her story, Christy initiated connections between herself and her mother. Following in her mother's footsteps, Christy claimed that she made too much money for government aid and was forced to work hours that prevented her from being at home with her family. By attributing her mother's absence to work, Christy was also able to assuage the guilt she felt about not always being able to appropriately mother Elijah. Although it became clear that Christy cared about and respected her own mother, it also became apparent that Christy blamed her mother's lack of guidance for many of the obstacles she encountered growing up:

> My mom was, as far as role models go, well she did the best she could. She never drank, but she smoked cigarettes. Now she doesn't, but she was never involved in substance abuse, which gives me hope. And like I said, her working hard all the time. My first job my mom got me at Mansion University because she was an usher at the football games and she helped me get a job there at age 14, working with her. I dated a biracial boy who was my first boyfriend and that kinda didn't make my family all that happy being from

the prejudice kind of background they are from and I got pregnant at fifteen and so that really kinda caused a lot of problems. I didn't have the baby. I had to get my mother's permission to have the abortion which she did give me, but she wouldn't go with me cause I think she wanted to put it up for adoption. I think that's what she thought was the best thing. I was fifteen, I was a freshman in high school, and a pompette and into diving and like I just couldn't see myself going full term. I mean I was a kind of a popular girl, kind of you know, and so in high school I was with the popular crowd for a while. Then, I got into theater and that kind of stuff and I started smoking pot in high school and I got in trouble with alcohol as well and got kicked off sports because I was at a party with alcohol. I appealed it, actually, and they let me stay on diving, but I didn't want to do pompettes anymore . . . I was abused by my brothers, I forgot to add that, I was sexually abused by them. Not like all the time but really it made a difference and when my dad died I confronted them. Well, I told my one sister and she told my one brother and he told my other brother and they confronted me about it, and so my brother Sam and I are on better terms now and I just recently called him trying to get him to hire one of my clients[8] but I'm just not close to my family. My mother, I am, I have more respect for my mother now that I have my own child and realize, oh my God, she did this how many times?

The horrible realities of Christy's childhood involved a family who rejected her, judged her, and sexually abused her. These were the circumstances in which she became indoctrinated into the meaning of *family* and unconditional love. Christy's resourcefulness and intelligence led her to find resources outside her family to support her as an adolescent attempting to enter adulthood:

When I was really young and we moved here, the Girls' Club was right next to Barnview School, it was like connected. So, everyday I would go to the Girls' Club and I loved it, you know, I did everything at the Girls' Club, every sport there was from like nine to thirteen . . . that was a big help for mother because I could hang out at the club, including on Saturdays. I did that almost everyday after school. That is actually how I got into college later. From about eighteen to twenty-three I was partying a lot. I was a baker for a while. You know a few jobs here and there. I'd work jobs for almost a year then quit and then at twenty-three I decided to try to figure out what the hell I was doing and the director, the ex-director at the Girls' Club, got me into college with a phone call . . .

Because her mother made a decent income and Christy was still considered a dependent at age 23, it appeared that Christy would be unable to attend college. However, at 23, Christy discovered the news that would drastically alter her life: "That's when I found out I was pregnant." With Elijah in utero, Christy became eligible for financial aid and was able to complete her degree in just 5 years.

At the age of 19, Christy met Mark, Elijah's father. Mark, a social worker, was described by Christy as a man who was "a very capable person, very char-

---

[8]Christy worked as a career placement employer.

ismatic, sensitive person." Christy's retelling of her 5-year relationship with Mark paints a picture of fire and ice, love and hate:

> *Mark is Elijah's dad. I met Mark when I, well wasn't twenty-one I know because we use to sit on top of the Redbird (local bar) and peek in at the band, so I must have been nineteen or twenty and things were pretty good for us for a while. Really, when I got pregnant, things were falling apart and Mark, Mark really didn't want me to have Elijah. He tried talking me out of having him and all this stuff, and so then we got back together a couple of different times. When Elijah was born we were sort of together but you know it has been a long time ago but I wasn't living with him. . . . We broke up a couple of times during Elijah's early years. And, then I moved back in with him when Elijah was four and this was the trailer that he lives in now, and things weren't meant to be. We were fighting and so I left home because it did get physical and that was kind of the last fight I wanted to have. And, Elijah adores his dad, like I said, so I left him in the home so Mark claimed abandonment, got custody for about four years, and that was like first through third grade.*

It appeared that Christy had little involvement with Elijah while he was under Mark's care for the 4 years. When Elijah entered the second grade, his father and teacher had him tested and labeled with attention deficit hyperactivity disorder (ADHD):

> *We had joint legal. Well the emergency petition was one thing but then we came up with an agreement and I was like o.k., because he was the social worker at the time, and made a lot more money than me, and I thought why fight it. But, then in first grade he had him in Union School, which was way out of his jurisdiction which was against the law, by the way, but he thought Union, a new school and it had all this new stuff, it would be better. That's when a teacher and Mark and maybe a psychologist, all unbeknownst to me, put my son on Ritalin. I didn't know anything about Elijah being diagnosed ADHD until, I don't know, how many months went by before Elijah told me he was taking Ritalin.*

To hide his ADHD label from his mother, Elijah would not take his medications on the weekends she had him. Christy was furious that Mark had not included her in the decision to label Elijah and place him on Ritalin, and she was very concerned about her child being dependent on a drug because of his family history of alcohol and drug abuse. Additionally, she didn't feel confident that the psychological evaluation was accurate. When Christy finally confronted Mark with her apprehension, she was hit with a frightening reality:

> *Psych eval was very generic. It was just like, "shows, exhibits fidgeting, shows all the classic symptoms, fill in the blanks and put kids name here, he's doing all the stuff. . . ."
> I've always been concerned about him taking medications for a lot of reasons; I don't want him depending on a pill, plus there is a history of amphetamine abuse on Mark's*

side. Like, Mark's mom took diet pills and stuff and she would give them to Mark so
Mark's drug of choice was speed . . . I was just always concerned about him taking any-
thing and I was working for getting him coping and all that stuff but Mark told me not
to worry about that because he was taking Elijah's Ritalin and that's when I started get-
ting sick to my stomach and I was like, "Oh my God, this guy's crazy! He's taking my
son's drugs and he's got my son lying to the doctor . . ."

After Mark shared his subterfuge, Christy panicked and contacted Elijah's doctor, working to gain full custody of Elijah:

I called the doctor, Dr. Manny, and he just sat there on the phone completely stupefied
and he said, "Not only is this wrong, he is also messing with my medical license!" I guess
the next time he (Mark) came in to get the prescription, Dr. Manny had him drug tested
and Elijah came up positive for Ritalin like he was suppose to be and Mark was nega-
tive. So, I could never prove that. I could never prove that just like now. There are seri-
ous substance abuse issues with Mark and I'm having a hard time proving it. So that's
when I started getting worried and I went and started getting really involved in his
school. He was at Anderson (elementary school) at that time so I went up to the social
worker and found out he had missed 30 days of school that year and was tardy all the
time. . . . God, I went over there one time, I went to the school and he wasn't there so I
was like o.k., so I go over there and there was some strange lady is in Elijah's bed, like
one of Mark's friends, smoking a cigarette and she looked like totally out of it, like out of
it, and Elijah was running back and forth from the kitchen to the bathroom filling up
water bottles. Just a kid thing, but he was just running around the trailer "Blub, blub,
blub, blah!" You know what I mean? Mark wasn't there, you know, so I really don't
know why all that happened, but I got custody back in third grade. . . . I got legal help
through the university, which took six to eight months for me to get anything for it . . .
but I was pretty lenient with visitation because I didn't want to traumatize him, which
now I'm regretting. Which I figured I would, but I always wanted to give Mark the bene-
fit of the doubt and Elijah, he acts like it's going to be this big traumatic thing, but the
truth is, he adjusted. . . . I regained custody, which was a big traumatic thing for Elijah
because he loves his dad. He loves him and he wants to be with his dad.

Christy's emotional oscillations were apparent as she discussed being torn between wanting to act in the best interest for Elijah's welfare and having to separate him from the father he adored.

Life for Elijah and Christy began together full time when Elijah was in the fourth grade. However, together for them created an oil-and-water combination: Elijah was used to being a pseudo-adult with little supervision; Christy's only true experience with parenting involved the role-modeling of her mother and Christy's own abusive relationship with her younger sister. As a single mother Christy worked to keep up with Elijah's school, care for him, and make enough money to support him. However, Elijah's personality and defiance issues made things exceptionally difficult, at which point Christy sought counseling from a nurse practitioner at a government-funded counseling service:

I think it was back when I regained custody of Elijah back in 2000, when all this stuff started happening and his defiance came out and stuff and she said something like, "What about ODD? I think he's ODD and he has a lot of stuff that goes with that." And I was like, "What's that?" and she explained it and it was like, I think he is more ODD than ADHD, I really do. I mean I don't know. I mean it's all about self-control really and I guess nobody has really proved anything that it is a brain thing but I don't know, I mean is it a total chemical imbalance, or a behavioral thing, or a combination?

Oppositional defiance disorder (ODD) is a label given in early adolescence to children who have become angry and hostile toward all adults and authority figures. The children then justify their disruptive, disrespectful, and aggressive behavior by attributing it to an overoppressive parent or teacher (4troubledteens Web site). In Elijah's case, he would often blame his mother for his actions, and this would carry into the classroom when he would refuse to complete assignments or follow teachers' directions. Christy felt that the abruptness by which Elijah was transferred from the freedom of his father's house to the restrictive atmosphere she attempted to run in her household was among several factors that led to Elijah's association with the label ODD:

I mean I've been doing a lot of reading on it (ODD) and I can see, well single parent families where you have two sets of rules, rules here and rules there, and the kid doesn't have to do either, and the fighting. When you have two parents fighting, that is going to create an angry child . . . you know when you have fighting parents and two separate households, and it's almost like too, he really has this fantasy about getting away with stuff. I mean a lot of kids have that anyways, but not to the extent that the kids that are labeled do. So, I think having no discipline at his fathers and also me being like, you know riding on him all the time cause I feel like . . . I'm swimming up stream as far as trying to get him to do what he's suppose to do. And, kind of that self-defeatist well I'm that kid so screw it, everyone thinks I'm a bad kid, I'm going to be in trouble anyways. But also, it's really not being taught respect for himself and for other people. Not having that consistent modeling of good parents, taking responsibility for themselves and making him take responsibility, having freedom with responsibility, not just having freedom with no responsibility, and that's what he's had. You don't have to work for this, you can just have it. I think that's a big, big contributing factor.

Amid his rule-breaking and fits of aggression, Elijah attempted to sell marijuana at Hometown Elementary to several students. Once again, Christy found herself in a situation with legal issues that she could not afford to take care of. Worst of all, she had to face the bitter facts that Elijah had found normalcy in drug usage through both herself and his father, and Elijah had most likely attained the drugs from friends of the father whom he admired:

I'm not going to pretend to be a perfect parent, I enjoy smoking pot. I don't have parties where people are sitting around passing a joint around, that's not smart. If I smoke with friends, when I did smoke pot, we'd go off into the other room but you know, kids pick up on that, they do. They smell it. So A-1, I can tell you that marijuana is my drug of choice. So, I've been a contributing factor to what has happened. I mean his dad going to the doctor, lying about drugs, I mean he's just known a lot more about drugs than a kid should know. And, I just don't know, I mean I think Mark treats him like a peer, versus a kid and kind of turns him on to the stuff he is doing. I know that when I found out Elijah was smoking I completely got everything out of my house. All the paraphernalia, so I know the pot was not from my house when he got busted. He says that he got it at Potter's Park but he also told the kids at home schooling that a friend of his dad's gave him the pot. Just gave it to him! O.K., so you know we've got a man (Mark), deeply depressed about his handicap, because of his right hand, he's got a toe on his hand . . . so he's so deeply depressed and now he's gotten more and more involved with harder things and I'm thinking that I was warned about this in 2001. A friend of mine came over and was like, "Christy, they're cooking up drugs and Elijah's watching everything!" I called social services at that point and it took them about six months to go up there and they didn't find anything. They substantiated neglect and poor conditions and I don't know how he explained himself. Like I said, I take some responsibility but I absolutely don't condone it, I mean he is way to young too be doing the stuff, and it certainly didn't come from me, I never passed a bowl to my kid, you know what I mean. I smoked and he knows it, and he figures hey, I'm a grown up too. It just makes me sick because now it's like this drug is normalized to this kid. I mean it will kill me if I ever find out Elijah has used other drugs.

After Elijah's arrest, Christy made every attempt possible to regain complete custody of Elijah, trying to get only supervised visitations for Mark, including completing the legal paperwork and representing herself in court. However, without an actual witness accusing Mark of supplying Elijah with drugs, or proof that Mark was partaking of drugs in front of Elijah, Christy had little power to regain total custody. Finally, she was able to prevent overnight visitation:

Family Preservation was assigned to the case and I requested them to be involved 'cause I really want Mark to get some help too. Elijah and I are going to take the anger management together and unfortunately that doesn't start until April. And then, I am doing a parenting class as well and I'm not sure what else for our family preservation. That's what was assigned, they may drug test him, they may drug test me, it's up to them to decide what they want to do as far as should Elijah stay in the home or should the kid be pulled out. I mean, they report to the judge. And then the court, the visitation thing there is going to be a mediator taking over that but Mark and I have to decide. I'm pretty much not bending on no overnight until he has legalized employment, good housing. You know, if he does that then I am more than willing to reinstate. I hope he does those things. The judge wanted me to produce a witness, and I'm like yea, let's get a bunch of junkies together and see who wants to stand up in court. I mean I don't think so. Although, his cousin did tell me that she thinks he's doing it. She was down here last year and said that she couldn't get Mark out of bed and that he was going to the bathroom for more than half an hour at a time. And, when he did get out of bed it was because a certain person called and maybe it was drug related, I don't know, but he was angry because this person didn't have any, or no money or whatever. But, when he got off the phone, Jenn said that he screamed at Elijah, making him feel like a worm. I don't know what he said exactly but he was really taking it out on Elijah and he was crying and Jenn felt really bad. That's another thing, they all support me but I didn't ask Jenn to come down and help me and all, and she didn't . . . but he went into the bathroom and she couldn't be sure. I don't know how long this has been going on either. I think it has been at least a year. I mean if I had more control over his environment than at least I would know he's not going to have it around him. At least he's going to have to go out to find it.

Two weeks after our interview, Christy called and informed me that Mark had been arrested and jailed on drug-related charges.

Before Elijah's drug arrest, he frequently felt as if he was "the bad kid," or that the other students would think he was behind in his schoolwork because of a lack of intelligence. It seems that, to distract others' attention from his self-perceived flaws, Elijah would go out of his way to create trouble or create excuses for not completing his assignments. Frequently, he would try to portray a persona of toughness so that his peers could not see his fragile emotional state and self-doubt. During counseling sessions at a behavioral care center, Christy attempted to get Elijah to describe himself and his relationships with other people:

So I try and keep pretty thankful for the relationships he has developed, at Hometown Especially . . . they all really care about him. I never doubted that. As far as the other kids . . . things were more personal than he wanted to be. That's what I'm talking about, character, I mean what kind of character are you Elijah? Who is the guy on the skateboard? You know what I mean? And, he says, "I'm a 'badass'!" and we didn't understand what that meant. We were like, what does that mean? Does that mean you are going to kick everybody's ass, or does that mean you're a great skateboarder, you know, you're a "badass" on the skateboard? Well, what that turned into was this thing that a "badass" friends loved them and they'll do anything for their friends, so it turned into this sort of peer acceptance kind of thing. I was Elijah are you compassionate? Are you funny? It turned into, "I want people to like me." Or, "I want people to think I'd do anything for them!" It was kind of confusing. That's what I'm trying to get him to understand, that you're not a badass, I mean do you want everybody to think you are a big bully? I mean cause we know he's a good kid. But, I mean he's told the counselors that he thinks he is dumb and he thinks other kids think that too, and stuff.

Elijah's issues with peer acceptance became even more pronounced after his arrest and expulsion from school. After bringing marijuana to school, the parents of many of Elijah's best friends did not allow their children to socialize with Elijah:

There were a couple of other kids involved, one of which was the one who told on him and there is the other kid who got suspended a while for not telling on him. Then there was his friend Garrett, who you know, best friend Garrett at school. And basically I think that Garrett's parents may be involved in smoking too, because Elijah's told me . . . but Garrett's parents won't let him hang out with him and he's been completely ostracized there for a while, because nobody's parents would let their kids hang out with him. The school is like, "You're kicked out and we don't have a place for you to go." Hanson (an alternative school) doesn't have a place for you yet. I mean he was completely ostracized. And he was down about that for a while, like, "I don't have any friends now." And my friend Bridget, she has a boy who is kind of like his brother. I mean they've grown up together, and he's a little bit younger than him and well I talked to Lance about everything and he was like shocked kind of like this isn't the Elijah that I know. I mean he will still hang out with him and stuff but Elijah came back and was like, "I can tell Lance is scared of me," and that kind of thing, which is good. I mean it is good for him to see his friends kind of going, "Hey, dude, you're freaking me out here!" But, he really has been ostracized a lot and I've kind of wanted to call Garrett's parents and be like, look, Elijah's on probation, he's not going to smoke any pot and I'd still like to see them hang out every once in a while. But, he's just really been ostracized through this particular thing.

Left with few options and wanting to give Elijah some kind of education for the semester he had been expelled, Christy was trapped between teaching her child or working to support herself and him. Even the local alternative school was unable to accept Elijah in the middle of the school year. Already behind academically due to absences during his first years of school, Elijah's fate looked bleak as far as having to repeat the sixth grade the next school year. However, through acquaintances, Christy happened on a home school mother, Ms. Shannon, who was willing to accept Elijah:

Mary and those kids out there, they've been home schooled their whole lives. They're out there in the country and they're isolated and they were jumping out of they're skins to have a new friend come out and be home schooled. Yea and I think you know his little rebellious attitude, I think in a way he thinks it's pretty cool, you know like, "I'm being home schooled. I'm different." I mean he respects Mary, so far so good. I've heard no complaints whatsoever since that first day and she has taught him respect; respect for other people's stuff, to not tear up other people's stuff, you know . . . and don't bring drugs into our home. And, we want you to be here and all that but she laid down the ground rules, right away. And I haven't heard one thing. Elijah's been having a little trouble with Matthew, which really surprises me since he's the oldest, but Elijah's little buddy-buddy with David and he is a little younger than him. And then there is five year old Luke who just jumps on Elijah like he is a big brother and that was my other hope, that he would see like a family structure, pecking order, the importance of sharing. I mean he's never had to do that. With this situation, that's what I was hoping for, I mean they are such tight family. And the kids, they are really smart, and they get into mischief and they razz each other and they get a little rough, but they don't get aggressive, you know what I mean? There's not that underlying aggression.

Christy's mood brightened as she spoke of Elijah's experiences in his new school. It was evident that the home school had resolved many of the issues she had to deal with on her own. Despite the 40-minute drive out to the Shannon home every weekday before work, Christy made sure Elijah was present and prompt for the remainder of the school year. Her love and dedication to her child stemmed from her expectations for him—expectations I never would have known had I not taken the time to interview her:

I'm not letting him quit school, that's for sure, and he's not leaving my home until he is 18! If it kills me! I mean he is saying that already, "I'm leaving when I turn 16!" I'm like let's get this straight right here, you're not leaving my home until you are 18. Well, I'm hoping that if he doesn't want to go to school, you know college, like academic college, that he will at least continue through some kind of trade, you know like dog grooming, I don't know. Right now, he's like I'm going to be a professional skateboarder and we're like, eh, that's like one in a million man and what would happen if you break your ankle? And I'd like him to think about his future, and think about what he likes but you can't expect someone to know what he likes and what he wants to do at such a young age. But I just hope that he finds a trade and acquires a work ethic. Like, even if he works in a kitchen that will be alright with me as long as he's working. That is all I hope for. I mean I don't want to seem like I'm not aiming high enough and all that I just think that we need to learn to like the simple things in life, it's either that and I'll feel like I've succeeded if Elijah's stayed out of jail.

I found it odd that she assumed her expectations for Elijah weren't high enough. Who should place a value on individuals doing what they enjoy?

You're probably not going to discover a whole lot more than what the books say. Because a lot of it's true, you know, it's passed down. Passed down, lack of parenting on my part too, you know from my parents to me and so on. But at the same time, from where I'm coming from I feel I've accomplished so much. I really didn't expect to go to college, I have a semi-professional job going on, and I don't think anyone expected that from me.

Throughout Christy's life, people expected little from her. In a society that continually tells her she isn't successful, Christy has found satisfaction in her own accomplishments, her greatest accomplishment being Elijah.

Fly Away Home

"Push out further! It really feels like flying!"

"Are you sure this is just dirt?"

"Well, dirt made out of cow crap, but it's not smelly anymore cause it's too old!"

Holding tight to the knotted nylon rope, I pushed away from the sharp incline, flying freely through the air. Thump! My feet slipped on the "old cow crap," so eloquently named by Elijah, and I rolled down the hill, laughing as I landed in the freezing creek below. Before I could even get my bearings, I found myself face to face with the underside of a crawdad, his feet and pinchers struggling and wiggling against the mud-covered fingers squeezing around its torso. "Check this out!" stated an enthusiastic Elijah. "He'll be perfect to clean the bottom of my fish tank!"

As I splashed around the creek, exploring with the four boys who were eagerly showing me various creek life they were able to catch, I thought to myself, "How ironic that Elijah's reward for completing the school work that he feels so imprisoned by is being able to fly." Concurrently, "How often had he felt like the crawdad, squirming under the inspection of assessment and scrutiny?"

The rope swing was not my first introduction to Elijah's home school environment, just an induction into the new world from where he now received his education. It became apparent just how different this world was from the children-filled halls of Hometown Elementary. I drove farther and farther away from the city, and the houses became farther and farther apart. I continued driving as the roads began to wind around pastures of cows and rolling hills, the concrete became gravel, and the gravel became dirt. Backing my vehicle up twice to gain speed to make it up the Shannon's driveway, I finally made it up over the hill and captured my first glimpse of Elijah's new school.

Surrounded by horses, dogs, rusty farm equipment, scrap wood, and fields sat the trailer home of the Shannon family. I watched as Christy and Elijah traversed grassy patches among muddy puddles, up the path to the Shannon's trailer. Christy had one arm resting on Elijah's shoulder, the other was used in defense to knock off rowdy dogs. As they walked together, I observed their actions with an overwhelming sense of the warm interactions between mother and son. Christy, a mother who loves and cares about her child with such compassion that she is willing to drive 40 minutes every day before work for her son to continue his education in an environment she respects. "Because a lot of it's true, you know it's passed down." I recalled Christy's own words because at that moment, the "passed down" that I witnessed was not the broken images of her childhood family, but images of a loving family, regardless of how small.

Cozy was the first word I wrote in my notes to describe the Shannon home. Space was limited and decoration consisted mainly of child-drawn dinosaurs, architectural house designs, and photos of the horses outside. A 1970s' style fabric curtain, donned with flowers, separated a computer from the otherwise very simple, family-friendly living area. The brown carpet, covered in mud from the feet of three active boys and their journeys out on the spring-softened ground, was covered by family clutter: log-cabin blocks, shoes, leftover dinner plates, Matchbox cars, and papers. As I stepped into the room, a tall gangly boy with wild, moppy brown hair and deep brown eyes to match held his hand out to me, and with a wide smile that was contagious to all, quietly said, "Hi. I'm Matthew!" I took his hand and looked up to see a declining stair step of two more boys that reminded me of Russian Mishawka dolls, each a smaller version of Matthew, both grinning sweetly. Elijah quickly introduced the younger Shannon boys to me, David and Luke, and I turned to shake hands with Elijah's new teacher, Mary.

Mary, who seemed little next to her oldest son, was dressed in a lengthy flowing skirt and a head scarf that covered her long hair that shone the same brown as her children's. She was very natural and welcomed me to her home with kind, smiling eyes. Everyone in the household had bare feet, and it was obvious that their home had never seen a stranger. Taking off my shoes, I plunked down in the middle of the floor with notepad and pen, prepared to take notes on the interactions and learning occurring within Elijah's new educational environment.

Mary pulled out a copy of *National Geographic* as the two older boys and Elijah pulled chairs into the living room. As they all sat down around Mary, except for Luke who was strumming a half-size guitar, she attempted to begin her lesson when Elijah spoke out.

Elijah: I thought we were doing other cultures? Why are we doing dinos?
Mary: It's about Africa. I got tired of doing the U.S. so I switched to other cultures.

As Mary flipped through the magazine to find the correct page, the boys began discussing a blue soccer shirt that Elijah offered to give to Matthew because he knew that he liked soccer.

Matthew: Maybe, do you want a blue shirt (to David)?
Elijah: No, just tell me keep your filthy, crappy, nasty shirt.
Matthew: That's not what I meant. It's just that blue is David's favorite color. If it were red I'd say yes.
Elijah: Yea right (looking at picture in *National Geographic* article they are beginning to read)! A dinosaur as big as Chicago! That's crap!

Within the first few moments of my observations, I could tell that Elijah was attempting to receive the acceptance of the oldest boy, Matthew. His frequent usage of the word *crap* also struck me because I remembered many times discussing appropriate language with Elijah when he was my student. I smiled as Mary casually ignored it or brushed it off with, "I know you need my attention right now and I will be there in a moment." Ignoring inappropriate language isn't a luxury in a classroom of 30 students.

Once again, Mary began reading the article for her lesson. While she read, Luke ran around strumming his guitar, and the other boys all rocked in their seats humming. Elijah then turned to me and with a grin whispered, "Get ready for mayhem!" At that point he turned and yelled at Luke to shut up and stop playing. The older brothers immediately stepped in and convinced Luke to put the guitar away. I began to wonder whether Mary would ever be able to complete the article, and I was unsure if the boys were actually listening until Elijah spoke up.

Elijah:	Wait a minute, I've never heard about that kind of dinosaur.
Mary:	It's pretty new.
Elijah:	I know about Allysoraus! We studied them at Hometown. Remember (he looked at me as I nodded in agreement)?
Mary:	Now each of you boys will read half a section.
Elijah:	Only half?
Mary:	Well, it's a pretty short article.

I looked on in amazement. Not only was Elijah paying attention amid the chaos, but he was also making connections to the reading and seemed willing to read out loud. Reading out loud was something that Elijah would never do in my classroom, and I never forced the issue. Here in the small-home structure, Elijah was willing to take risks and read willingly, looking for help from Mary for difficult words. While the other boys read, Elijah appeared distracted, but continually made relevant comments about the passage until it was Matthew's turn to read.

Elijah:	Yo man! I've got some good news! I got a mower and we can take the engine out of it!
David:	Is it a riding or a push mower?
Elijah:	Riding.
David:	Then we should just ride it around how it is.
Matthew:	Yea, take the mower blade off of it and it will cruise! I bet it can do at least 60!
David:	Yea! Just leave the motor in it!
Mary:	Let's go into details later.

I watched Elijah try to talk his way into being accepted by Matthew. The reading resumed until Mary read the final sentence, "This is only the beginning."

David:	Well, if it's just begun, why did they end the article?
Elijah:	Yea, that's the beginning, so "The end!"
Mary:	You have your notebook right Lijah?
Elijah:	I always have my notebook. I never fail!
Mary:	(Unconvincingly, Mary muttered) Umm-hmm.

Together it appeared that David and Elijah had formed a bond of friendship, almost in the shape of a brotherly relationship. Mary had shortened Elijah's name in an endearing nickname, and Elijah would hop up during study time to make himself a sandwich or boil water for tea. It was obvious that Elijah felt very "at home" with the Shannons, and the caring he felt for them was reciprocated. However, as soon as situations teetered on the brink of being too emotional, Elijah would throw up his wall of words in an effort to lash out and prove that he did not need the support of others.

Elijah:	What's this (points to a pot on the furnace)?
Matthew:	You know that dried up apple?
Elijah:	You stuck it in there?
David:	Yea and it expanded and the bottom exploded out and it made the whole room smell nice!
Elijah:	You guys are the strangest family! Let's put an old smelly apple on the stove!
David:	It smelled nice and we thought we could sell it to a perfume company.
Elijah:	Oh yea, that's a great idea! New from Glade, Old smelly man! Do you see this math book here (holds up a Carson-Dellarosa fifth-grade math skills book)? If you ever decide to home school your kids, don't get this book! (Then to Mary) It'd make me regret having you for a mom even more!
Mary:	(Smiling) It's just a basic math skills book.

By calling the family strange and insulting Mary's mothering skills, Elijah attempted to distance himself from the connections he was feeling. Additionally, he did not want me to see that he was enjoying learning. I watched as he continued to sway back and forth between displaying affection and showing off as a rebel who needed no one.

Mary:	We really need to do grammar today.
Elijah:	Please, please, please don't make us do grammar!
Matthew:	Please, please, please shut up!
Elijah:	Would you like to switch me pencils?
Matthew:	Yea, thanks.
Mary:	(Turning to me) That was David's pencil.
Matthew:	Yea, I found it in the library.

As the boys took out their notebooks to begin their grammar lessons, David walked off to the back room, Matthew leaned back in his chair and propped his book up on his knees, Luke ran around making zooming noises as he drove imaginary cars, and Elijah slumped over his paper as Mary approached him.

Elijah:	Mrs. R (referring to me), you have to check out the rope swing before you leave. Man, the one day we finally run out of this stuff (math sheets) we have to do grammar (starts to walk off).
Mary:	Wait Lijah, don't hide. Do you know what we're looking for here?
Elijah:	Yes, proper nouns. But I don't want to sit in that chair anymore. It hurts and it's too little.
Mary:	That's fine. We can sit on the floor. You know I don't have a problem with sitting on the floor.
Genell:	Am I distracting here?
Mary:	No, this is normal.
Elijah:	Man, am I going to have to use this in real life?
Mary:	Yes, if you want people to speak to you and listen to you, you have to speak and write well.
Elijah:	I speak well, I just don't write well.
Mary:	You need to be able to do both. And if you want to learn a different language, like Chinese, you need to understand your own language first.
Elijah:	I thought about Spanish.
Mary:	Spanish? You sat here all semester with that opportunity and you said, "No, I don't want to learn Spanish!"
Elijah:	Well, I was bored and I didn't want to mess with it!

With much guidance from Mary, Elijah finally finished his work similarly to how he worked in my classroom. He would drop his pencil, pick it up, stand up, erase a word, drop his pencil, pick it up, play with his shoe, and so on. I noticed that Mary spent the entire grammar time sitting right next to Elijah to help him stay focused. This was yet another luxury very seldom afforded to me in a typical fifth-grade classroom.

David returned approximately 30 minutes later, handing his grammar to Mary for her to check. As he walked by Elijah, he gave him a high five.

Mary:	(To David) Get Luke some juice while I check this over.
David:	Sure. How'd I do?

Mary showed David some corrections and he spotted some on his own, then took the paper back to fix it. I watched as he handed his little brother a cup full of juice, then tousled Luke's hair. Elijah watched as well, and I wondered how often had he observed brothers being affectionate or siblings helping out their mother? What a priceless lesson he was learning.

Once grammar was finished, the boys went straight to their math lessons. Math had always been a difficult subject for Elijah, and I could tell he still felt uncomfortable exposing his weakness. While the other boys worked independently, Elijah flopped around on the floor, twiddled his pencil, and strummed on the guitar with Luke. Seeing this, Mary started to walk over to where Elijah was supposed to be working. Elijah darted back across the room and slid onto the floor, then, grabbing his math book, slammed his head into it and mumbled, "Nighty-night!" At that point, David walked by on his way outside, the reward for completing his assignments.

Elijah:	Are you going to the rope swing?
David:	Yea, I'll wait for you there.
Elijah:	Yea I guess. I have all this math and crap! Do I have to do this math today?
Mary:	Yes.
Elijah:	Please just let me do some that you write on a sheet for me.
Mary:	No, do the math that your mom bought you and wants you to do. It's just addition and subtraction. Have you done this before?
Elijah:	Yea, but it was at Hometown and I sucked so I hated it. Do I have to do what the book says? What will happen if I don't? Will a great big hand reach out and choke me or something?
Mary:	(Looks at her hand and smiles jokingly) It just might!

Elijah moaned and began to attempt some of the problems. Mary moved over to Matthew's work and looked over it. With his mother's permission, Matthew threw on his shoes and started making toast. Mary then approached Elijah again.

Mary:	Let me check it over, I wasn't watching the last part.
Elijah:	Well, if there is anything wrong with it don't tell me, just hit me in the arm and that'll be good—just hit me! Or yell at me! I get yelled out enough that I can take anything a man or a woman can dish out.
Mary:	There is just one little thing . . .
Elijah:	I know! I know! The money signs. I'm waiting till the end to put them on. Did you notice I knew exactly what you were talking about before you even said it?
Mary:	That's because you've listened to me enough times.
Elijah:	Luke! Shut Up!
Mary:	Luke, please quiet down.
Elijah:	Luke, for the love of everything holy, stop! PLEASE! Am I almost half way done? (Looks up at the fish tank) Woah! Why are all those fish crowded behind there? You know, if he plays around on that

(referring to Luke on the guitar) while he is little, he'll be really good when he is older, like a little Jerry Garcia. You know Jerry only had three fingers and he was the greatest acoustic guitar player ever. You could have the next Jerry Garcia!

Mary: Yea, I guess so . . .

Elijah: I'm kind of sick today.

Matthew: You're sick every day.

Elijah: I hope you're not saying something bad about me Matthew, I'd hate for something bad to happen to you! Mrs. R, do you remember when I jumped off the monkey bars and my knee hit my nose?

Genell: Yes, that was one of many incidents, but I remember. You were very active!

Elijah: Well, that's a nice way of saying that, "Very active!" Man, I'm so tired. I'm not doing anything technical right now! I've already done a bunch of these.

Mary: Well, now you can do a bunch more.

Elijah: Oh good (sarcastically)! Is this a hexagon?

Mary: Yes.

Elijah: Hey Matthew, do you know that skate park the city said they were going to build at Clinton Park? Well, my dad and I went by and we saw some lumber and stuff but dude, they didn't have anything built yet! Stupid mayor! I'll choke him! This stupid city never does anything it says it's going to. They'll probably just say someone stole the wood then, "Oh sorry, we can't build the park now!" Hey, what if I didn't finish this last one?

Mary: A job done in halves is a job not done.

Elijah: What? A half-ass job?

Mary: No, a job done in halves . . .

Elijah: I know what you said, I just wanted to cuss.

Mary: I know.

Elijah: These problems are why I hate math.

Mary: It's just a process and once you learn the process it's easy.

Elijah: Yea! The process of why I hate math.

Watching Elijah interact was like watching a magician at work. It was difficult to keep your eyes on his trick hand as he distracted you with every illusion possible. From cussing, blaming the government of conspiracy, to threatening the other boys, Elijah tried again and again to move away from school work and upset Mary. These were the same tactics that he used in the classroom and the same tactics that could not be as easily pushed aside within the restrictions of the public school setting. Mary impressed me with her skill and patience and later informed me that, "This was pretty much the norm, although he does a little more work every day."

Finally finished with his math and with the approval of Mary, 3 hours after his arrival to their home, Elijah was allowed to go out and play. Elijah had achieved freedom, and Mary was able to help him learn; learn about class work, learn about family—learn about respect. While he put on his shoes, he began to ask me questions about his friends at Hometown.

Elijah:	Have you been to Hometown lately?
Genell:	No.
Elijah:	Well, after everything, Garrett's parents wouldn't let me talk to him or anything but I ran into him downtown and his dad was like, "Are things getting better?" And I said yea, and he said, "Good, you can give us a call sometime."
Genell:	I'm sure that made you feel good?
Elijah:	Yea cause he was my only friend there so if you go by Hometown and you see him tell him I'll stop by his house. (Turned to Mary) You know my dad may be getting out this week.
Mary:	Really?
Elijah:	Yea cause Aunt Jenn is suppose to be coming down with the money this week to get him out.
Mary:	Cool.

There it was, a child's unwavering desire to belong; belong to his family, belong to his father, belong to his friends. Even after his father was put in jail, Elijah still felt the need to defend him. Even though Elijah committed a crime, being able to spend time with his friends was first priority on his mind. Elijah's eyes may have contained the experiences of an adult, but his heart was still that of a child.

Finding Home

When the bristles of the painter's paintbrush collect small particles of dust, it often streaks across the freshly painted wall, tainting the pure color desired. After Elijah's arrest, he was seen as the dust collecting in the paintbrushes of the children around him. Many have heard the old adage, "One rotten apple can ruin the whole bunch." In an effort to keep from spoiling the entire bunch, Elijah was removed. While writing Elijah's story, I couldn't help but notice the amount of exclusion in his life: exclusion from family, exclusion from friends, exclusion from school. For this reason, I looked into the lessons of education that his story was shaped around: (a) consequences of school expulsion, (b) power relationships in school settings, and (c) benefits of alternative schooling.

Expulsion.   What messages are schools sending out when they expel children? During the *No Child Left Behind* (U.S. Department of Education) movement, it appears that it is still acceptable to leave behind the children who need education the most. President George W. Bush stated that, "When it comes to the education of our children . . . failure is not an option" (nochildleftbehind Web site). By not offering an alternative education for students who have been expelled, what option other than failing is left? "When school districts have no choice but to expel students, the long-term implications for the individual and for society as a whole become a matter of serious concern" (Glaze, 2001, p. 44). In Henry Levine's (1972) "The Cost to a Nation of Inadequate Education," he discussed the consequences of the public school systems not providing quality education to all students, some of which include an increase in the demand for social services and an increase in crime (as cited in Glaze, 1996). Without a school to attend and without any form of guidance, what should one assume Elijah would have done with his time? Christy noted that Elijah used marijuana when he "felt stressed, was around it, and was bored." Certainly, expulsion from school could induce all of those. Concurrently, expulsion from school added to Elijah's feelings of being left out, of not being included with his peers, and "peer rejection, in turn, leads to more undesirable behavior" (Henry, 2000, p. 100). Therefore, undesirable or oppositional behaviors by a student may truly be a proper response to an oppressive educational system (Kohl, 1994).

Power.   Oppressive educational systems create unequal balances of power among administrators, teachers, and students. "All institutions by their very nature create an atmosphere which in turn regulates the attitudes and behavior of those who work within them . . . The atmosphere in most public elementary schools results in feelings of estrangement, not only between staff and students, but also between the students themselves" (Goodman, 1992, p. 94). Although I attempted to create an atmosphere of community within my classroom, many aspects and restrictions of the school day and the institution often made it difficult for student voices to be heard. As one person responsible for 30 children, many of my communications with the students were "notions of management, control, and discipline, that is, concepts common to groups of strangers rather than people who are working together as a community" (Goodman, 1992, p. 96), and much of my attention was directed toward quick solutions to avoid escalations of further chaos in a rigid, unbending schedule. For a child like Elijah, I would often have to focus on muting his inappropriate language or send him to the hall to keep him from getting other students off track. I regret that it was not always easy to focus on his charisma or natural leadership ability. Although I knew a small portion of Elijah's life experiences, it was dim in comparison to what I know now—a fact that prevented much of my pedagogy from giving him the time and space for "imagination, for trans-formation of the given" (Polakow, 1993, p. 151).

Larry Cuban (1989) discussed how the culture of school often degrades or ignores family and community backgrounds, promoting a curriculum that serves to crush the self-esteem of poor students and neglects the strengths they bring to the school. Nevertheless, as Barone (1989) wrote, "Restructuring that gives teachers the time, the resources, and the motiva-tion to learn about the individual worlds of their students will be only a be-ginning. Empathy alone is not enough . . . empowering teachers (and stu-dents) in this way may require more resources than our society is willing to provide" (p. 188). One always wishes for hindsight as the ancient saying goes: "If I only knew then what I know now." Had I known the story of Elijah when I had him as a student, I could have provided him with a more pro-ductive education. "It takes teachers and administrators who through the dynamics of power between themselves and their students cultivate chil-dren's self-esteem, help children realize that they are not alone in the world (demonstrate that people do sincerely care for them), and teach children that caring for others is as important as caring about oneself" (Goodman, 1992, p. 117). It appeared as I observed him in a setting of alternative edu-cation, a home school, that Elijah was better able to flourish in a more equal power dynamic.

Alternative.   Many families are resorting to alternative schooling for their children because the meanings and values embodied in public educa-tion are typically middle-class, monocultural, and lacking in religious ideol-ogy, which are not the ones that parents want articulated to their children. Elijah was sent to home school for a lack of other options. However, I watched as he acquired positive social interactions, unconditional caring, self-esteem, and the opportunity to practice self-regulation and self-control.

From the beginning of his education with Mary, she made it clear to Eli-jah that he was no longer a labeled kid; he was included in their family. Re-gardless of the efforts I made in the classroom, the large social structure was artificially manufactured, unlike that of siblings. "Sibling interactions flow from a context of expectations for bonding and unconditionally accepting relationships. . . . By contrast, school-based peer relationships . . . interac-tions are required to occur regardless of the existence of any relationship and will probably determine the nature of the relationships to be formed" (Harry, Day, & Quist, 1998, p. 297). Elijah's closest friend in school, Gar-rett, was alienated because of Elijah's poor choices. In his new home school situation, Elijah was included in a family structure as if he were a sibling. He was treated fairly, consistently the same as the other Shannon boys, and given the same restrictions and privileges. Mary explained that he was not going to be ostracized for his mistakes, but that they would work through them together if he was willing to respect her and her family. Because of this, Elijah appeared comfortable and confident in the Shannon's home. "Children's true individuality (rather than self-indulgence) can grow only within a community structure in which there are restrictions and expectations placed upon the individual by that community" (Goodman, 1992, p. 102). Elijah was given restrictions and expectations in his new educational situation, expectations different than the "dominant ideology, and the meritocratic view" that public schools placed on him, and his mother, with the assumptions "that all are trying to achieve broadly the same aims in life" (Willis, 1977, p. 147). In the alternative school setting, Elijah was able to excel not only in the educational knowledge set by today's national standards, but, more important, as a person.

No Place Like Home

The oxymoron I have presented is one of inclusion in a story that is mostly about exclusion. Do not walk away feeling as if there is little hope for public education or that home school is the only option. The concern is mainly that we, as educators, have only "concentrated our energies in schools on 'achievement' and 'effective teaching strategies' " (Payne, 1998, p. 143). What are we doing to children if our main concern is a test score, rather than their ability to share their talents and function successfully within our society? If many people feel that education is the lifeblood of democracy, then educating and understanding children should be our goals. These goals can only be achieved by taking the time to learn about the life experiences of young people like Elijah; a frightened boy, carried by his teacher through the hallways of the school, balled up in the fetal position, scared eyes, crying for his mother as the police walked in to take him out the doors.

Those eyes.

Once again I looked through my notes, and thumbing through my yearbook, covered in student handwriting is my entire class in their costumes of Oz. "*There's no place like home. There's no place like home.*"

I felt the same sense of nostalgia creep over me. The thesaurus lists the following synonyms for nostalgia: wistfulness, longing, melancholy, *homesickness.* I tried to make my classroom a second home. If the public schools turn education into a second home for children, into second families, would it truly be like that place "somewhere over the rainbow"?

After all, there's no place like home.

REFERENCES

Barone, T. (1989). Ways of being at risk: The case of Billy Charles. In T. Barone (Ed.), *Aesthetics, politics, and educational inquiry: Essays and examples* (pp. 182–189). New York: Peter Lang.

Baum, L. F. (1900). *The wonderful wizard of Oz.* Chicago: George M. Hill Co.

Cuban, L. (1989, June). The at-risk label and the problem of urban school reform. *Phi Delta Kappan,* pp. 780–782.

Four troubled teens. (April 28, 2003). www.4troubledteens.com

Goodman, J. (1992). *Elementary schooling for critical democracy.* New York: State University of New York Press.

Harry, B., Day, M., & Quist, F. (1998). He can't really play: An ethnographic study of sibling acceptance and interaction. *Journal of the Association for Severe Handicaps, 23*(4), 289–299.

Henry, D. B. (2000). Peer groups, families, and school failure among urban children: Elements of risk and and successful interventions. *Preventing School Failure, 44*(3), 97–105.

Kohl, H. (1994). *I won't learn from you: And other thoughts on creative maladjustment.* New York: New Press.

Payne, R. K. (1998). *A framework for understanding poverty* (rev. ed.). Highlands, TX: RFT.

Willis, P. (1977). *Learning to labor: How working class kids get working class jobs.* New York: Columbia University Press.

Chapter 9

Winners Need Losers:
The Basis for School Competition
and Hierarchies

Ellen Brantlinger
Indiana University, Bloomington

Research confirms that children from lower income and/or minority families consistently score lower on educational outcome measures than their higher income counterparts (Jencks & Phillips, 1998). Although the common implication is that these students are less smart or have a poor work ethic, there are a number of other reasons for the outcome disparities. First, despite valuing education, viewing it as the avenue to occupational mobility, and having relatively high aspirations for educational success (Brantlinger, 1985, 1993), low-income students and parents have low expectations for educational and occupational attainment because they are realistic in realizing that they cannot afford higher education or other enabling school advantages (Demerath, 2003; R. Ryan, Sheldon, Kasser, & Deci, 1996). Second, because poor children rarely benefit from school's competitive structure, school competition does not play the same motivating role (i.e., incentive to do better) in urban or poor schools as it does in the suburbs (Brandau & Collins, 1994). However, poor children do benefit from supportive academic push and access to advanced curriculum and programs (Gamoran & Hannigan, 2000; Oakes & Guiton, 1995; Reynolds & Wolfe, 1999). Unfortunately, these conditions rarely exist for them in their ghetto schools or low-track classrooms. Third, the ubiquity of poor and minority people's experiences with biased treatment and barriers to school and societal success has a cumulative effect on their morale and energy. The struggles associated with living in poverty and depression related to failures result in a resignation to the probability of future unfavorable circumstances and, subsequently, alienation from mainstream institutions (Brantlinger, 1985, 1993; Mickelson, 1993). Fourth, the insightful students and parents are angry about inequities and humiliations, and hence tend to reject dominant ideologies and engage in resistant and oppositional behaviors. Such defiance inevitably results in retaliation by those in charge and a subsequent worsening of life chances (Ray & Mickelson, 1990; Willis, 1977).

The fifth and clearly most important reason for class-related achievement disparities is that the education of poor, immigrant, and minority children has always been hampered by their vastly inferior school and community conditions (Kozol, 1991, 2001; Seiler & Tobin, 2000; Wenglinsky, 1998). Orfield (2000) reported almost total segregation by race/ethnicity and social class in urban school districts and "mass chaos and disorganization" with "high rates of administrator turnover so that consistency is terribly low in anything they do." Hence, poor children and children of color get "subtractive" schooling, meaning that their schooling may do more harm than good and students are excluded from mainstream settings (Noddings, 2000; Valenzuela, 2001). Time spent in school is often agonizing for poor and working-class children (Brantlinger, 1993), as it has been for generations. Kliebard (1986) cited the 1913 case of a factory inspector in Chicago, who questioned children of immigrants about whether they would choose to continue working long hours in sweat shops or go to school. Of 500 interviewed, 412 preferred factory labor to the monotony, humiliation, and sheer cruelty they experienced in school. Poor people do not choose inadequate schools for their children, however, policy failure means urban residents have little control over the quality of their community schools (Anyon, 1997). Moreover, they do not have the power of the pocketbook to live in neighborhoods known for good schools (Brantlinger, 2003). Even in school choice situations, there are economic and institutional barriers to their attendance at high-quality schools (Apple, 2003).

Until recently, students who stuck it out in school and successfully completed certain required courses, which frequently were adapted to their achievement levels, received a high school diploma. Hence, the majority of students who stayed in school for 12 years graduated. Regardless of students' postschool plans, the high school diploma has been a valued credential. Furthermore, graduation has been a rite of passage to adulthood for American adolescents. In the past decade, things have changed. An increasing number of states have instituted high-stakes graduate exit exams (also known as gateway, certification, and competency exams), which limit secondary students' eligibility for a diploma to those who pass the test (Langenfeld, Thurlow, & Scott, 1997). As of January 2001, eighteen states had legislated requirements for students to pass a uniform, large-scale assessment to receive high school diplomas, and six more planned to adopt one within 3 years (O'Neill, 2001). If statistics elsewhere are similar to those in

Indiana, between a third and a half of sophomores initially fail the test; of those remaining in school until their senior year, 14% fail the test and so do not receive diplomas (Lane, 2000). Currently, up to 50% of adolescents drop out of school in large urban areas, compared with fewer than 25% in suburban and small town areas (Urban Institute, 2004). Indeed Urban Institute statistics indicate that in some particularly impoverished urban areas the dropout rate is more than 75%. National test scores and dropout figures reveal who is failing—or being failed—in American schools.

The educational Zeitgeist of the late 20th and early 21st century is accountability. Accountability is to be realized through the adoption of tightly defined standards and a host of standardized tests designed to measure whether these high standards have been met. The consequence of failure to score well or meet standards is the enforcement of rather severe sanctions not only on students, but on teachers, administrators, schools, and school districts. This tough love approach to purportedly improve school outcomes is also billed as the way to raise local, state, and national economic outcomes. Although low-income people seem unaware that they hold the fate of nations in their hands, the popular rhetoric of politicians would have us believe that the indigent among us are to blame not only for tough times in schools, but also in the country. This target for blame is not new. It has been the traditional focus of scholars who study low-income and minority students and families to explain, and supposedly reverse, school failure (Ryan, 1971; Valencia, 1997; Wright, 1993). Researchers who look for deficits in students and families, however, will never find the key to social class-related distinctions in school performance because they are turning their scholarly gaze in the wrong direction. To understand educational outcome difference, it is necessary to cast the scholarly gaze upward and research those who succeed in school and control the conditions that result in school success and school failure.

GRAMSCI'S ADVICE TO STUDY WHO BENEFITS
FROM ANY SOCIAL PRACTICE

To discern reasons behind the spate of official state and federal mandates for high-stakes testing as well as other stringent standards and accountability measures, in this chapter, I turn to what Italian Marxist Antonio Gramsci (1971/1929–1935) called the perennially essential question to ask related to understanding social phenomena: Who benefits? In terms of recent state and federal educational accountability legislation, I make the case that they are popular because they retain and strengthen various established forms of dominance. I identify losers as those who fail the test and remain at the bottom of hierarchies. More important, I identify a coalition of winners who retain or improve their position at the top of hierarchies through these competitive educational initiatives.

CREATING STANDARDS, CREATING OTHERS[1]

To gain a monopoly of winning positions, dominant groups must set, get consensus for, and enforce normative standards that are used to designate themselves as competent and Others as inadequate. There are theories about how powerful, dominant groups shape unequal relations that marginalize and oppress Others. Ericka Apfelbaum (1999), a German Jewish refuge who moved to France during World War II, claims that central groups create myths about human characteristics and establish norms that reflect their own groups' strengths. They promote these traits as the standard for all and hold subordinate groups accountable for attaining the standards regardless of whether it is possible and without evidence that their norms serve a worthwhile purpose either for themselves or for Others. Individuals and groups who fail to achieve dominant standards are identified (marked, labeled, branded) with stigmatizing names (e.g., failure, disabled, at-risk) and sent to separated locations (special education rooms, low tracks, vocational schools). These distinction-making[2] processes create a binary of (dominant) insiders and (subordinate) outsiders. It is implied that there is a homogeneity of characteristics within the collective who meet the standards as well as in those who do not (Shanahan & Jones, 1999). When dominant groups portray themselves as adequate and normal, peripheral groups become inadequate and abnormal. Maximum power is held by dominant individuals when distinctions between "us" and "them" are believed to be extreme, fundamental, and irreversible.

Groups declared outside the central collective for reasons related to appearance, ability, behavior, gender, race/ethnicity, language usage, social class, or sexual orientation are relegated to subordinate status. Subordinate status is inevitably associated with such oppressions as exploitation, humiliation, harassment, cultural imperialism (in which Others' attributes are denigrated), bodily violence (intimidation, genocide, mercy killing, physical attack, forced sterilization), segregation, and banishment (Eagleton, 1990; Young, 1990, 2000). Based on a meta-analysis of anthropological studies, Brown (1991) reported that, to varying degrees, all peoples create hierarchies that correspond to power and status relations. He further claimed that the privileging of central (mainstream, powerful) groups is wide-

---

[1]When Other is capitalized, it denotes the referent is perceived as different and inferior.

[2]See also Bourdieu's (1984) theories regarding the significance of distinction-producing actions in social class relations.

spread, even universal. With predominantly White personnel and deeply entrenched Eurocentric traditions, American schools have a history of unfavorable relations with people of color. Subordinates inevitably are segregated into low, marginalized positions and have little access to goods and services (Nielsen, 1997). Evidence about the overrepresentation of poor children and children of color in special education and low-track placements confirms Nielson's assertion (Artiles & Trent, 1994; Connor & Boskin, 2001; Harry & Anderson, 1995; Losen & Orfield, 2002; Patton, 2004).

PURPOSEFUL HIERARCHIES

Hierarchies are not purposeless, passive rankings, but represent important interdependent relations among people of different ranks. Indeed the role, status, and perhaps even *raison d'etre* of dominant groups hinge on the existence of Others who can be designated as inferior and less worthy; domination depends on subordination, superiority needs inferiority. Drawing on Lacan's idea of signification in her analogy of empire building, Bellamy (1998) claimed that the identity of colonizers is based on a lack that can only be filled by colonized Others. Related to this chapter, for example, competitive schooling is based on the premise that, for some students to pass and excel, Others must do poorly and fail. Routines of the accountability and standards movement rely on a dynamic of some teachers and schools judged as excellent models of best practice, while others are declared incompetent and failing.

CONTRIVING LEGITIMACY FOR HIERARCHY: THE ROLE OF IDEOLOGY

Dominant groups justify their negotiations for advantage through circulating certain liberal and neoliberal[3] ideologies that contrive legitimacy for high-stakes measures and social hierarchies. According to Gramsci (1971/ 1929–1935), because those who dominate are faced with constant resistance from subordinates, they must continuously exert effort to retain their power. Historically, force has been used to gain and retain power. However, it is nicer and more effective if powerful people can convince those in low positions of the legitimacy of status hierarchies and material disparities. To rule in supposed democracies, dominant groups must have some degree of permission from Others. They gain consensus for their goals by circulating ideologies that obfuscate power imbalances. Thompson (1990) defined *ide-*

---

[3]Neoliberals have an atavistic faith in free enterprise and the rationality of the market (Harvey, 1996).

ology as meaning in the service of power. Inscribed in language (Bakhtin, 1981) and institutions (Tyack & Tobin, 1994), ideologies permeate thought and action (Zizek, 1994), thus mystifying interpersonal rankings (Thompson, 1984). Ideologies serve to prevent resistance by those at the losing end of status orderings. Nevertheless, when subordinates get wise to status or material distinctions, new legends must be brought forward to convince them of their legitimacy. Gramsci defined *hegemony* as a dynamic process of ideology circulation in which subordinates are continuously offered new persuasive evidence to interpret experience in ways favorable to dominant interests.

One form of ideology is storytelling. Cultural deprivation explanations for distinctions in school outcomes was a story debunked decades ago (Keddie, 1973; W. Ryan, 1971). Nevertheless, such stories are still relied on to explain why poor and Black children do less well in school and, correspondingly, why intergenerational poverty and income gaps exist. Versions of victim-blaming narratives are told by lay persons as well as prominent social scientists (see reviews by Brantlinger, 1997, 2003; Valencia, 1997; Wright, 1993). Human agency versus social structure explanations for differential school outcomes divide educational theorists. Those who espouse deprivation accounts see personal immorality (not caring, not trying) and bad families (not aspiring, not supporting)—that is, problems in human agency—as the root of failure. Informed ethnographers such as McDermott and Varenne (1996) see caring among the poor set against a breakdown of opportunity. Bowles and Gintis (1976) and Bourdieu (1984) provided structural accounts to explain intergenerational poverty. They maintain that schools are deliberately structured to maintain the advantage or hegemony of the powerful.

Despite that structuralist sociologists believe that schools maintain the existing social class structure, the American Dream of social mobility ideology, combined with tales of school as a fair meritocracy, result in both achieving and failing students believing that the playing field is level. The view that those who excel to do so by virtue of natural talents and those who fail lack the necessary attributes to succeed becomes common sense. Such ideological persuasions lead people to believe that high achievers are entitled to rewards and low achievers deserve negative school and life outcomes. A popular impression (ideological story) held by the middle class is that poor people choose to fail in school, attend schools with inadequate resources, and live in poverty (Brantlinger, 1993, 2003). Such narratives expurgate the poor while constructing the worthiness of people, like themselves, who "aspire" and "try" (see Thompson's [1990] ideas about the nature of ideological operations). Because affluent people are distanced geographically and psychologically from the poor, their impressions of these Others have little connection to reality. Regardless of cultural myths and stereotypes (ideological narratives), actual empirical evidence indicates that poor people share the middle class' reverence for education and desire for the good life as well as the perception that social mobility depends on school achievement and attainment (Brantlinger, 1985; Kozol, 2001; Lauder & Hughes, 1999; MacLeod, 1987).

SUPPOSED RATIONALE FOR HIGH-STAKES TESTING

An official reason for mandating graduation exit exams is that, without setting a cut-off standard that prevents low-performing students from earning a diploma, schools do not guarantee that graduates have even minimal basic skills, literacy, and general knowledge. It is claimed that without an achievement baseline determined by criterion-referenced tests,[4] the diploma conveys little about high school graduates' competencies, and therefore has little credibility or value as a credential. Test proponents believe the diploma is worth more if access to it is limited.

Another official rationale touted for requiring high-stakes tests is that the possibility of failure and denial of the diploma provide necessary incentives for students to work harder (FairTest, 1999–2000a). A discourse (common ideology) of societal decline purports that some people do not pull their weight, hence burden others and pull society down. Stringent standards and punitive sanctions are billed as tough love remedies for dealing with corrupted adolescents, neglectful parents, and inept teachers. Such measures are to provide a reality check to warn, and supposedly motivate, students to attend school, behave themselves, and try in their courses. In terms of the effectiveness of tests in motivating failing students to improve scores, Berliner (2003) documented that, despite the substantial human and monetary expense of high-stakes tests, such initiatives have little or no impact on measured achievement.

The stakes connected with the testing movement are not leveled exclusively at students. Schools, school districts, and personnel are judged (and penalized) according to aggregate test scores. Mortimore and Mortimore (1999) claimed that accountability proponents portray teachers as lazy, incompetent, and lacking motivation to excel. Although teachers may now "teach to the test," whether by choice or district mandate, they may not be effectively implementing practices they value. Some school personnel are

---

[4]Test companies and department of education officials claim that high-stakes are criterion referenced. In actuality, cutoff scores for failure are based on norms and tend to be set at about the lowest third or quartile. Perhaps it is no coincidence that about a third of U.S. children live below the poverty level and it is mostly these children who fail. The claim that failing students are not working at grade level is flawed. "Grade level" is a statistical average (norm). If some children work above grade level, others' achievement must be below grade level.

so pressured by punitive aspects of accountability trends that they feel driven to cheat (Associated Press, 2000, June 8).

Regardless of their recent popularity, "get tough" approaches (e.g., zero tolerance suspension and expulsion rules, grade retention) have not demonstrated a constructive impact on target students. Indeed such punitive practices as low grades, stigmatizing placements, and castigating discipline inflict symbolic violence, further alienating students from schooling (FairTest, 1999–2000a). Similar "for your own good" rationales are often used to justify violence in childrearing (Miller, 1986). Because it is claimed that such mandates are in students' best interest, despite their dire consequences for vulnerable students, test promoters and governmental officials who vote for them advertise themselves as concerned and caring about poor and minority children. *No Child Left Behind* legislation is infused with a beneficent politician ideology. If initiatives fund compensatory programs for students who fail, politicians also claim generosity.[5] Governing bodies routinely tout the need to discipline or close doors to students and families when they institute what they call *opportunities*. The first special education class I taught was called an "Opportunity Room"—a misnomer that fooled nobody, especially my students. Students required to attend compensatory classes and summer school or retake tests are unlikely to understand these practices as beneficial. Rather, they are seen as further evidence that schools are not designed in their own best interests.

WHO FAILS? WHO LOSES?

A short period of time after the exit exams were adopted, it became clear that poor and minority children were the ones who would fail them. In major urban districts across Indiana, minority failure was higher than 50% (Associated Press, 2000, April 30)—rates similar to Blacks and Latinos in Texas (FairTest, 1999–2000a). Racial disproportions must have been anticipated; Black students inevitably score lower than White students on all achievement measures (Jencks & Phillips, 1999). Because of the history of race and class discrimination, any informed educator would expect class- and race-related score disparities. A Texas judge acknowledged that graduation tests had a "legally meaningful and disparate impact against African American and Latino students" (FairTest, 1999–2000a, p. 1), yet concluded that "test-based discrimination is not illegal because only a high stakes exam can force students and educators to work hard enough and be focused enough

---

[5]In Indiana and elsewhere, reforms have not been funded both because of state budget crises and lawmakers intentionally removing funding requirements for educational reform bills to get the support of fiscal conservatives (Associated Press, 16 September, 2002).

to learn the 'basic skills' measured" (p. 11). Educators also could have predicted that the tests would raise further obstacles to poor students' school success and limit their access to an enriched or even mainstream general education curriculum. Despite evidence of the negative effects of grade-level retention, "anti-social promotion policy" is now "intertwined with standards-based school reform via high-stakes testing" (Valencia, 2002, p. 14). A new Florida policy bases promotion largely on tests, with the result that five times as many youngsters were forced to repeat third grade than the previous year. Opposed to the practice in which promotion depends on a mandated test score criterion, Senator Frederica Wilson, a former elementary school principal who works in a dropout prevention program, predicts: "These children will either become so angry they're going to be aggressive and discipline problems or be so demoralized and heartbroken and depressed. I know that these children are going to drop out" (Associated Press, 2003, August 24, p. A10).

The statistics regarding who fails high-stakes tests should not be surprising—they are the same students who fail in other school enterprises: score below average on all tests, have low grade point averages, have high rates of grade-level retention, have more punished infractions, have poor school attendance records, and have high dropout rates. Some are identified as disabled, were disabled in the past but currently are not classified, or barely miss cutoff criterion for disability classification. In the first year of the test, more than 1,000 diploma-track seniors with identified disabilities failed Indiana's Graduation Qualifying Examination and thus were not eligible to receive high school diplomas (O'Neill, 2001). The American Civil Liberties Union (ACLU) brought forward a class-action lawsuit charging that gateway tests violated special education students' constitutional rights (Associated Press, 2000, April 30).[6] Others who fail graduate exit exams are not in special education, but have been singled out for other forms of compensatory or remedial interventions. "Risk" has previously referred to poor school performance and potential for grade retention or dropping out—or being pushed out—of school (Fine, 1991). Indeed high school dropouts can be identified for that inevitability as early as third grade. Now risk encompasses the probability of students not passing gateway tests and not receiving diplomas even if they have remained in school for the full 12 years.

Given the high rates of failure on high-stakes tests, a public or at least student and parent outcry might have been expected. Yet little stakeholder or grassroots opposition has surfaced in my locale. A few critical letters to the editor appeared, but they were written in a calm and tentative tone by edu-

---

[6]O'Neill (2001) reported the judge upheld the law claiming that the state has a public interest in "ensuring that an Indiana high school diploma is worth more than the paper it is printed on" (p. 195). The appeal was still pending at the time this chapter was written.

cators. A more animated complaint arose when someone learned that those denied a diploma due to exam failure would be ineligible for admission to technical and vocational colleges. Because of the devastating consequences of the test for a large percentage of the student body, the lack of public outrage might be puzzling. Given the high correlations between all forms of school failure (i.e., the stability of ranked orderings of achievement over time and across measures), however, a viable explanation for the lack of public opposition to the gateway exams is that this is one more instance of failure for students who always fail. The negative impact is on students already on the losing end of school evaluative and status continua and bottom rung of hierarchies. Disproportionately poor, of color, and/or English language learners, their low, powerless place in school mirrors their family's societal status. They live an impoverished, ghetto existence (Conley, 1999; Ehrenreich, 2001; Oliver & Shapiro, 1995) and attend schools and classes with the fewest resources (Anyon, 1997; Kozol, 1991, 2001) and least academic push (Chazan, 2000). Perhaps those who fail the gateway test are too worn out and demoralized by life circumstances to have the energy or incentive to fight this particular battle.

FOCUSING ON WHO PASSES RATHER THAN WHO FAILS HIGH-STAKES TESTS

In contrast to the deleterious outcomes for low-income students, students who readily pass gateway tests on the first try are White and middle class. Educated in suburban schools or high-ability groups in comprehensive elementary schools, then in honors, gifted/talented, or advanced or accelerated sections during their secondary years, students who readily pass these new tests have high grade point averages and score above average on other tests. It is well documented that middle- and upper class students are always on the winning end of ranked orderings. Again given that test scores inevitably sort students along social class lines, and based on what is known about correlations between tests, the class- and race-linked outcomes certainly could have been anticipated.

There are numerous insider (to the class) explanations for middle-class students' success, including they: "come from genetically superior stock," "acquire cultural capital from educated families," "internalize parental values and caring about school," "are raised to believe that educational achievement and attainment are the epitome of success," "receive respectful home treatment that nurtures the high self-esteem necessary for competence," "live in emotionally supportive conditions that allow them to concentrate on learning," and "are not subjected to the distracting tensions of substance abuse or antisocial or criminal lifestyles" (see Brantlinger, 2003).

Such lay and professional reasoning attributes middle-class success to superior student and family characteristics—again to the personal traits rather than the structural distinctions in institutional response to members of each class.

In addition to middle-class people's perceptions of the strengths of their class, there are other explanations for affluent students' school success that are not based on stereotypes about who is or is not intelligent. One theory is that humans behave rationally. Thus, middle-class students' efforts are due to their conviction that K–12 achievement is necessary for admission to higher education and, in turn, that college degrees permit access to professional jobs with salaries high enough to maintain their customary affluent lifestyles. Students who engage in status maintenance behaviors are aware that sufficient family funds are available to facilitate their attaining middle-class goals. This assurance provides the incentive to make an effort in school. It must be acknowledged that high aspirations are only likely to enhance achievement when combined with expectations of sufficient resources for advanced education. Given the conducive conditions of monetary support and parental knowledge regarding higher education, students of the educated middle class are on a college-bound track from the time they are born.

Another neutral explanation for class-related school success rates is that middle-class people of Euro-American heritage are in control of social institutions and design them so that they mirror their home culture while excluding Others' cultures (Bourdieu, 1977; Delpit, 1995; Ladson-Billings, 1998). One way to look at this is that arbitrary historical circumstances have resulted in an Anglo-oriented American school system and immigrant groups that followed British settlers have had to assimilate to Anglo customs. Some believe the cultural mismatch with poor and minority group is temporary, surmountable, and unintentional. Ogbu (1995) made a compelling case that certain involuntary immigrants, especially ones who do not blend in because of skin color or lasting cultural differences due to continuing segregation, have not been able to break the cultural barriers to be successful in American schools and society.

Another version of the cultural difference hypothesis is that White, middle-class people are reluctant to give up their hegemony. According to this theory, in both their professional and parent advocacy (for their own children) roles, college-educated people determine the curricular and pedagogical factors that privilege children of their class (Apple, 1993; Brantlinger, 2003). They insist on Eurocentric curriculum and achievement-differentiated school structures. Henry (1995) wrote of replacing Eurocentric curricula as important to anticolonial struggle even in institutions within the borders of colonial powers. Perhaps most important to the ubiquitous affluent class school advantage is that American voters never choose to equalize expenditures; they always override school funding policies that confront dependence on local property taxes and, hence, disparate school circumstances.

My assertion about the neutrality of these reviewed social class reproduction theories might be challenged. Consistent with Marxist accounts of domination and oppression, these theories highlight how social relations and societal institutions are stratified along class lines. Yet even critical theories become neutral when highly abstract language is used that does not translate into practice. Scholars often convey resignation to stratified relations or fail to be introspective about their own role in reproducing them (Brantlinger, 1999a, 1999b). They do not declare or notice which side they are on (Becker, 1963). In this sense, critical scholars may do as much harm as mainstream scholars who follow technorational agendas of exacting classifications for low-achieving students or offering make-shift remedies for failure. Bracey (1997) criticized academics who make careers of collecting grants to fix problems. Sleeter (2000) argued that, "researchers from dominant groups have a long history of producing knowledge about oppressed groups that legitimates their subordination" (p. 10). Few scholars turn their gaze upward (inwards) to understand why dominant classes consistently win and continuously create new measures to guarantee their inevitable domination of hierarchies.

I dub theories neutral when they do not pinpoint human intentionality. When leftist or postmodern theories identify culture as a stock of commonsense beliefs about what is right, natural, and normal (Rochon, 1998), see tacit knowledge as visceral and internal (Vygotsky, 1978), or see the body/subject as socially inscribed and managed (Shapiro, 1999), it is implied that those who benefit are mere puppets controlled by external forces. In these theories, deliberate intention and informed, anti-oppressive agency remain invisible. Yet if there are no intentions, there is no responsibility (or accountability), and hence little possibility for equitable change.

Although nothing is neutral (Zizek, 1994), I use the term *political* as an honorific for theories that pinpoint the intentionality and self-serving actions of dominant classes and connect to direct agendas for transformative action. Within these parameters, I ask such questions about the widespread adoption of exams as: If existing evaluative measures already ranked students, why were additional tests needed? If who fails and who passes the gateway test is the same as for all school measures, hence predictable, what is the exam's purpose? Who needs them? Who wants them? Why are they so popular among legislators and voters? On what social meanings do these tests depend? Real answers to such questions are complex, interactive, and definitively political because they focus on the agency and intentional acts of those who dominate in school and society. If Gramsci were here, he might ask, "If gateway tests do not benefit students they disqualify from high school graduation, then who do they benefit?"

WHO BENEFITS?

Because practices mandated by the standards and accountability movement, in general, and the high school exit exams, in particular, are expensive financially and in terms of time spent by teachers and students, it is important to understand why people endorse them and why government officials legislate them. It seems reasonable to conclude that a number of parties reap rewards from increased educational competition. Turning to Gramsci's idea of hegemony (that powerful groups in society strive to maintain and strengthen their dominance by offering new evidence to justify it), it is plausible to assume that high-stakes tests facilitate the win/lose situations that justify hierarchical social relations and dominant groups' material and status advantages. In the remainder of this chapter, I identify various winners and conjecture about how they benefit in the competitive milieu of the current high-stakes testing, accountability, and standards movements.

Benefits for Test Producers

The most obvious response to the "Who benefits?" question is that gateway tests are a good source of revenue for test merchants. Through connections to the media, test producers announce declining achievement rates for American students and link these rates to downward national economic trajectories—current, foreseen, or imagined. Economic doomsday narratives scare the public into compliance with regulations that require the adoption of yet another expensive accountability measure, if not to gauge students' achievement, then to assess teachers or preservice teachers. According to this explanation, the burgeoning use of exams results from a conspiracy designed to keep money flowing in the direction of test producers, especially CEOs of such supposedly not-for-profit companies as ETS. Dependency on objective tests as the sole criterion of educational performance also benefits the companies that shape textbooks containing the specific knowledge required for tests. So among the winners in the high-stakes testing movement are vendors who design and market tests and produce official textbook knowledge.

Hysteria about achievement inadequacies has resulted in proliferation of tests for students at every level of education as well as for preservice and inservice teachers. When I started as a teacher educator in the late 1970s, graduating from a teacher education institution translated into state certification. Now teacher education graduates must pass several tests, including one for each age level they teach as well as each subject area and/or disability category of certification. If teachers want certification in another state, they must take a different set of tests conveniently customized for that state. Similarly, a few years ago, our institution admitted students to teacher education based solely on their GPAs in prerequisite courses. Some programs required evidence of experience with children. Presently, we have dropped the experience requirement, but students must pass admission tests to get into programs. This testing expansion has meant a boom for test and textbook industries as well as for organizations that provide tutorial courses or materials aimed at helping students improve test scores. It should be no surprise, then, that these companies are part of corporate conglomerates with connections to the media and prominent politicians (Metcalf, 2002). It is likely that these affiliates deliberately circulate knowledge about educational crises and then market remedies purportedly to improve literacy and other forms of achievement (McNeil, 1995, 2000).

Benefits to Transglobal Capitalists

Capitalism is based on maximizing profits, hence the endless pursuit of opportunities to enhance revenue for corporations and stockholders. It is not surprising that those who benefit most from capitalism's free market enterprise would eschew public institutions. That capitalist controlled mass communication would publicize low scores, condemn teachers, construct students/workers as intellectually and morally inferior, and recommend business-oriented measures to correct problems they identify is also not unexpected. By clever use of their media, capitalists create themes that resonate with ideologies of neoliberals, neoconservatives, authoritarian populists, and the new middle class (Apple, 2003). Alliances formed through groups' supposed mutual interests allow politicians who endorse the agendas of rich people and powerful corporations to get elected. Certainly, reducing public spending and giving tax breaks to the wealthy are their high priorities. To sway the system to advantage current elites, voters and their representatives must be convinced that certain citizens are unworthy of receiving government spending. When the public believes that test scores are the key criterion for judging human worth, then it is opportune to prove students and teachers deficient and schools dysfunctional based on low scores. Corporate executive officers (CEOs) have gotten widespread public concurrence that certain citizens are undeserving and that welfare safeguards and other public services and accommodations for some citizens unduly burden other taxpayers. They have also advertised that increasing school finances is simply throwing money away.

Defective school and deficient worker narratives also provide CEOs with the excuse and public endorsement for maintaining low wages. Such narratives distract public attention from unethical corporate and labor practices, business welfare, and self-serving actions of elites. They divert attention that concerned citizens should have about the worldwide colonization of land and people by Western transglobal corporations (H. Martin & Schumann, 1997; Sleeter, 2000). While blaming illiterate U.S. workers, CEOs insist that for their industries to stay afloat they must relocate abroad, opportunely to places with low-wage structures and lax environmental standards. Meanwhile, they claim to transfer companies to Third World countries for the sake of the U.S. economy—to stay ahead of global competition for production and markets. Corporate leaders, and the politicians who endorse their agendas, insist on literacy standards, but reject plans aimed at setting standards for environmental protection or living wages. Unions are busted while CEOs do the "necessary" downsizing that creates national unemployment and underemployment and decimates fringe benefits for the working class. Meanwhile, they upsize their own salaries and return huge profits to corporate shareholders. Transnational corporations have managed to dismantle governmental restrictions so they have infinite unregulated power (Sleeter, 2000). Nation states have lost control of transglobal corporations, hence are unable to autonomously regulate living standards and welfare needs of their population (Medovoi, 2002; Sassen, 1998). It is little wonder that those with power over economic conditions like to believe in the inferiority of American workers and the neutrality and inevitability of market trends.

Perhaps the most interesting aspect of the intensification of testing and standards that have marked schools and workers as defective is the disconnect between reality and fiction about achievement and its links to the economy. Although current achievement among U.S. students is relatively high (Berliner, 2000), this has not prevented jobs with sustainable salaries from disappearing for Americans (Wilson, 1996). If inferior workers actually were the cause of corporation departures, then companies would not move to countries whose citizens have lower literacy levels. A credible reason for the onslaught of tests is that corporations have used low scores to convince the public of student/worker inadequacies and pinpoint these failures as the reason for their low wages and existing salary discrepancies between managers and workers. By constructing low scorers as personal losers, corporations have a convenient scapegoat for social problems and a diversion from personal blame. Low test scores provide proof that the poor (previously the working class) are inferior and undeserving. Constructing market dynamics as systemic inevitabilities, corporate owners deny their own intentionality and avoid being held accountable for contributing to the dire outcomes of the modern American working class.

Benefits to Media Moguls

Media enterprises sustain themselves by engaging the attention of potential consumers of products sold by press or network advertisers. In the past, independent presses and radio stations were owned by individuals of various political persuasions, and hence had diverse perspectives that influenced readers (voters) in myriad ways (McChesney, 1999). A flourishing populism meant working- and middle-class voters had some leverage over who got elected, and hence how politicians regulated capitalist enterprise and were responsive to constituencies. Organized nationally and locally, labor action forced capitalists to pay relatively high working-class wages and provide fringe benefits. Times have changed. International communication networks are now controlled by fewer than two dozen enormous profit-making corporations (McChesney, 1997, 2001). Responsive to those in power, media serve a master (McChesney, 1999; McLeod & Hertog, 1999). Dominant value messages (ideologies) that distort the reality of modern life advantage business and bureaucratic institutions (Viswanath & Demers, 1999). Corporate control of the media results in public expenditures being *the problem* and business and unregulated free markets being *the answer*, so business-oriented measures are recommended to solve their versions of educational and national problems. In this media monopoly, those who protest the capitalist system are ignored, excluded, or negatively portrayed (Glasser & Bowers, 1999).[7] In snippets of coverage of the massive protests against the World Bank and World Trade Organization in Quebec City, Switzerland, Seattle, and Washington, DC, protesters were portrayed as rabble-rousing miscreants with no legitimate gripes.

At the same time that media ownership became centralized under corporate control, concern about societal decline and students not measuring up to earlier standards heightened. During the Sputnik era, hysteria arose about losing the cold war to Russia, in particular, and communism, in general. Working-class Americans were persuaded to associate with free market capitalism and disassociate with anything socialist. After the breakup of the Soviet Union and opening of China to the West, concern about the communist threat shifted to worry about losing out in the economic competition to dominate world markets. Announcements about educational mediocrity, inadequate workers, and the United States losing in global competition prevailed. These mostly undocumented sound bites coalesced into a discourse of school and societal decline that convinced the public of the

---

[7]Britzman (1992) called the highly publicized idea of declining teacher quality an "arranged, slippery history that hides its interestedness and politics of selection" (p. 73).

need to raise standards and hold public schools accountable for improvements in educational—and economic—outcomes. *The Nation At Risk* legislation framed the rationale for concentrating on measurable academic achievement, and *No Child Left Behind* reemphasized similar goals under the guise of concern for the fate of poor and minority children.

A plausible explanation for the publicity about social and academic deterioration is that it gains and retains audiences. Media moguls know that people have personal experiences with and an interest in schools. Education coverage filled the space left when the communist threat dissipated. It still provides filler when natural disasters, crimes, or international conflicts are unavailable to the newspaper pages or air waves. A form of cold war logic lurks behind the fear that America must better educate its workers to win in global markets or on battlegrounds. This crisis mentality about the state of education and the economy is not unique to Americans. Hyperbolic concern about literacy tied to fears of workforce collapse and national vulnerability is apparent in England (Ball, Kenny, & Gardiner, 1990; Whitty, 2000) and Australia (Taylor, Rizvi, Lingard, & Henry, 1997). Apparently sensationalism surrounding declining achievement and social conditions has gained media coverage internationally.

A compelling case has been made against the validity of arguments of school decline or inferior workers. Bracey (2000) detected flaws in statistics that purport to document American students' comparative weakness. Rothstein (1999) concluded that, regardless of reports to the contrary, student achievement has consistently improved. The agitation about academic decline and the United States losing ground to other nations has been called a *manufactured crisis* (Berliner & Biddle, 1995). In terms of education's responsibility for depressing the U.S. economy, the case has been made that, even if achievement were declining, tougher standards for student performance would not improve either schools or the economy (Kohn, 1998; Kozol, 2001; Meier, 2000; Ohanian, 1999; Starratt, 1994). Others reject the argument that schools can or should be engines for economic restoration (Smyth & Schacklock, 1998). Regarding apprehension about the scarcity of graduates competent in technical fields—see *Nation at Risk* (U.S. Department of Education, 1983) and *America 2000* (U.S. Department of Education, 1991)—contradictory evidence exists of high unemployment rates among graduates with advanced degrees, especially in mathematics, science, and technology (Boutwell, 1997; Noddings, 1994; O'Brien, 1998).

Benefits for Politicians and Political Pundits

At this point in history, undoubtedly due to the clever manipulation of media moguls, the public as well as political parties have learned to dwell on leaders' personal traits rather than substantive issues. Intense and bitter party rivalries are constant. Such contention is ironic given that differences between Democrats and Republicans—the only parties with a chance to win in modern American elections—are barely discernible. Politicians seem to fear that anything other than the articulation of bland, conformist agendas will alienate voters. Fueled by the educational crisis mentality and avoiding real issues, various politicians espouse their own versions of high educational and accountability standards. They join the bandwagon of politicians who bill themselves as "education" presidents, mayors, governors, or legislators. Bureaucrats gain political capital from being messengers of the popular doom and salvation rhetoric regarding education. Because these measures seemingly are instituted for students' sakes, concern about educational failure allows politicians to advertise themselves as caring about children and the country.

Politicians have nothing to lose and much to gain from pursuing "improve education" agendas. In the first place, running for public office is expensive, so inevitably politicians are affluent. Members of affluent, educated classes are the ones who benefit most from the social hierarchies created and intensified by standardized tests. Mandates for high-stakes tests and accountability measures officially sanction existing hierarchical relations by rewarding cultural capital and avoiding the equity or redistributive reform that would undermine their privilege. In addition to the personal gain of their children and grandchildren rising to the top of academic competition, thus having access to advantaged school conditions, some politicians own stock in test and textbook companies (Metcalf, 2002). Such conflicts of interest are covered in alternative media with small circulation, however, they are not published in mainstream circuits. Hence, the fact that certain politicians engage in illegal and unethical behaviors goes relatively unnoticed by the general public.

Bourdieu (1998) equated neoliberalism with dominant discourse of political submission to economic rationality, undivided reign of the market, and withering away of state regulation of business. Wells (2000) contended that neoliberalism undergirds free market rationale for school choice policy (e.g., charter school development, public vouchers for private schools), which she saw as a backlash against redistributive reforms aimed at decreasing disparities in education and society. Bourdieu claimed that in the mode of consensus, people collectively have an "atavistic faith in the historical inevitability of productive forces" and "utter a fatalistic discourse that transforms economic tendencies into destiny." He warned that "flagrant inadequacies of the market are undermining the public interest and liquidating the gains of the welfare state," and condemns the French public for judging the "political candidates according to narrow-minded, regressive, security-minded, protectionist, conservative, xenophobia" (p. 18).

BENEFITS FOR CONSERVATIVES

In contrast to the goals of democratic and grassroot reform that gained ground during the 1980s, current reform initiatives advocate top–down control of education. An impetus for the groundswell of concern about education and subsequent onslaught of high-stakes legislation is that conservatives fear that democratic, progressive, transformative school reform would diminish their power and advantage. Test-driven educational standards direct educators away from democratic and multicultural reform and back to a monolithic, western European-centered, subject matter, discipline-oriented curriculum. For high performance on objective tests, teachers and students must concentrate on the standard academic content provided in commercial texts. Again it must be emphasized that textbook and test-producing companies are owned by the same transglobal corporations (Metcalf, 2002).

Religious conservatives have long been troubled by the prospect that public school personnel teach secular values that are not consistent with or drawn from their own religious tenets. Some fundamentalist parents have taken their children out of public schools to be home schooled. Others are determined that if public schools will not be shaped by Christian content, curriculum must be restricted to academic subject matter. Academic conservatives, who believe in the superiority of western European culture, are alarmed by the multicultural encroachment on traditional educational content. Because test content drives teachers to cover the conservative curriculum that will be on the test, these conservatives approve of high-stakes testing.

Benefits for Advocates of School Privatization

Capitalist conservatives appear to advocate for more and more tests to prove the general inadequacy of public schooling. Earlier high-stakes initiatives had an impact only on failing schools—that is, low-income, minority school populations. *No Child Left Behind* (NCLB) regulations exert control over all schools by insisting they document continuous annual progress. Although, constitutionally, education has been deemed a state responsibility, NCLB has vastly extended federal power over education. This coincides with corporations' global level of control and capitalist plans to privatize the world. True believers who have faith in the rationality and benefits of pure market economy eschew anything public. They demand private ownership of industry, national resources, health, welfare, and education. Evidence of public school failure provides an incentive for privatization. NCLB offers the condition that families can move their children from failing to successful schools, including private ones. Thus, the federal government mandates that vouchers be provided for private schools. Although their agenda for privatization is less encompassing and not founded on free market ideology, the fundamentalist religious right and racial separatists join in on public school bashing to fund the parochial and/or segregated schools of their choice. The pluralist, democratic dream of diverse children coming together in comprehensive public schools is forsaken.

Benefits for Enterprising School Superintendents

High-stakes tests have distinctive outcomes for various school districts. Given the high correlation between social class/race and achievement outcomes, it is evident that school districts with the lowest percentage of children on free and reduced lunch will have higher scores and will look best when test outcomes are publicized. Administrators and teachers in high-income school catchment zones tend to believe that higher scores are due to their management and instructional competencies (Brantlinger, 2003). Such deceptive boasting is not as corrupt as the deliberate manipulation of the student test pool done to make a district and its administration look good. In an article graphically entitled, "Flunk 'em or get them classified," McGill-Franzen and Allington (1993) exposed administrators' practice of classifying students as disabled to eliminate them from the test pool and retaining students ineligible for classification so their scores could be averaged into a lower grade level. These actions result in dramatic improvement in school or district test scores, but have negative consequences for retained and classified students.

Benefits for Professionals and the Professions

Educated professionals both receive and award the credentials that give their class power over much of social life (Bourdieu, 1996; Eagleton, 1990). Historically, expanding numbers of specialists and technical experts correspond to burgeoning numbers of abnormalities and pathologies (Caplan, 1995; Capshew, 1999; Kutchins & Kirk, 1997). Special education provides evidence of proliferating disability categories and swelling ranks within them. Many concur that high-incidence disabilities (e.g., learning disability, emotional disturbance, attention deficit hyperactivity disorder [ADHD]) have more to do with the nature of schools than the nature of individuals (Apter, 1996; McDermott & Varenne, 1996; Mercer, 1973; Smith, 1997). Expert classification of certain children lead to their outgroup status (Goffman, 1963). Poor children and children of color are overrepresented in special education (Artiles & Trent, 1994; Brantlinger, 1986, 1993; Connor

& Boskin, 2001; Harry, 1994; Patton, 1998), as they are in low tracks (Ansalone, 2001). Psychologists have been criticized for naturalizing oppressive standards for social adjustment (Schnog, 1997) and calling difference "deviance" when it is located in Others. They also see traits as fixed rather than influenced by school structure and practice (e.g., social determinism in the *Bell Curve*).

Some question the expansion of specialized fields (Brown, 1995; Danforth, 1996; Gordon & Keiser, 1998) and the ever-tightening standards that secure professional monopoly of the highest ranks (Gouldner, 1979; Wright, 1985). Troyna and Vincent (1996) called the elevation of social service professions a "reign of experts." As professionals gain authority, autonomy is reduced for others (Bourdieu, 1996; Eagleton, 1990; Mills, 1943). Foucault (1977) theorized that middle-level bureaucrats in schools, penal institutions, and other social agencies use the major disciplinary instruments of hierarchic surveillance, normalizing sanctions, and examination—mechanisms recognizable in the adoption of high-stakes tests and other components of the accountability and standards movement. Professional norms are made to appear universal and objective through technical and scientific (ideological) story-telling. The pretense of knowledge as authorless, disinterested, and value-free is what Nagel (1986) called the "view from nowhere." Apfelbaum (1999) located such knowledge in those at the powerful center of social life. Foucault (1980) noted that universal intellectuals have been replaced by specific intellectuals who have credentials to use technical expertise and work in disciplines. Such "faceless professionals" are "competent members of a social class going about their business" (p. 7). Martin (1998) reminded readers of Gramsci's observation that even working-class intellectuals cease to serve their original class interests and play a conservative role by supporting the status quo.

In modern times, social divisions are institutionalized. Social class formation intersects with the structure of social agencies (education, welfare, judicial, penal, mental health), which are regulated by governmental acts. Legislators pass laws and professionals develop protocols for practice that comply with the laws. Most of these regulations have a differential impact on high- and low-income people. Official regimentation depersonalizes human actions while solidifying hierarchical relations. For example, the Individuals with Disabilities Education Act (1990) authorizes disability categories and due process guidelines for treatment supposedly to ensure equal and appropriate treatment. States mandate high-stakes tests and accountability measures apparently for the purpose of bringing low achievers up to speed. So as officials monitor those under their control, doling out rewards and sanctioning failure, personnel at each bureaucratic level simply comply with established procedures to "do their jobs." Power imbalances between local actors do not appear to be the result of intentional acts. Thus, be-

tween class power disparities and hierarchies are disguised as they are perpetuated. All the while, professionals do benefit from ever-tightening standards to secure their monopoly of high ranks.

In the end, professionals have a social class position. E. O. Wright (1985)
postulated that what he called the *new middle class* is a contradictory class
that does not benefit from corporate profits to the same extent as elite
classes, and yet their financial and social interests are still tied to the market. Hence, they gain from market economy and market thinking (Dale,
2001; Rizvi & Lingard, 2001). The current trend in teacher education is to
expect professors to fall in line with political and business agendas (Pinar,
2002). Bourdieu (1996) maintained that with its material power and ideological control, affluent people use schools to sanctify social divisions—to
impose the symbolic violence of ranking and segregating. Subordinates are
positioned as educational consumers in need of services, whereas dominant
classes are promoted as experts who provide service. For professionals to
work, there must be constituencies to serve. A professional class would still
be employed in egalitarian societies, yet the swelling of an underclass "at
risk" or "with needs" means employment security and extended job opportunities for credentialed professionals who have the expertise needed in
the expanding social service bureaucracies.[8]

Benefits for Members of the Educated Middle Class

Although U.S. schools have always relied on standardized tests to chart student progress, under the standards and accountability movements, testing
has intensified and the stakes for failing and passing have increased. A
close-to-home explanation for the onslaught of tests is that they provide opportunity for those who do well on tests to prove their superiority. Disparate
test results reaffirm commonsense notions that positive personal attributes
account for school success—that middle-class children are intellectually superior and/or have better work ethics. Documenting poor children's inadequacies reaffirms the belief that their relegation to lesser school circumstances is necessary and not discriminatory. The stronger the measures
used to prove inferiority and more replications of Others' extensive flaws,
the more credible the arguments about status differentials, hence the more
justification for distinguishing practices that separate advanced children
into exclusive neighborhood schools and high-ability groups and tracks
(Brantlinger, 2003). Because middle-class children typically have no trou-

---

[8]An exception is when the gap between affluent and poor widens so much that the middle
class is squeezed out and has no role—a phenomenon referred to as *Brazilianization*. This happened most recently in Argentina.

ble passing tests (doing better than low-income children), they do not need to worry about the graduate exit exam hurdle. Indeed they benefit from the diploma's scarcity. When every student earns a diploma, it has little value as a credential. To have worth, status markers must be scarce. Adults of this class vote to limit access to diplomas and other enriched school conditions—they legislate measures and control institutions in ways that perpetuate distinctions; plainly put, they "hog resources" (Sleeter, Gutierrez, New, & Takata, 1992, p. 173). Rorty (1997) complained that "suburbanites, who know social mobility advanced their parents' fates, see nothing wrong with belonging to a hereditary caste," having a "secession of the successful" by preventing the mobility of Others (p. 86). Disparate test scores explain school inequities as related to school proficiencies to both the *haves* and the *have nots*—that is how hegemony works.

Although educated middle-class people may believe they have nothing to gain from high-stakes tests, they have social and material advantage in school and postschool situations. One answer to the question of who benefits from gateway exams is that those who win in education and occupation seek increasingly conclusive evidence of their superiority to justify taking home larger and larger shares of the national economic pie. It is no coincidence that those found to be inadequate are the least powerful citizens. At a time of rising wages for the educated middle class (U.S. Census, 2001), stratified outcomes strengthen the image of others' faults and justify uneven wage structures and growing income gaps. The affluent need evidence of their worth to provide a grounding for privilege. Dominant classes depend on storied reasons (ideologies) for Others' failures because cut-throat competition and slanted playing fields are not admired or condoned. Selfishness and greed are subject to approbation by religious and secular standards (Bersoff, 1999). According to Baumeister (1996), "The desire to think well of oneself is one of the most fundamental and pervasive motivation in human psychological function" (p. 27). Draconian measures adopted to document Others' inferiority can be understood as attempts to maintain, restore, or improve the self-evaluation of perpetual winners.

Although the United States is the largest imperial power in history, this fact is rarely mentioned, nor do Americans refer to themselves as capitalists (Kailin, 2000). When capitalism is addressed, as with other neoliberal discourses, it is not framed as imperialism, but rather in democratic or Enlightenment terms as *individual rights, freedom,* and *progress* (Sleeter, 2000). This viewpoint ignores issues of power and does not name who is and who is not advantaged (Epstein & Steinberg, 1997). Ahmad (1992) claimed that economic realities surround and saturate us, and corporate repressions and the rise of a compliant bourgeoisie (college-educated, managerial class) and strengthened market mentality regarding schools are interrelated.

The Really Essential Question: Does Anybody Win?

Americans naively believe that modernity means a progression of peoples and countries toward independence and general improvement in material and social conditions. Development of democratic market economies is generally perceived as an unquestionable public good. Yet economic and political/social goals diverge. Liberty in the market has not meant liberty for most people. Corporate global control has diminished rather than increased national or personal independence (Appadurai, 1997; Rose, 1996). Capitalism's global rampage has gone mostly uncontested as transglobal corporations negotiate away national governments' regulations. Carlson and Apple (1998) referred to Gramsci's theory that advanced capitalist societies are in an era of factory mass production in which consumerism has emerged to drive industrialization and public institution organization. Consumption patterns caused by relative affluence have decimated the world's forests, which has disastrous consequences for indigenous peoples, wild life, and global ecology, including global warming and consequent volatile weather patterns. In reference to the tremendous growth of suburbs and extensive use of cars, Kunstler (2000) tallied up the economic, environmental, social, and spiritual costs that America pays for its consumer-crazed lifestyle. Globalization has meant an increasing concentration of extreme wealth in relatively few international families and increasing poverty and hopelessness among large sectors of world society (Anyon, 2000; Garmarnikow & Green, 2000).

In thinking about recent political and economic trends, "drift" captures the idea that things happen without public deliberation or conscious planning on the part of a broad base of citizens. By claiming that declining environmental and social conditions are inevitable, transglobal corporations deny their intentionality and avoid being held accountable for contributing to dire social and natural outcomes. Class inequalities have not been made a pressing national concern by either party—indeed they are barely acknowledged (O'Brien, 1998). Yet Rorty (1997) claimed that the citizen self-respect needed for participation in democratic deliberation is incompatible with large social divisions. Disparate economic and social conditions pit citizens against each other; the struggle is less often between classes than within them. Elites compete with each other for the rewards of high-paying and high-status positions (Newman, 1998). Subordinates struggle among themselves over limited resources and access to power. Internal strife among impoverished people—whether based on racism[9] or convenient

---

[9]For example, White working-class men hold Blacks accountable for their own economic insecurity and conditions of job fragility (Weis & Fine, 1996).

outlets for expressions of anger and frustration—does not benefit anyone. It is based on false consciousness of class interest and misperception of one's enemy.

Not coincidentally, the burgeoning development of transglobal corporations has occurred simultaneously with the schools' emphasis on dispensing only knowledge valued by business. With this market agenda for education, teachers are to be "passive, objective, and efficient distributors of technical information" (Leistyna, 1999, p. 7). Teacher education focuses on preservice teachers learning an aggregate of measurable skills that are consistent with standards, thus becoming a conservative determinant of teacher practice (Brantlinger, 1996; Hatton, 1997). Knowledge is standardized and commodified so it can be assessed by high-stakes measures and translated into credentials and differentiated status (Saavedra, 2000). Bourdieu (1984) claimed that school knowledge is mainly useful as cultural capital that produces social class distinctions. Thus, knowledge is power (Foucault, 1980). Labaree (1997) argued that, under current conditions of schooling, students can succeed (pass tests, get good grades) without learning. Carlson and Apple (1998) warned that the narrow academic focus of modern curriculum has negative effects on identity formation, so both successful and unsuccessful students pay a price for schools' excessive competition and strict emphasis on credentialing. Osbourne (1996) argued that the unfair sorting of technocratic education has a negative impact on unsuccessful students; like Rorty, he claimed when inequalities escalate, democracy is under threat internally. Unregulated and expansive business development, corporate intervention in schooling, and attempts to legislate control over school outcomes result in a reproduction of the current social class and wage structure that bind students to the existing social order (Bartlett, Frederick, Gulbrandsen, & Murillo, 2002; Neill, 2000; Sleeter, 2000).

Kailin (2000) argued that high-stakes testing, retention, and accountability standards are new ways to create notions of failure and keep the masses back. She questioned how such reforms can be constructive when, for example, in the city of New Orleans, 91 out of 103 schools, are considered below adequate (failing) schools, in which the official response is to subject students, teachers, and administrators to stringent repercussions. Neill (2000) called high-stakes tests "a bad reflection of even the better parts of standards." He delineated that this testing movement causes: (a) a narrowing of curriculum through the elimination of curricular depth because tests cover general factual knowledge; (b) increased student dropout or pushout rates; (c) a weakening of constructive test purposes; (d) speeded-up or intensified mechanistic school (busy) work; (e) bureaucratized, centralized school power; (f) disempowered teachers; (g) alienated students; and (h) standardized minds.

CONCLUSION: OPPOSING HIGH-STAKES TESTING
(AND DOMINANCE)

My big picture view of who benefits from high-stakes testing frames winners
in a way that challenges the neutrality of educated middle-class people. This
framing may shed light on the lack of effective resistance to standards and accountability initiatives despite widespread discontent about them (note the
preponderance of critical presentations on the 2003 American Educational
Research Association annual meeting program). Prominent educators and
scholars have taken a stand against the high-stakes juggernaut. Meier (1994)
asked that the purpose and nature of schools be examined to better align
their means to their ends; she insisted that high-stakes measures are not the
answer to achievement disparities (Meier, 2000). Others warn that implementing differentiating educational policies and practices force certain children into debilitating roles (Mehan, Hubbard, & Villanueva, 1994; Noddings, 2000; Oakes, Quartz, Ryan, & Lipton, 2000). McNeil (2000) urged
educators not to consent to punitive measures advocated by a corporate elite
whose main concern is personal profit and not children. Kohn (1998) insisted that administrators "respect the moral bottom line" and not give into
requests of self-centered school patrons. The unnamed Editors of *Rethinking
Schools* (2000) recommend that schools should: be responsible to communities not the marketplace, be actively multicultural and antiracist, willing to
promote social justice for all, be geared toward learning for life and the
needs of democracy, receive adequate and equal resources, and collaborate
with parents and community members. Looking beyond schools, they insist
that communities be revitalized.

In considering what might work to increase equity in modern times, general principles can be drawn from such intellectuals as Polanyi (1957), who
claimed that reciprocity—the giving and receiving according to need—the
dominant mode of exchange in traditional societies should be the principle for modern ones. Rawls (1971) recommended distributive justice so the
neediest in society are first to get scarce resources. Kittay (1999), the
mother of a disabled child, looked at the dependency work of women and
wrote that her aim is to "find a knife sharp enough to cut through the fiction of our independence" (p. xiii). Similarly, Koggel (1998) suggested
that, instead of asking what independent, autonomous agents need, a relationship approach to equality asks what moral persons embedded in relationships of interdependency should have to flourish.

Due to the routinized forms of noninvolvement of teachers in real decision making and the disruption of top–down high-stakes reform pressures,
Herr (2000) advocated asking teachers to name their own concerns. Saavedra (2000) recommended that teachers: not privilege external expert
knowledge aligned with corporate interests, refuse to become disempow-

ered technicians, quit allowing themselves to be pathologized, discontinue unhealthy competitiveness with each other, and fight oppressive control forced on them by somebody else's idea of reform. Seeing the need for solidarity and authentic partnerships among teachers, Saavedra suggested they join teachers' movements. An example of teacher activism is the Florida teachers who traveled 6 hours to return their bonuses (for students' high scores) to Governor Jeb Bush to focus attention on what they see as a misuse of the Florida Comprehensive Achievement test to rank schools (FairTest, Winter 1999–2000b). Teachers' fight for equity and social justice must be joined by others. For activism to succeed, it must have the critical mass necessary for an effective social movement (Marwell & Oliver, 1993; Meyer & Tarrow, 1998; Tarrow, 1998). Activism requires commitment, hard work, and especially the bravery to leave the privileged center of mainstream life and confront it. Social movements are necessarily extra institutional; for durable change, they must disrupt rather than interrupt dominant practice (Katzenstein, 1998).

Although I assign a thinking and theorizing role broadly to all humans, it is necessary that those paid to set trends in academia or lead in schools should be held most accountable for deep, critical thinking about improving life circumstances for citizens. For Gramsci, intellectuals are consciously reflective social analysts (who interrogate their own tacit knowledge and class-embedded ideologies), and the test for intellectual production was the extent to which it fused with the life of the masses, mobilizing them to think critically about their circumstances (Martin, 1998). Freire (1973, 1985, 1989) infused consciousness raising into literacy instruction. Said (1994) claimed that real intellectuals are moved by metaphysical passions about disinterested principles of justice and truth—they denounce corruption, defend the weak, and defy imperfect or oppressive authority. Mills' (1963) intellectuals had impassioned social visions. Scatamburlo (1998) echoed Marx's call for ruthless criticism of everything that exists—that is not afraid of its own conclusions nor of conflict with existing power relations. Harvey (1996) argued that, although it is dangerous in academia to confess to being meta about anything, he believes the grand, metanarratives about social equity (e.g, Marxism) and Enlightenment ideals of equality and justice are relevant to today's society. Walkerdine (2000) recommended creating new spaces in which people can reinvent themselves (and Others) in more positive ways. She noted that as subject positions change for women, men must be prepared to cope with the loss of a particular kind of masculinity. In a similar vein, new roles and identities must be developed for the traditionally oppressed and the traditional oppressors.

Hence, those of us in the center of mainstream social life must be willing to give up material and status advantage so that egalitarian ideals might be realized. We scholars should not be exempt from our own critical insights

(Bourdieu, 1998). In terms of readiness for change, Harvey (1996) asserted: "It transpires that there is not a region in the world where manifestations of anger and discontent with the capitalist system cannot be found" (p. 430). Rather than drifting passively (Eliasoph, 1998), it is time to take stock of trends and make deliberate democratic decisions about the future (Elster, 1998). Oettingen (1996) suggested that people generate positive fantasies and mental images depicting future events and scenarios; that optimism has beneficial effects on motivation, cognition, and affect. Schudson (1998) advocated the need to capture the national imagination with a large moral mission. In this chapter, I have asked who benefits from high-stakes testing. I have shown how we, as members of the educated class, are complicit in hierachies. I ask readers to join a countermovement to oppose stratifying measures and work to overcome hierarchical and excluding relations in school and society.

REFERENCES

Ahmad, A. (1992). *In theory: Classes, nations, literatures.* London: Verso.

Ansalone, G. (2001). Schooling, tracking, and inequality. *Journal of Children & Poverty, 7,* 33–47.

Anyon, J. (1997). *Ghetto schooling: A political economy of urban educational reform.* New York: Teachers College Press.

Anyon, J. (2000, April 25). *Political economy of an affluent suburban school district: Only some students get the best.* Paper presented at the American Educational Research Association annual meeting, New Orleans, LA.

Apfelbaum, E. (1999). Relations of domination and movements for liberation: An analysis of power between groups. *Feminism & Psychology, 9,* 267–272.

Appadurai, A. (1997). *Modernity at large: Cultural dimensions of globalization.* Minneapolis, MN: University of Minnesota Press.

Apple, M. W. (1993). *Official knowledge.* New York: Routledge.

Apple, M. W. (2003, April 21). *Education the right way: Markets, standards, God, and inequality.* Paper presented at the American Educational Research Association annual meeting, Chicago, IL.

Apter, T. (1996). Expert witness: Who controls the psychologist's narrative? In R. Josselson (Ed.), *Ethics and process in the narrative study of lives* (pp. 22–44). Thousand Oaks, CA: Sage.

Artiles, A. J., & Trent, S. (1994). Overrepresentation of minority students in special education: A continuing debate. *Journal of Special Education, 27,* 410–437.

Associated Press. (2000, April 30). Summit to address failure rates among black students. *Bloomington Herald Times,* p. C3.

Associated Press. (2000, June 8). Cheating teachers increasingly common: Emphasis on top test scores fuels adult deception, critics say. *Bloomington Herald Times,* p. A4.

Associated Press. (2002, September 16). Review finds lack of commitment to school reform. *Herald Times,* p. A5.

Associated Press. (2003, August 24). Thousands of Florida kids held back because of test. *Hoosier Times* p. A10.

Bakhtin, M. (1981). *The dialogic imagination* (C. Emerson & M. Holquist, Trans.). Austin, TX: University of Texas Press. (Original work published 1975)

Ball, S., Kenny, A., & Gardiner, D. (1990). Literacy, politics, and the teaching of English. In I. Goodson & P. Medway (Eds.), *Bringing English to order* (pp. 47–86). London: Falmer.

Bartlett, L., Frederick, M., Gulbrandsen, T., & Murillo, E. (2002). The marketization of education: Public schools for private ends. *Anthropology and Education Quarterly, 33*, 5–29.

Baumeister, R. F. (1996). Self-regulation and ego threat: Motivated cognition, self-deception, and destructive goal setting. In P. M. Gollwitzer & J. A. Bargh (Eds.), *The psychology of action: Linking cognition and motivation to behavior* (pp. 27–47). New York: Guilford.

Becker, H. (1963). *Outsiders: Studies in the sociology of deviance.* New York: The Free Press.

Bellamy, E. J. (1998). "Intimate enemies": Psychoanalysis, Marxism, and postcolonial affect. In R. Miklitsch (Special Issues Ed.), *Psycho-Marxism: Marxism and psychoanalysis late in the twentieth century* (pp. 341–359). *South Atlantic Quarterly, 97*(2).

Berliner, D. (2000, November 14). *What business ought to be concerned about in American education.* Indiana University School of Education Distinguished Lecture Series.

Berliner, D. (2003, April 22). *A state-by-state analysis of the impact of high-stakes accountability policies on academic performance.* Paper presented at the American Educational Research Association annual meeting, Chicago, IL.

Berliner, D. C., & Biddle, B. J. (1995). *The manufactured crisis: Myths, fraud, and the attack on America's public schools.* Reading, MA: Addison-Wesley.

Bersoff, D. M. (1999). Explaining unethical behavior among people motivated to act prosocially. *Journal of Moral Education, 28*, 413–428.

Bourdieu, P. (1977). *Outline of a theory of practice.* Cambridge, England: Cambridge University Press.

Bourdieu, P. (1984). *Distinction: A social critique of the judgement of taste.* Cambridge, MA: Harvard University Press.

Bourdieu, P. (1996). *The state nobility: Elite schools in the field of power* (with M. de Saint Martin; L. C. Clough, Trans.). Stanford, CA: Stanford University Press.

Bourdieu, P. (1998). *Acts of resistance against the tyranny of the market.* New York: New Press.

Boutwell, C. E. (1997). *Shell game: Corporate America's agenda for schools.* Bloomington, IN: Phi Delta Kappa.

Bowles, S., & Gintis, H. (1976). *Schooling in capitalist America.* New York: Basic Books.

Bracey, G. W. (1997). *The truth about America's schools: The Bracey reports, 1991–1997.* Bloomington, IN: Phi Delta Kappa.

Bracey, G. W. (2000). The TIMSS "final year" study and report: A critique. *Educational Researcher, 29*, 4–10.

Brandau, D. M., & Collins, J. (1994). Texts, social relations, and work-based skepticism about schooling: An ethnographic analysis. *Anthropology & Education Quarterly, 25*, 118–136.

Brantlinger, E. A. (1985). What low-income parents want from schools: A different view of aspirations. *Interchange, 16*, 14–28.

Brantlinger, E. A. (1986). Making decisions about special education: Do low-income parents have the information they need? *Journal of Learning Disabilities, 20*, 95–101.

Brantlinger, E. A. (1993). *The politics of social class in secondary schools: Views of affluent and impoverished youth.* New York: Teachers College Press.

Brantlinger, E. A. (1996). The influence of preservice teachers' beliefs about pupil achievement on attitudes toward inclusion. *Teacher Education and Special Education, 19*, 17–33.

Brantlinger, E. A. (1997). Using ideology: Cases of non-recognition of the politics of research and practice in special education. *Review of Educational Research, 67*, 425–460.

Brantlinger, E. A. (1999a). Class moves in the movies: What *Good Will Hunting* teaches about social life. *Journal of Curriculum Theorizing, 15*, 105–120.

Brantlinger, E. A. (1999b). Inward gaze and activism as moral next steps in inquiry. *Anthropolgy & Education Quarterly, 30*, 413–429.

Brantlinger, E. (2003). *Dividing classes: How the middle class negotiates and rationalizes school advantage.* New York: Routledge Falmer.

Britzman, D. P. (1992). Teachers under suspicion: Is it true that teachers aren't as good as they used to be? In J. L. Kincheloe & S. R. Steinberg (Eds.), *Thirteen questions: Reframing education's conversation* (pp. 73–80). New York: Lang.

Brown, D. E. (1991). *Human universals.* Philadelphia: Temple University Press.

Brown, D. K. (1995). *Degrees of control: A sociology of educational expansion and occupational credentialism.* New York: Teachers College Press.

Caplan, P. J. (1995). *They say you're crazy.* Reading, MA: Addison-Wesley.

Capshew, J. H. (1999). *Psychologists on the march: Science, practice, and professional identity in America, 1929–1969.* Cambridge: Cambridge University Press.

Carlson, D., & Apple, M. W. (1998). Introduction. In D. Carlson & M. W. Apple (Eds.), *Power/knowledge/pedagogy: The meaning of democratic education in unsettling times* (pp. 1–38). Boulder, CO: Westview.

Chazan, D. (2000). *Beyond formulas: Mathematics and teaching: Dynamics of the high school algebra class.* New York: Teachers College Press.

Conley, D. (1999). *Being black, living in the red: Race, wealth, and social policy in America.* Berkeley: University of California Press.

Connor, M. H., & Boskin, J. (2001). Overrepresentation of bilingual and poor children in special education classes: A continuing problem. *Journal of Children & Poverty, 7,* 23–32.

Dale, R. (2001). Globalization and education: Demonstrating a "common world educational culture" or locating a "globally structured educational agenda"? *Educational Theory, 50,* 427–448.

Danforth, S. (1996). Autobiography as critical pedagogy: Locating myself in class-based oppression. *Teaching Education, 9,* 3–14.

Delpit, L. (1995). *Other people's children: Cultural conflict in the classroom.* New York: New Press.

Demerath, P. (2003). Negotiating individualist and collectivist futures: Emerging subjectivities and social forms in Papua New Guinean high schools. *Anthropology and Education Quarterly, 34*(2), 136–157.

Eagleton, T. (1990). *The ideology of the aesthetic.* Oxford: Basil Blackwell.

Editors of *Rethinking Schools* (2000). A vision of school reform. *Rethinking Schools, 14,* 27.

Ehrenreich, B. (2001). *Nickel and dimed: On (not) getting by in America.* New York: Henry Holt.

Eliasoph, N. (1998). *Avoiding politics: How Americans produce apathy in everyday life.* Cambridge: Cambridge University Press.

Elster, J. (1998). Introduction. In J. Elster (Ed.), *Deliberative democracy* (pp. 1–18). Cambridge: Cambridge University Press.

Epstein, D., & Steinberg, D. L. (1997). Love's labours: Playing it straight on the Oprah Winfrey show. In D. L. Steinberg, D. Epstein, & R. Johnson (Eds.), *Border patrols: Policing the boundaries of heterosexuality* (pp. 32–65). London: Cassell.

FairTest (1999–2000a, Winter). Court rules for high-stakes Texas test. *Examiner, 14*(1), 11.

FairTest (1999–2000b, Winter). Florida teachers refuse bonuses for high test scores. *Examiner, 14,* 5.

Fine, M. (1991). *Framing dropouts: Notes on the politics of an urban public hihh school.* Albany: State University of New York Press.

Foucault, M. (1977). *Discipline and punish: The birth of the prison.* Harmondsworth: Penguin.

Foucault M. (1980). *Power/knowledge: Selected interviews and other writings 1972–1977* (Colin Gordon, Ed.) New York: Pantheon.

Freire, P. (1973). *Education for critical consciousness.* New York: Seabury.

Freire, P. (1985). *The politics of education: Culture, power, and liberation.* South Hadley, MA: Bergin & Garvey.

Freire, P. (1989). *Pedagogy of the oppressed.* New York: Continuum.

Gamoran, A., & Hannigan, E. C. (2000). Algebra for everyone? Benefits of college-preparatory mathematics for students with diverse abilities in early secondary school. *Educational Evaluation and Policy Analysis, 22,* 241–245.

Garmarnikow, E., & Green, T. (2000, April 25). *Social capital, social class, citizenship and educational policy under new labor.* Paper presented at the American Educational Research Association annual meeting, New Orleans, LA.

Glasser, T. L., & Bowers, P. J. (1999). Justifying change and control: An application of discourse ethics to the role of mass media. In D. Demers & K. Viswanath (Eds.), *Mass media, social control, and social change: A macrosocial perspective* (pp. 399–418). Ames, IA: Iowa State University Press.

Goffman, E. G. (1963). *Stigma: Notes on the management of spoiled identity.* Englewood Cliffs, NJ: Prentice-Hall.

Gordon, M., & Keiser, S. (Eds.). (1998). *Accommodations in higher education under the Americans with Disabilities Act.* New York: Guilford.

Gouldner, A. W. (1979). *The future of intellectuals and the rise of the new class.* New York: Seabury.

Gramsci, A. (1971/1929–1935). *Selections from the prison notebooks* (Q. Hoare & G. N. Smith, Eds.). New York: International Publishers.

Harry, B. (1994). *The disproportionate representation of minority students in special education: Theories and recommendations.* Alexandria, VA: National Association of State Directors of Special Education.

Harry, B., & Anderson, M. G. (1995). The disproportionate placement of African American males in special education programs: A critique of the process. *Journal of Negro Education, 63,* 602–619.

Harvey, D. (1996). *Justice, nature and the geography of difference.* Cambridge, MA: Blackwell.

Hatton, E. (1997). Teacher educators and the production of bricoleurs: An ethnographic study. *Qualitative Studies in Education, 10,* 237–257.

Henry, A. (1995). Growing up black, female, and working class: A teacher's narrative. *Anthropology & Education Quarterly, 26,* 279–305.

Herr, K. (2000, April 26). *Creating change from within: One school's dance with district mandates and school-wide inquiry.* Paper presented at the American Educational Research Association annual meeting, New Orleans, Louisiana.

Herrnstein, R. & Murray, C. (1994). *The Bell Curve.* New York: The Free Press.

Jencks, C., & Phillips, M. (Eds.). (1998). *The Black–White test score gap.* Baltimore, MD: Brookes.

Kailin, J. (2000, April 27). *The hidden dimensions of liberal racism: An anti-racist response.* Paper presented at the American Educational Research Association annual meeting, New Orleans, LA.

Katzenstein, M. F. (1998). Stepsisters: Feminist movement activism in different institutional spaces. In D. S. Meyer (Ed.). *The social movement society: Contentious politics for a new century* (pp. 195–216). Lanham, MD: Rowman & Littlefield.

Keddie, N. (1973). *The myth of cultural deprivation.* London: Penguin.

Kittay, E. F. (1999). *Love's labor: Essays on women, equality, and dependency.* New York and London: Routledge.

Kliebard, H. (1986). *The struggle for the American curriculum: 1893–1958.* Boston: Routledge & Kegan Paul.

Koggel, C. M. (1998). *Perspectives on equality: Constructing a relational theory.* Lanham, MD: Rowman & Littlefield.

Kohn, A. (1998). Only for my kid: How privileged parents undermine school reform. *Phi Delta Kappan,* pp. 569–577.

Kozol, J. (1991). *Savage inequalities: Children in America's schools.* New York: HarperPerennial.

Kozol, J. (2001, April 25). *Book review: Ordinary resurrections.* CSPAN, Primetime.

Kunstler, J. H. (2000, May 20). *Can America survive suburbia?* Talk at Bloomington Convention Center. Sponsored by Bloomington Restorations, Bloomington, IN.

Kutchins, H., & Kirk, S. A. (1997). *Making us crazy: DSM. The psychiatric bible and the creation of mental disorders.* New York: The Free Press.

Labaree, D. F. (1997). *How to succeed in school without really learning: The credentials race in American education.* New Haven, CT: Yale University Press.

Lane, L. (2000, April 7). ISTEP results. *Bloomington Herald Tribune,* pp. A1, A9.

Langenfeld, K., Thurlow, M., & Scott, D. (1997). High stakes testing for students: Unanswered questions and implications for students with disabilities. *NCEO Synthesis Report, 26.*

Lauder, H., & Hughes, D. (1999). *Trading in futures: Why markets in education don't work.* Buckingham: Open University Press.

Leistyna, P. (1999). *Presence of mind: Education and the politics of deception.* Boulder, CO: Westview.

Losen, D. J., & Orfield, G. (2002). *Racial inequality in special education.* Cambridge, MA: Harvard University Press.

MacLeod, J. (1987). *Ain't no making it: Leveled aspirations in low-income neighborhoods.* Boulder, CO: Westview.

Martin, H. P., & Schumann, H. (1997). *The global trap.* New York: Zed Books.

Martin, J. (1998). *Gramsci's political analysis: A critical introduction.* New York: St. Martin.

Marwell, G., & Oliver, P. (1993). *The critical mass in collective action: A micro-social theory.* Cambridge: Cambridge University Press.

McChesney, R. W. (1997). *Corporate media and the threat to democracy.* New York: Seven Stories Press.

McChesney, R. W. (1999). *Rich media, poor democracy.* Champaign, IL: University of Illinois Press.

McDermott, R. P., & Varenne, H. (1996). Culture, development, disability. In R. Jessor, A. Colby, & R. A. Shweder (Eds.), *Ethnography and human development: Context and meaning in social inquiry* (pp. 101–126). Chicago & London: University of Chicago.

McGill-Franzen, A., & Allington, R. L. (1993). Flunk 'em or get them classified. *Educational Research, 22,* 19–22.

McLeod, D. M., & Hertog, J. K. (1999). Social control, social change and the mass media's role in the regulation of protest groups. In D. Demers & K. Viswanath (Eds.), *Mass media, social control, and social change: A macrosocial perspective* (pp. 305–330). Ames, IA: Iowa State University Press.

McNeil, L. (1995). Local reform initiatives as national curriculum: Where are the children? In L. McNeil (Ed.), *The hidden consequences of a national curriculum* (pp. 13–46). Washington, DC: American Educational Research Association.

McNeil, L. (2000). The educational costs of standardization. *Rethinking Schools, 14,* 8–13.

Medovoi, L. (2002). Globalization as narrative and its three critiques. *The Review of Education, Pedagogy, and Cultural Studies, 24,* 63–75.

Mehan, H., Hubbard, L., & Villanueva, I. (1994). Forming academic identities: Accommodation without assimilation among involuntary minorities. *Anthropology & Education Quarterly, 25,* 91–117.

Meier, D. (1994, Winter). A talk to teachers. *Dissent,* pp. 80–87.

Meier, D. (2000, June 12). Interview: Do tests hurt poor kids? *Newsweek,* p. 79.

Mercer, J. R. (1973). *Labeling the mentally retarded.* Berkeley: University of California Press.

Metcalf, S. (2002, January 28). Reading between the lines: The new education law is a victory for Bush and for his corporate allies. *The Nation, 274,* 18–22.

Meyer, D. S., & Tarrow, S. (1998). *The social movement society: Contentious politics for a new century.* Lanham, MD; Rowman & Littlefield.

Mickelson, R. A. (1993). Minorities and education in plural societies. *Anthropology & Education Quarterly, 24,* 269–276.

Miller, A. (1986). *For your own good: Hidden cruelty in child-rearing and the roots of violence.* New York: The Noonday Press.

Mills, C. W. (1943). The professional ideology of social pathologies. *American Journal of Sociology, XLIX,* 165–180.

Mills, C. W. (1963). *Power, politics, and people: The collected essays of C. Wright Mills* (I. L. Horowitz, Ed.). New York: Ballantine.

Mortimore, P., & Mortimore, J. (1999). The political and the professional in education: An unnecessary conflict? In J. S. Gaffney & B. J. Askew (Eds.), *Stirring the waters: The influence of Marie Clay* (pp. 221–238). Portsmouth, NH: Heinemann.

Nagel, T. (1986). *The view from nowhere.* New York: Oxford University Press.

Neill, M. (2000, April 28). *The nature and consequences of high-stakes testing in a time of global reaction.* Paper presented at the American Educational Research Association annual meeting, New Orleans, LA.

Newman, K. (1998). *Falling from grace: The experience of downward mobility in the American middle class.* New York: Vintage.

Nielsen, H. D. (1997). Preface. In H. D. Nielsen & W. K. Cummings (Eds.), *Quality education for all: Community-oriented approaches* (pp. ix–x). New York & London: Garland.

Noddings, N. (1994). Foreword. In C. M. Brody & J. Wallace (Eds.), *Ethical and social issues in professional education* (pp. ix–x). Albany: State University of New York Press.

Noddings, N. (2000, April 27). *Address to Division B annual meeting.* At the American Educational Research Association annual meeting, New Orleans, LA.

Oakes, J., & Guiton, G. (1995). Matchmaking: The dynamics of high school tracking decisions. *American Educational Research Journal, 32,* 3–33.

Oakes, J., Quartz, K. H., Ryan, S., & Lipton, M. (2000). *Becoming good American schools: The struggle for civic virtue in school reform.* San Francisco: Jossey-Bass.

O'Brien, J. (1998). Introduction. In J. O'Brien & J. A. Howard (Eds.), *Everyday inequalities: Critical inquiries* (pp. 1–39). Malden, MA: Blackwell.

Oettingen, G. (1996). Positive fantasy and motivation. In P. M. Gollwitzer & J. A. Bargh (Eds.), *The psychology of action: Linking cognition and motivation to behavior* (pp. 236–259). New York: Guilford.

Ogbu, J. U. (1995). Understanding cultural diversity and learning. In J. A. Banks & C. A. Banks (Eds.), *Handbook of research on multicultural education* (pp. 582–593). New York: Macmillan.

Ohanian, S. (1999). *One size fits few: The folly of educational standards.* Westport, CT: Heinemann.

Oliver, M. L., & Shapiro, T. M. (1995). *Black wealth/white wealth.* New York: Routledge.

O'Neill, P. T. (2001). Special education and high stakes testing: An analysis of current law and policy. *Journal of Law & Education, 30,* 185–221.

Orfield, G. (2000, April 27). *What have we learned from school reconstitution?* Paper presented at the American Educational Research Association annual meeting, New Orleans, LA.

Osbourne, A. B. (1996). Practice into theory into practice: Culturally relevant pedagogy for students we have marginalized and normalized. *Anthropology & Education Quarterly, 27,* 285–314.

Patton, J. M. (1998). The disproportionate representation of African Americans in special education: Looking behind the curtain for understanding and solutions. *The Journal of Special Education, 32,* 25–31.

Patton, J. M. (2004). The disproportionate representation of African Americans in special education: Looking behind the curtain for understanding and solutions. In S. Danforth & S. Taff (Eds.), *Crucial readings in special education* (pp. 164–172). Upper Saddle River, NJ: Pearson.

Pinar, W. (2002, September 9). *What is curriculum theory? Anti-intellectualism in schools of education.* Miller Lecture Series, Indiana University.

Polanyi, K. (1957). *The great transformation.* Boston: Beacon.

Rawls, J. (1971). *A theory of justice.* Cambridge, MA: Harvard University Press.

Ray, C. A., & Mickelson, R. A. (1990). Corporate leaders, resistant youth, and school reform in Sunbelt City: The political economy of education. *Social Problems, 37,* 178–190.

Reynolds, A. J., & Wolfe, B. (1999). Special education and school achievement: An exploratory analysis with a central-city sample. *Educational Evaluation and Policy Analysis, 21,* 249–269.

Rizvi, F., & Lingard, B. (2001). Globalization and education: Complexities and contingencies. *Educational Theory, 50,* 419–426.

Rochon, T. R. (1998). *Culture moves: Ideas, activism, and changing values.* Princeton, NJ: Princeton University Press.

Rorty, R. (1997). *Achieving our country: Leftist thought in twentieth-century America.* Cambridge: Harvard University Press.

Rose, N. (1996). The death of the social? Refiguring the territory of government. *Economy and Society, 25,* 327–356.

Rothstein, R. (1999). *The way we were? The myths and realities of America's student achievement.* A Century Foundation Report.

Ryan, R. M., Sheldon, K. M., Kasser, T., & Deci, E. L. (1996). All goals are not created equal: An organismic perspective on the nature of goals and their regulation. In P. M. Gollwitzer & J. A. Bargh (Eds.), *The psychology of action: Linking cognition and motivation to behavior* (pp. 7–26). New York: Guilford.

Ryan, W. (1971). *Blaming the victim.* New York: Random House.

Saavedra, E. (2000, April 27). *Teacher study groups as contexts for transformative learning and practice.* Paper presented at the American Educational Research Association annual meeting, New Orleans, LA.

Said, E. (1994). *Representations of the intellectual: The 1993 Reith lectures.* London: Vintage.

Sassen, S. (1998). *Globalization and its discontents.* New York: New Press.

Scatamburlo, V. L. (1998). *Soldiers of misfortune: The New Right's culture war and the politics of political correctness.* New York: Peter Lang.

Schnog, N. (1997). On inventing the psychological. In J. Pfister & N. Schnog (Eds.), *Inventing the psychological: Toward a cultural history of emotional life in America* (pp. 3–16). New Haven, CT: Yale University Press.

Schudson, M. (1998). *The good citizen: A history of American civic life.* Cambridge, MA: Harvard University Press.

Seiler, G., & Tobin, K. (2000, April 26). *Students' perceptions of repression, social justice, and failure to learn science in an inner city high school.* Paper presented at the annual meeting of the American Educational Research Association, New Orleans, LA.

Shanahan, J., & Jones, V. (1999). Cultivation and social control. In D. Demers & K. Viswanath (Eds.), *Mass media, social control, and social change: A macrosocial perspective* (pp. 31–50). Ames, IA: Iowa State University Press.

Shapiro, S. B. (1999). *Pedagogy and the politics of the body: A critical praxis.* New York: Garland.

Sleeter, C. E. (2000, April 28). *Keeping the lid on: Multicultural curriculum and the organization of consciousness.* American Educational Research Association annual meeting, New Orleans, LA.

Sleeter, C. E., Gutierrez, W., New, C. A., & Takata, S. R. (1992). Race and education: In what ways does race affect the educational process? In J. L. Kincheloe & S. R. Steinberg (Eds.), *Thirteen questions: Reframing education's conversation* (pp. 173–182). New York: Lang.

Smith, T. J. (1997, March). *Storying moral dimensions of disordering: Teacher inquiry into the social construction of severe emotional disturbance.* Paper presented at American Educational Research Association annual meeting, Chicago, IL.

Smyth, J., & Shacklock, G. (1998). *Re-making teaching: Ideology, policy and practice.* London & New York: Routledge.

Starratt, R. J. (1994). *Building an ethical school: A practical response to the moral crisis in schools.* London: Falmer.

Tarrow, S. (1998). *Power in movement; Social movements and contentious politics* (2nd ed.). Cambridge: Cambridge University Press.

Taylor, S., Rizvi, F., Lingard, B., & Henry, M. (1997). *Educational policy and the politics of change.* London and New York: Routledge.

Thompson, J. B. (1984). *Studies in the theory of ideology.* Berkeley: University of California Press.

Thompson, J. B. (1990). *Ideology and modern culture: Critical social theory in the era of mass communication.* Stanford, CA: Stanford University Press.

Troyna, B., & Vincent, C. (1996). "The ideology of expertism": The framing of special education and racial equality policies in the local state. In C. Christensen & F. Rizvi (Eds.), *Disability and the dilemmas of education and justice* (pp. 131–144). Philadelphia: Open University Press.

Tyack, D., & Tobin, W. (1994). The "grammar" of schooling: Why has it been so hard to change? *American Educational Research Journal, 31,* 453–479.

Urban Institute. (2004, February 26). Http://www.urban.org/

U.S. Census. (2001, Sept. 25). Poverty rates up as income inequality increases. *The Herald Times,* p. A4.

U.S. Department of Education (1983). *A nation at risk.* Washington, DC: Author.

U.S. Department of Education. (1991). *America 2000.* Washington, DC: Author.

Valencia, R. (Ed.). (1997). The evolution of deficit thinking: Educational thought and practice. London & Washington, DC: Falmer.

Valencia, R. (Ed.) (1997). *The evolution of deficit thinking: Educational thought and practice.* London and Washington, DC: Falmer.

Valencia, R. R. (2002). The plight of Chicano students: An overview of schooling conditions and outcomes. In R. R. Valencia (Ed.), *Chicano school failure and success: Past, present, future* (2nd ed., pp. 3–51). London & New York: Routledge Falmer.

Valenzuela, A. (1999). *Subtractive schooling: U.S.–Mexican youth and the politics of caring.* Albany: State University of New York Press.

Viswanath, K., & Demers, D. (1999). Mass media from a macrosocial perspective. In D. Demers & K. Viswanath (Eds.), *Mass media, social control, and social change: A macrosocial perspective* (pp. 3–30). Ames, IA: Iowa State University Press.

Vygotsky, L. S. (1978). *Mind in society.* Cambridge, MA: Harvard University Press.

Walkerdine, V. (2000, April 26). *Feminist and critical perspectives on education and psychology.* Paper presented at the American Educational Research Association annual meeting, New Orleans, LA.

Weis, L., & Fine, M. (1996). Narrating the 1980s and 1990s: Voices of poor and working-class white and African American men. *Anthropology & Education Quarterly, 27,* 493–516.

Wells, A. S. (2000, April 26). *When local control meets the free market: School choice policy for the new millennium.* Paper presented at the American Educational Research Association annual meeting, New Orleans, LA.

Wenglinsky, H. (1998). Finance equalization and within-school equity: The relationship between education spending and the social distribution of achievement. *Educational Evaluation and Policy Analysis, 20,* 269–283.

Whitty, G. (2000, April 25). *Schooling and the reproduction of the English middle classes.* Paper presented at the American Educational Research Association annual meeting, New Orleans, LA.

Willis, P. (1977). *Learning to labor: How working class kids get working class jobs.* New York: Columbia University Press.

Wilson, W. J. (1996). *When work disappears: The new world of the urban poor.* New York: Knopf.

Wright, E. O. (Ed.). (1985). *Classes.* London/New York: Verso.

Wright, S. E. (1993). Blaming the victim, blaming society, or blaming the discipline: Fixing responsibility for poverty and homelessness. *The Sociology Quarterly, 34,* 1–16.

Young, I. M. (1990). *Justice and the politics of difference.* Princeton: Princeton University Press.

Young, I. M. (2000). *Inclusion and democracy.* Oxford: Oxford University Press.

Zizek, S. (1994). Introduction: The spectre of ideology. In S. Zizek (Ed.), *Mapping ideology* (pp. 1–33). London/New York: Verso.

Chapter 10

Conclusion: Whose Labels? Whose Norms? Whose Needs? Whose Benefits?

Ellen Brantlinger
Indiana University, Bloomington

IDENTITY RESOURCES FOR OTHER PEOPLE'S CHILDREN

In studying a comprehensive girls school in England, Benjamin (2002) found that the students identified as disabled had few positive identity resources available to them. Given the oppressive nature of American schools for poor children and children of color, it is difficult for them to acquire an acceptable identity that recognizes their strengths, is located in reality, joins them with others, reflects their inner being, and leads to the realization of their potential. Clearly, for children in subordinate positions, these unresolved identity issues cause conflict, stress, and crisis (Erikson, 1968; Maslow, 1970). The problem with identity construction is that, regardless of individuals' identity aspirations, identity is never entirely under their personal control. Identity is "socially bestowed, socially sustained, and socially transformed" (Berger, 1963, p. 98). Studying how labeling dynamics fix identity categories, Becker (1963) contended that privileged social groups maintain their status by creating rules (norms) by which outsiders' behaviors are seen as infractions constituting deviance and those seen as deviant are labeled with stigmatizing names. Labeling is about politics, power, and representation. Hudak (2001) noted that, from a clinical perspective, labeling results in a "false" (imposed, rejected) self (identity) that is "personally dislocating and fragmenting" (p. 21). Children fight the stigma and pain of denigrating labels to feel "real and alive, not isolated and alienated" (p. 19).

A widespread discourse with powerful effects that remains obscured by normative practice is ableism (Hehir, 2002). Ableism is assumed and rather obscure norms that provide the basis for labeling children as disabled. Disability cannot be extracted from the social world that produces it (McDermott & Varenne, 1996; Mehan, 1992). Unfortunately, American professionals are oriented toward distinction-making; they compulsively stress the importance of normality and are crazy about labeling (Armstrong, 1993; Caplan, 1995; Capshew, 1999; Kutchins & Kirk, 1997). Given the prevalence and popularity of the medical model that situates problems in students rather than systems and structures, Armstrong (1993) conjectured that once medical-scientific language is used to talk about emotional or behavioral issues, professionals begin to believe that they know what they are talking about when they are actually speaking in tongues. That children are unhappy with labels and about being stuck in special education has been well documented (Brantlinger, 1993; Rodis, Garrod, & Boscardin, 2001; T. J. Smith & Danforth, 2000). Yet the harmful side effects of labeling are largely ignored in professional communities. Because much special education scholarship is focused on delineating the nature and causes of disability and on perfecting remedial interventions, Disability Studies scholar Oliver (2004) argued that special education research has had little constructive influence on policy and has made no contribution to improving the lives of people with disabilities. Rather, such research has been alienating for them as well as for researchers. Oliver uses alienation in the original Marxist sense to refer to the process whereby workers become estranged from products they produce. Disability is alienating for the person so labeled as well as those with the power to classify.

Addressing teachers' "unintended cruelties," T. J. Smith and Danforth (2000) cited letters written by adolescents and adults to former teachers whose instructional and interactional styles made them feel uncomfortable, unworthy, and angry. Their criticism generally was aimed at teachers' use of evaluation as a tool of stratification and ways they found deficits in them. Using the phrase *ability profiling* for the overrepresentation of children of color in special education, Collins (2003) described the case of a fifth-grade African-American boy in a southern rural school who was angry about his learning disability classification and exclusion from the general classroom. He struggled to be seen as competent after receiving his stigmatizing label. A. Smith (2001) illustrated how identity emerges as a construct of language and how classifications create a kind of fiction that alienates people from the complex interplay of differences within themselves and between themselves and others. She included poignant narratives of a second-grade African-American boy, identified and placed as emotionally disturbed, who desperately wanted out of special education. Early and continuing problematic experiences, stereotyping, labeling, and tracking influence African-American males' achievement and coping strategies (Ferguson, 2000; Swanson, Cunningham, & Spencer, 2003). Such negative educational practices constitute violence against children (Block, 1997). The damage is cognitive as well as affective. Dewey (1910) wrote of

> children who begin with something to say and an intellectual eagerness to say it are sometimes made so conscious of minor errors in substance and form that the energy that should go into constructive thinking is diverted into anxiety not to make mistakes, and even, in extreme cases, into passive quiescence as the best method of minimizing error. (p. 186)

Kaufman (2001), a college professor, told of her "personal experience of oppression" when she was held back in first grade because of social immaturity. Kaufman *knew* it was her "own fault," but ironically it was "this consciousness of agency" that made her feel powerless (p. 47). A sense of loss of self kept her from taking risks—she did not want to expose herself as stupid. Controlling others' perceptions of her and containing feelings of insecurity became driving forces in her grade school life. The "toxic runoff" from the stigma of flunking shaped how she came to know the world. Kaufman argued that, "learning and information are commodified in schools. Students acquire information (rather than knowledge) in order to acquire grades, not to participate increasingly in the larger communities of which they are members" (p. 50). Labaree (1997) claimed that in the consumerist public school system, parents see schools as an investment in their children's future and achievement as a marketable commodity. In such schools, personnel are forced to concentrate on grading, sorting, and selecting students as the means for children to distinguish themselves from others.

As with any hegemonic relation (Gramsci, 1971/1929–1935), subordinates internalize the negative messages about themselves that have been constructed by the actions and ideologies of dominant class individuals. Some lack the power and stamina to protest, so passively fit into degrading and damaging routines. Others resist with actions that are counterproductive to their learning, social adjustment, and future prospects (Willis, 1977). Although most professionals accept the status quo of differential achievement and adjustment and attribute problems to the oppressed (DuBois, 1965; Ryan, 1971; Valencia, 1997; Wright, 1993), others successfully use a Freirian consciousness-raising approach to help students analyze and dismiss damaging views of themselves (see Freire, 1973). Fleischer (2001) studied four special education students in a New York City high school who were caught in webs of discursive official and unofficial formations of violence against themselves comprised of name-calling, blaming, and putdowns. Fleischer learned that, given a trusting environment, with literature

critical of hegemony (dominant group norms), his students became coun-
terhegemonic theorizers who spoke to ways they are stigmatized and marginalized in and by special programs. They could also imagine alternatives
to the system that had humiliated them. Pruyn (1999) used similar teaching
methods with Los Angeles youth.

UBIQUITY OF THE NEED TO NAME AND SORT

During years of going to inner-city schools with preservice teachers for a se-
mester-long practicum, I noticed that teachers had what my students and I
came to call *the bad boy chair*—an isolated desk located in the back of the
room, immediately adjacent to the teacher's desk, or facing the opposite
direction from other children's desks. This was not a temporary time-out
chair, but a permanent seating arrangement for a child considered to
be abnormal. Given the high rate of student attrition in this urban district, we found that if the isolate left the classroom (often to be placed in a
self-contained special class), another child soon became the designated
outcast. Teachers seemed to need to identify someone as not part of the
normal group or find exemplars of bad behavior to isolate, ostracize, and
condemn. It may be that students began to reject certain children and
teachers focused on an easy target. Whatever the origin of children's outsider status, once identified, oddballs or pariahs were fair game for bullying, which starts early in schools and is rarely stopped by adults (Bochenek
& Brown, 2001; Ferguson, 2000; Olweus, 1993).

In a middle-school study, Eder, Evans, and Parker (1995) found a rigid
ranking system acted out in spatial segregation in the cafeteria. Cross-group
shunning and within-group teasing were ubiquitous. Youths felt a high degree of insecurity about their own social standing. By joining a group's ridicule, certain students were able to redirect their insecurities outward and
deflect potential negative attention toward themselves. Although some students did not approve, few intervened to protect victims. Isolates experienced considerable stress. A low-income girl assigned to work in the lunchroom had such a strong fear of ridicule or mistreatment that she went to
great lengths to avoid high-status students. Scapegoats were special education students and/or students felt to be unattractive or overweight. Athletes
were particularly prone to using degrading terms about homosexuality and
weak (feminine) behavior.

Wanting and expecting conformity (normativity) and having little tolerance for difference is conjectured to stem from deep psychological needs.
Powers of Horror: An Essay in Abjection (1982) by French linguist and psycho-
analyst Kristeva is an insightful book, but a hard read, so I rely on T. J. Smith
and Danforth's (2000) interpretation of her ideas. Abjection is offered as a
possible explanation for the way apparently healthy and well-adjusted indi-

viduals participate in forms of group-based fear, hatred, and oppression. People engage in intense self-creation work and defend their identity boundaries by constructing exclusionary social codes and a symbolic cultural order that assigns lesser identities to such groups as the poor, women, ethnic minorities, persons considered to have disabilities, gays, and lesbians. In abjection, individuals project impure and offensive nonidentity elements (that's not me!) onto certain Others—either groups or individuals. Within the daily operations of language and culture, humans express loathing and disdain toward Others, producing a regularity of rejection in the social order (discussion adapted from T. J. Smith & Danforth).

In terms of privileging whiteness and racial exclusion (making it normal), Lipsitz (1998) applied an abjection hypothesis to what he called a *possessive investment in Whiteness*. Because Whiteness remains unmarked, White people escape the scrutiny of, and definition by, people of color. This outward gaze serves the vital function of maintaining White privilege by externalizing difference, defining difference from Whiteness as inferiority, and resisting self-examination and critique. White hegemony (racial domination) is maintained by using externalizing and decentering strategies that direct gaze at Others (McLaren, Carrillo-Rowe, Clark, & Craft, 2001).

THE FLAWED LOGIC OF AVERAGE EXPECTATIONS

Why everyone is expected to be the same—or average—is puzzling. Garrison Keillor brags that all Lake Wobegon children are above average, although test experts with faith in the Bell Curve would argue that Minnesota children's high status is a geographical anomaly that cannot be generalized to other states. That educators find Keillor's announcement ludicrous is strange because many educational practices hinge on the premise that children who are not average have risks, special needs, or disabilities. Students who exceed the statistical average are perceived as needy because of their special gifts and talents. Professional life and educational practice revolve around convoluted norms that identify certain children as having needs, risks, and disabilities simply because they are different from others.

The dilemma of expecting all children to be average is that it is an unobtainable goal. Averages can be temporarily fixed on normed tests, yet by definition averages are unstable. If the test scores of children currently behind in skills and knowledge do improve as mandated by *No Child Left Behind* (2001), the average gets pushed up. As the average rises, children who previously had somewhat higher scores as well as ones with improved test scores will still and again be behind. The requirement for children to be average is illogical. No one recommends withholding education from advanced children to reduce their scores to be closer to average. It is ill-advised and counterproductive for low achievers to be penalized with stigmatizing names and isolating placements because their achievement is not as respectable as that of other children. The paradox for low-achieving children is that they are not able to get a general education until they are normal (average), but can never be normal if they are boxed into special education spaces with dummied-down curricula (Ansalone, 2001; Dunn, 1968; Gatto, 1992; Reynolds & Wolfe, 1999; Wells & Crain, 1992). Colucci (2000) found that instructional effects were strongly dependent on track placement. When placed in low tracks, students' achievement gains diminish over time, thus producing further inequality (Carbonaro & Gamoran, 2002). It must be noted that the special education continuum constitutes a highly legalized track system. It is not only wrongheaded for a nation to expect all children to score the same on achievement tests, but counterproductive to give them stigmatizing names, retain them, assign them to differentiated achievement tracks, or deny them such standard rewards as a high school diploma.

A truth that is ignored by some school personnel and most politicians is that averages and norms are theoretical, statistical constructs not meant to define particular children and especially not *all* children. It is normal for children to achieve at various levels, hence children who place anywhere on an achievement continuum are normal. Although it is great for children to be above average in desirable traits and below average in undesirable ones, it is also fine for them to be average. In fact for some to be above average, others must be below average, which should not mean that those below are abnormal. Yet in our present educational ranking systems, some have to be considered subnormal for social hierarchies to survive.

Consensus about the importance of achievement, and imperative of average achievement, is confirmed by the burgeoning of test-prep programs (Brandon, 2003). Previously, cramming was limited to preparing high school students for exams for college admission. Now the private test-prep business has hit grade schools. Testprep curriculum is chosen by nervous personnel at high-achieving schools; it is mandated for the failing public schools largely attended by Other people's children. Brandon claimed that materials designed to prepare third graders for California's standardized test (sold by Kaplan, a leader in the test-preparation industry) are among the most detailed of a new generation of guides for elementary schools. Meeting the demands to be average turns out to be costly and stressful for some and profitable for others.

ABNORMAL PROFITS/PROPHETS

Given the onslaught of tests, test-prep programs, and standardized curriculum packages, it is imperative to ask who benefits from them. Kohn (2003) and Metcalf (2003) exposed how politicians and their networks of cronies benefit from the push for commodified and privatized schooling. Kohn claimed that the financial rating service owned by McGraw-Hill offers to evaluate and publish the performance, based largely on test scores, of every school district in requesting states. Michigan purchased this service for more than $10 million. With pressure to look good on tests, personnel in low-scoring districts feel compelled to purchase heavily scripted commercial curricular packages designed to raise scores. McGraw-Hill is a major manufacturer of standardized tests and instructional materials (Open Court, Reading Mastery, Direct Instruction). It is no coincidence—and should be no surprise—that the Bush and McGraw families have been friends for three generations (Metcalf, 2003). Sizable profits are made by the companies that develop and score virtually all standardized tests to which students and prospective teachers are subjected. Politicians uncritically accept the goals and methods outlined by the private sector, and there is public consensus about the economic rationale for schooling. School-to-work programs endorsed and produced by these corporations are based on ideologies that pave the way for privatizing schools. Miner (2003) argued that privatization is couched in rhetoric that extolls the ability of the marketplace to unleash creativity and innovation. Although skeptical of those claims, Miner argued that privatization is a way companies get their hands on a big share of the $350 billion K–12 education industry. Metcalf pointed out the irony of the political party that once called for the abolition of the Education Department now grappling for a radically enhanced federal (and commercial) presence in public schools.

Inspirational posters aimed at encouraging hope for the future in children with dyslexia and their parents often list important historical figures thought to have had learning disabilities. The current American president has been put in that category by satirists Begala (2000) and Miller (2001). Classified as dyslexic, slow, and backward, the president acted with legislators to endorse the *No Child Left Behind Act* (2001), which demands that all children make annual yearly progress toward the grade-level average. If children designated as failures do not improve, there are serious sanctions for them as well as their teachers, schools, and communities (Worfel, unpublished manuscript). At the same time, Bush's educational plan promises to be a bonanza for testing and literacy product companies.

THOSE AT RISK TO LOSE THEIR NORMAL EDGE

There is evidence that fitting too firmly into normal positions restricts divergent (and logical) thinking and is detrimental to further intellectual development. Dweck (2002) studied what causes smart people to do dumb things and fall behind mentally over time. She concluded that when people are too invested in being smart and think smartness is something they have and others do not have, they concentrate on looking smart rather than on challenging and stretching themselves and expanding their skills in ways needed to continue to learn and grow mentally over time. Dweck noted this happens when intelligence is viewed as a highly valued commodity.

Schmidt (2000) lost his job as an editor of a science journal when he made the charge that typical professional life is not intellectually challenging and allows only the most constrained creativity. He further contended that professional socialization into the normative foundational knowledge of disciplines causes stagnation in both intellect and originality. Pinar (2002) similarly accused education schools of having an anti-intellectual climate. Rather than stimulating creative and original thinking, the expectation in teacher education is that teachers and professors should apply what is already known and packaged in available professional resources. Focusing on similar issues, Silberman (1971) wrote that what is mostly wrong with public schools is not due to indifference or stupidity, but to mindlessness. He claimed that only a handful of professionals ask why they are doing what they are doing and think seriously or deeply about the purposes or consequences of education. These scholars indicate that adults in schools may be subjected to unexamined meanings in the same way that students learn the hidden curriculum—the "unstated norms, values, and beliefs transmitted through the underlying structure of meaning in the formal content and the social relations of school and classroom life" (Giroux, 1988, p. 23). It seems that it would be best for both adults and children to unlearn mindless and meaningless content. Older readers might find these claims reminiscent of Ivan Illich's (1971) contentions in *Deschooling Society.* Organizational stagnation is a related issue. If professional and public gazes become normatively fixed, the institutions they oversee become inflexible and irrational. Foucault (1973) claimed that the institutional gaze is bounded by geographical and experiential space so that organizations are vested with relatively stable orientations and resources for humans to use in interpreting themselves.

WHY NOT ACTUAL ISSUES AND VALUED STUDENT CHARACTERISTICS?

While pondering the irrationality of wanting everyone to be average, it is also important to understand why intellectual (racial, behavioral, linguistic) uniformity is valued. Norms and values overlap in meaning and function, "values are the currently held normative expectations underlying individual and social conduct" (Laungani, 1999, p. 191), so "values, like air, pervade our cultural atmosphere, and we imbibe them often without a conscious awareness of their origins" (p. 192). Given the intertwining of norms and values, it is important to think about why school achievement and people who attain high educational levels are so admired and advantaged. Because there is not room at the reified, hence actual, top for everyone, it is curious why socially comprehensive schools' sole focus is on college preparation and advanced educational attainment. Most students feel that much of academic learning—especially that measured on high-stakes standardized tests—is dull and boring (Burkett, 2001). The current test-oriented curriculum is fairly useless to humans in their roles as workers, family members, friends, neighbors, and seekers of enjoyment and fulfillment. Rather than insisting on normal, routine, and homogeneous academic outcomes, it seems that a realistic problem-solving curriculum focused on actual social, medical, and environmental issues would be far better. Plenty of societal problems exist that need attention and undoubtedly will continue to exist because they are not currently being resolved by citizens.

Another major task for comprehensive public schools should be to redistribute rewards for students. Instead of centering on a monolithically and ethnocentrically defined ideal student, schools should be sites where diversity is valued and effective border crossing and cross-border interaction is learned. Diversity makes life interesting. Various kinds of people are needed for diverse societal roles. Unfortunately, schools have long devalued the working class and ignored essential services this class provides. School settings should be designed to enable students to take pride in varied occupations and recognize their respective contributions to communities. Sharp and Green (1975) recommended centering schools' goals on humanistic practices that benefit rather than hinder children. T. J. Smith and Perez (2000) claimed this might be done by relying on teachers' stories about what is good and bad—morals that can be explored from within the contexts of particular lives.

DISCERNING OPPRESSIVE PRACTICE AND ITS FALLOUT

The authors included in this book have tried to disentangle the concept of normal and challenge the ways certain children's needs are established as special. In cutting a wide swath, we trouble entrenched customs and accuse multiple agents—many in high places—of benefiting from policies, practices, and ways of thinking that harm others, and particularly children who do not do well in school. Discourses from within and beyond education are brought together as we attempt to make the point that special educators often unwittingly collude in a complex of disturbing practices that do not benefit those we claim to help. We recommend that school personnel think hard about practices that harm, and turn to a morality of social reciprocity and distributive justice in which the school and life circumstances of the most vulnerable are considered first. By doing this, professionals can work together to transform traditional commodified, hierarchical educational structures and practices. Like Benjamin (2002), we are "interested in sustainable change based on the egalitarian concept of redistribution instead of schools taking part in the production of winners and losers in the games of global capital" (p. 134)

Until ideal children can be cloned, student variation is inevitable. Unless there is support for a justice that equally distributes material resources and social advantage, the norm of cultural/social variation should be expected. Fraser (2003) hypothesized that if economic disparities between individuals and families were reduced, then certain sociocultural distinctions would diminish and perhaps disappear. Relatedly, I. M. Young (2000) discussed the importance of social inclusion to the democratic functioning of societies. A melding of traits and universal inclusion would be an equitable and democratic way to achieve human uniformity. So instead of rushing headlong into the race to be (or exceed) average, the quagmire of children left behind might be resolved if students, parents, teachers, and administrators deliberately avoid the temptation to perceive average as flawed. If solidarity were garnered around everybody being normal, success might be attainable for more children. School might be a gentler, more communal place. Aspiring to be average and ordinary might be valued as democratic.

Among the most troubling aspects of modern education is its increasing dependence on norms and norm-based policies and practices. Indeed norms have come to take precedence over values and intellect in educational decision making. Using test scores and achievement norms to compare and sort children, and rigidly structured curriculum to routinize knowledge, is the order of the day. This control ethos in modern educational bureaucracies privileges the standardization of ethnocentric norms (Brown, 1995). One evident fallout from excessive reliance on norms is the establishment of social class, race, gender, and professional/lay markers that are so strongly fixed that cross-border relations and border crossings—in and out of school—are exceedingly difficult (Lease, McFall, & Viken, 2003). Voices of people who cry out for humane interactions and democratic goals are condemned for "not being objective" or "not conforming" to the economic enhancement purposes of education. The literature is replete with inspiring treatises that recommend socially inclusive communities for children and collaboration among school personnel. Yet Achinstein (2002) found a conflict-filled reality in which schools were poorly coordinated and personnel struggled because of ideological conflicts. She found state and local administrators managed teachers' work culture in a way that made idealistic practices impossible.

Teachers had low and powerless status in a bureaucratic system in which there was a rising trend toward centralization of control through standards, tests, and mandated curriculum requirements.

Critical educators argue that political impositions that insist on systematic surveillance of students and teachers results in their socialization into regimes of boredom. Similarly, mapping children onto rigid and counterproductive psychometric classification grids invents deskilled, classed, and gendered cultures (Luke & Luke, 1995). Luke and Luke credited M. Young (1971) for beginning an ideological critique of the organization and status of school knowledge, and for countering functionalist claims about the neutrality and objectivity of curricular content, cultural transmission, and intensified testing. Leistyna (1999) pointed out that "traditional, conservative, technocratic models that dominate mainstream practice . . . embrace depersonalized methods that often translate into the regulation and standardization of school practice" (p. 7).

Despite the widely circulated postmodern discourses in which it is understood that human thought/language/behavior is multileveled, shifting, and inevitably infused with values, ideology, and subjectivity, people—including scholars who by now should be informed by these discourses—find it necessary to establish a nameable, stable, and controllable world and so subscribe to archaic foundational knowledge and legislate stultifying bureaucratic policy. By succumbing to normative discourses that inscribe thoughts and script actions as they comply with the normative routines of schooling (Tomkins, 1995), people ignore deep human values and needs and allow themselves to be stripped of agency. Pinar (2002) criticized the anti-intellectual climate that predominates schools and schools of education. Taylor, Rizvi, Lingard, and Henry (1997) contended that education "is no longer discussed in terms of broad visions and ideals but according to what governments believe to be possible and expedient" (p. 3). Hence, educational policy replaces theory as a source of guidance for practitioners. Taylor and colleagues included poignant stories of teachers and principals who had been happy in their professions, but were increasingly frustrated by the plethora of policies that were thrown at them without their being consulted. Such policies prescribe certain practices so that professionals are not allowed to make difficult moral decisions on a child-by-child basis. Whether the tendency to fix the world concretely and reductively is essential to humans or due to less universal, but still well-established, trends socialized over generations, people in Western societies are now dependent on predetermined ways to name the world and preordained paths to follow. Daily life is turned over to normative gods of conformity.

Our attack on the current overreliance on norms (rather than values and creative intellect) is not based on a naive notion that social life can be free of norms. Norms naturally develop in social contexts and are shaped by language, traditional institutions, and everyday social relations. Norms script people's interactional patterns and mold their expectations. People cannot escape normative influences, yet to some extent critically reflective agents can understand and control the way norms structure their individual or collective life circumstances. New customs and ways of thinking can evolve in response to cultural dissonance and perceived negative practices and outcomes. In other words, people can work to intentionally shape norms. Received knowledge is tenacious; however, humans can question and refuse to comply with socialized patterns that they perceive as not constructive. Through critical inspection—and introspection—norms can be made transparent enough to be confronted and modified. The trick is to get people to reach consensus that particular norms are dysfunctional. People might agree that normative practice is flawed when it causes people pain and grief. Because vast social inequalities are especially egregious in democractic societies, it seems that educators might be convinced to be attuned to the feelings and needs of Other people's children. If they embrace a social reciprocity morality and work toward that morality's ends, the material and status discrepancies between elites and the disadvantaged might be reduced.

REFERENCES

Achinstein, B. (2002). *Community and diversity and conflict among school teachers: The ties that blind.* New York: Teachers College Press.

Ansalone, G. (2001). Schooling, tracking, and inequality. *Journal of Children & Poverty, 7*(1), 33–47.

Armstrong, L. (1993). (1993) *And they call it help: The psychiatric policing of America's children.* Reading, MA: Addison-Wesley.

Becker, H. (1963[1973]). *Outsiders.* New York: The Free Press.

Begala, P. (2000). *"Is our children learning?": The case against Prezident George W. Bush.* New York: Simon & Schuster.

Benjamin, S. (2002). *The micropolitics of inclusive education: An ethnography.* Buckingham: Open University Press.

Berger, P. (1963). *Invitation to sociology.* Garden City, NY: Doubleday.

Block, A. A. (1997). *I'm only bleeding: Education as the practice of violence against children.* New York: Peter Lang.

Bochenek, M., & Brown, A. W. (2001). *Hatred in the hallways: Violence and discrimination against lesbian, gay, bisexual, and transgender students in U.S. schools.* New York: Human Rights Watch.

Brandon, K. (2003). Test-prep pressure hits grade schools. In A. Kohn & P. Shannon (Eds.), *Education, Inc.: Turning learning into a business* (pp. 58–62). Portsmouth, NH: Heinemann.

Brantlinger, E. A. (1993). *The politics of social class in secondary schools: Views of affluent and impoverished youth.* New York: Teachers College Press.

Brown, D. K. (1995). *Degrees of control: A sociology of educational expansion and occupational credentialism.* New York: Teachers College Press.

Burkett, E. (2001). *Another planet: A year in the life of a suburban high school.* New York: Harper-Collins.

Caplan, P. J. (1995). *They say you're crazy.* Reading, MA: Addison-Wesley.

Capshew, J. H. (1999). *Psychologists on the march: Science, practice, and professional identity in America, 1929–1969.* Cambridge: Cambridge University Press.

Carbonaro, W. J., & Gamoran, A. (2002). The production of achievement inequality in high school English. *American Educational Research Journal, 39*(4), 801–827.

Collins, K. M. (2003). *Ability profiling and school failure: One child's struggle to be seen as competent.* Mahwah, NJ: Lawrence Erlbaum Associates.

Colucci, K. (2000). Negative pedagogy. In J. L. Paul & T. J. Smith (Eds.), *Stories out of school: Memories and reflections on care and cruelty in the classroom* (pp. 27–44). Stamford, CT: Ablex.

Dewey, J. (1910). *How we think:. How we think, a restatement of the relation of reflective thinking to the educative process.* Boston: D.C. Heath.

DuBois, W. E. B. (1965). *Souls of Black folk.* New York: Avon.

Dunn, L. M. (1968). Special education for the mildly retarded: Is much of it justifiable? *Exceptional Children, 35,* 5–22.

Dweck, C. S. (2002). Beliefs that make smart people dumb. In R. J. Sternberg (Ed.), *Why smart people can be so stupid* (pp. 24–41). New Haven, CT: Yale University Press.

Eder, D., with C. C. Evans & S. Parker. (1995). *School talk: Gender and adolescent culture.* New Brunswick, NJ: Rutgers University Press.

Erikson, E. (1968). *Identity: Youth and crisis.* New York: Norton.

Ferguson, A. A. (2000). *Bad boys: Public schools in the making of Black masculinity.* Ann Arbor: University of Michigan Press.

Fleischer, L. E. (2001). Special education students as counter-hegemonic theorizers. In G. M. Hudak & P. Kihn (Eds.), *Labeling: Pedagogy and politics* (pp. 115–124). New York: Routledge Falmer.

Foucault, M. (1973). *The birth of the clinic.* London: Routledge.

Fraser, N. (2003). *Redistribution or recognition?: A political-philosophical exchange.* London & New York: Verso.

Freire, P. (1973). *Education for critical consciousness.* New York: Seabury.

Gatto, J. T. (1992). *Dumbing us down: The hidden curriculum of compulsory schooling.* Philadelphia: New Society Publishers.

Giroux, H. A. (1988). *Teachers as intellectuals: Toward a critical pedagogy of learning.* Amherst, MA: Bergin & Garvey.

Gramsci, A. (1971/1929–1935). *Selections from the prison notebooks* (Q. Hoare & G. N. Smith, Eds.). New York: International Publishers. (Original work published, 1929–1935)

Hehir, T. (2002). Eliminating ableism in education. *Harvard Educational Review, 72,* 1–31.

Hudak, G. M. (2001). On what is labeled "playing": Locating the "true" in education. In G. M. Hudak & P. Kihn (Eds.), *Labeling: Pedagogy and politics* (pp. 9–26). New York: Routledge Falmer.

Illich, I. (1971). *Deschooling society.* New York: Harper & Row.

Kaufman, J. S. (2001). The classroom and labeling: "The girl who stayed back." In G. M. Hudak & P. Kihn (Eds.), *Labeling: Pedagogy and politics* (pp. 41–54). New York: Routledge Falmer.

Kohn, A. (2003). Introduction: The 500-pound gorilla. In A. Kohn & P. Shannon (Eds.), *Education, Inc.: Turning learning into a business* (pp. 1–11). Portsmouth, NH: Heinemann.

Kristeva, J. (1982). *Powers of horror: An essay in abjection.* New York: Columbia.

Kutchins, H., & Kirk, S. A. (1997). *Making us crazy: DSM. The psychiatric bible and the creation of mental disorders.* New York: The Free Press.

Labaree, D. F. (1997). *How to succeed in school without really learning: The credentials race in American education.* New Haven, CT: Yale University Press.

Laungani, P. (1999). Cultural influences on identity and behavior: India and Britain. In Y. T. Lee, C. R. McCauley, & J. G. Draguns (Eds.), *Personality and person perception across cultures* (pp. 191–212). Mahwah, NJ: Lawrence Erlbaum Associates.

Lease, A. M., McFall, R. M., & Viken, R. J. (2003). Distance from peers in the group's perceived organizational structure: Relation to individual characteristics. *Journal of Early Adolescence, 23*(2), 194–217.

Leistyna, P. (1999). *Presence of mind: Education and the politics of deception.* Boulder, CO: Westview.

Lipsitz, G. (1998). *The possessive investment in Whiteness.* Philadelphia: Temple University Press.

Luke, C., & Luke, A. (1995). Just naming? Educational discourses and the politics of identity. In W. T. Pink & G. W. Noblit (Eds.), *Continuity and contradiction: The futures of the sociology of education* (pp. 357–380). Cresskill, NJ: Hampton.

Maslow, A. (1970). *Motivation and personality.* New York: Harper & Row.

McDermott, R. P., & Varenne, H. (1996). Culture, development, disability. In R. Jessor, A. Colby, & R. A. Shweder (Eds.), *Ethnography and human development: Context and meaning in social inquiry* (pp. 101–126). Chicago & London: University of Chicago.

McLaren, P., Carrillo-Rowe, A. M., Clark, R. L., & Craft, P. A. (2001). Labeling Whiteness: Decentering strategies of white racial domination. In G. M. Hudak & P. Kihn (Eds.), *Labeling: Pedagogy and politics* (pp. 203–224). New York: Routledge Falmer.

Mehan, H. (1992). Understanding inequality in schools: The contribution of interpretive studies. *Sociology of Education, 65*, 1–21.

Metcalf, S. (2003). Reading between the lines. In A. Kohn & P. Shannon (Eds.), *Education, Inc.: Turning learning into a business* (pp. 49–57). Portsmouth, NH: Heinemann.

Miller, M. C. (2001). *The Bush dyslexicon: Observations of a national disorder.* New York: W. W. Norton.

Miner, B. (2003). For-profits target education. In A. Kohn & P. Shannon (Eds.), *Education, Inc.: Turning learning into a business* (pp. 131–139). Portsmouth, NH: Heinemann.

No Child Left Behind Act of 2001, 20 U.S. C.§ 6301 et seq.

Oliver, M. (2004). Changing the social relations of research production. In S. Danforth & S. Taff (Eds.), *Crucial readings in special education* (pp. 138–147). Upper Saddle River, NJ: Pearson.

Olweus, D. (1993). *Bullying at school: What we know and what we can do.* Oxford: Blackwell.

Pinar, W. F. (2002, September 10). *What is curriculum theory?* Talk presented in the Beatrice S. and David L. Miller Education Seminar Series, School of Education, Indiana University, Bloomington, IN.

Pruyn, M. (1999). *Discourse wars in Gotham-West: A Latino immigrant urban tale of resistance and agency.* Boulder, CO: Westview.

Reynolds, A. J., & Wolfe, B. (1999). Special education and school achievement: An exploratory analysis with a central-city sample. *Educational Evaluation and policy Analysis, 21*(3), 249–269.

Rodis, P., Garrod, A., & Boscardin, M. L. (2001). *Learning disabilities and life stories.* Boston: Allyn & Bacon.

Ryan, W. (1971). *Blaming the victim.* New York: Random House.

Schmidt, J. (2000). *Disciplined minds: A critical look at salaried professionals and the soul-battering system that shapes their lives.* Lanham: Rowman & Littlefield.

Sharp, R., & Green, A. (1975). *Education and social control.* London: Routledge & Kegan Paul.

Silberman, C. (1971). *Crisis in the classroom.* New York: Vintage.

Smith, A. (2001). The labeling of African American boys in special education: A case study. In G. M. Hudak & P. Kihn (Eds.), *Labeling: Pedagogy and politics* (pp. 109–114). New York: Routledge Falmer.

Smith, T. J., & Danforth, S. (2000). Ethics, politics, and the unintended cruelties of teaching. In J. L. Paul & T. J. Smith (Eds.) *Stories out of school: Memories and reflections on care and cruelty in the classroom* (pp. 129–152). Stamford, CT: Ablex.

Smith, T. J., & Perez, S. (2000). The morals of teachers' stories. In J. L. Paul & T. J. Smith (Eds.), Stories *out of school: Memories and reflections on care and cruelty in the classroom* (pp. 105–127). Stamford, CT: Ablex.

Swanson, D. P., Cunningham, M., & Spencer, M. B. (2003). Black males' structural conditions, achievement patterns, normative needs and "opportunities." *Journal of Urban Education, 38*(5), 608–633.

Taylor, S., Rizvi, F., Lingard, B., & Henry, M. (1997). *Educational policy and the politics of change.* London & New York: Routledge.

Tomkins, S. (1995). Script theory and nuclear scripts. In E. K. Sedgwick & A. F. Frank (Eds.), *Shame and its sisters: A Sylvan Tomkins reader* (pp. 179–195). Durham, NC: Duke University Press.

Valencia, R. R. (Ed.) (1997). *The evolution of deficit thinking: Educational thought and practice.* London & Washington, DC: Falmer.

Wells, A. S., & Crain, R. L. (1992). Do parents choose school quality or school status? A sociological theory of free market education. *Sociology of Education, 65*(1), 616–618.

Willis, P. (1977). *Learning to labor: How working class kids get working class jobs.* New York: Columbia University Press.

Worfel, P. (n.d.). *Friendly fire, collateral damage, and rules of engagement: A casualty of "No Child Left Behind."* Unpublished manuscript.

Wright, S. E. (1993). Blaming the victim, blaming society, or blaming the discipline: Fixing responsibility for poverty and homelessness. *The Sociology Quarterly, 34*(1), 1–16.

Young, I. M. (2000). *Inclusion and democracy.* Oxford: Oxford University Press.

Young, M. (1971). *Knowledge and control.* London: Macmillan.

Author Index

249

Subject Index